CULTIVATING CREATIVITY

CULTIVATING CREATIVITY

Iain M. Robertson

NEW VILLAGE PRESS · NEW YORK

Published in the United States by New Village Press.

bookorders@newvillagepress.net

www.newvillagepress.org
New Village Press is a public-benefit, nonprofit publisher.

Distributed by NYU Press.

Hardcover ISBN: 978-1-61332-119-5

EBook ISBN: 978-1-61332-120-1

Publication Date: January 2022

First Edition

For their support of this publication we wish to thank Furthermore, a division of the JM Kaplan Fund.

Furthermore:
a program of the J.M. Kaplan Fund

Production Editor: Kristina M. Park

Design: Kristina M. Park & Paula Airth

We wish to thank Hady De Jong for her steadfast participation and passion to push this book to completion.

PERMISSIONS

Excerpt from *Ivor Cutler: Y'Hup* by Natasha Hoare is reprinted by courtesy of Goldsmiths Press.

Excerpt from "Ash Wednesday" by T.S. Eliot from *Selected Poems* by T. S. Eliot is reprinted by permission of Faber and Faber Ltd., Canada.

Excerpt from "Ash Wednesday" from COLLECTED POEMS 1909-1962 by T.S. Eliot. Copyright © 1936 by Houghton Mifflin Harcourt Publishing Company, renewed 1964 by Thomas Stearns Eliot. Reprinted by permission of Mariner Books, an imprint of HarperCollins Publishers, USA. All rights reserved.

Excerpt from "I Am Waiting" by Lawrence Ferlinghetti, from *A Coney Island of the Mind*, copyright ©1958 by Lawrence Ferlinghetti. Reprinted by permission of New Directions Publishing Corp.

Excerpts from

"Lucy In The Sky With Diamonds" Words and Music by John Lennon and Paul McCartney Copyright (c) 1967 Sony Music Publishing LLC Copyright Renewed.

"Nowhere Man" Words and Music by John Lennon and Paul McCartney Copyright (c) 1965 Sony Music Publishing LLC Copyright Renewed All Rights Administered by Sony Music Publishing LLC, 424 Church Street, Suite 1200, Nashville, TN 37219
International Copyright Secured.
All Rights Reserved.

Reprinted by Permission of Hal Leonard LLC

Photo of author Iain Robertson (p. 243) by Mike Siegel, *The Seattle Times*

Library of Congress Cataloging-in-Publication Data

Names: Robertson, Iain M., author.

Title: Cultivating creativity / Iain M. Robertson.

Description: First edition. | New York, N.Y.: New Village Press, 2022. | Summary: "The product of over three decades of teaching design studios and creativity seminars primarily at the University of Washington, this book provides exercises and strategies for encouraging creative expression in and out of the classroom. In addition, it offers full-color illustrations, participant reflections, pedagogical reflection, and guidance on creating new exercises"—Provided by publisher.

Identifiers: LCCN 2021025245 | ISBN 9781613321195 (hardcover)

Subjects: LCSH: Creative ability—Study and teaching. | Creative thinking—Study and teaching.

Classification: LCC LB1590.5 .R62 2022 | DDC 153.3/5--dc23

LC record available at https://lccn.loc.gov/2021025245

To Hady, Alex, and Johanna
with love and gratitude

CONTENTS

FOREWORD

Creativity, often promoted as an essential tool for problem solving, is rarely well articulated or tested. In the following chapters, Iain offers simple, affordable, and successful methods to foster creativity. Relying on the simple acts of reflection, discourse, adventure, and spontaneity, or simply by changing the learning environment, Iain Robertson demonstrates how creative thinking can be nurtured and encouraged.

These methods can be applied in the classroom or used by individuals to shift perspectives and unfasten imaginations. Are students realizing their full potentials, is education stifling or inspiring? How do we learn through exploration? These and other crucial issues are discussed, and solutions offered to experience the elation students have discovered in transformative exercises, in a bus, at a coffeeshop, or by confronting a messy table top! As Iain repeatedly clarifies in the text, these tools are not just for those engaged in design education, but also for those in aligned and seemingly divergent fields, including those teaching, studying, and practicing business, education, and technology. In these pages all educators will find inspiration and techniques that can be applied to their own unique foci.

The writing found in the following pages is undoubtedly Iain's. His brilliant ideas are expressed through his unique Scottish humor and his deep affection for literary craftmanship and for words, puns, and double entendres, all of which are woven throughout the practical, reflective, and inspiring content of this book.

As he has done for so many, Iain changed my life trajectory. Upon arriving in Seattle in 1989, I began to hear many stories about Iain Robertson. I was first employed in the landscape architecture firm The Portico Group, founded by alumni of the firm Jones and Jones, where Iain practiced before teaching at the University of Washington. He was often referenced in conversations, and it was clear he was highly admired and memorable. Later while jogging through the university campus, I would run into him on campus. He often stopped and chatted with me. At one point he suggested I think about teaching a construction course as a lecturer. This became a reality. Then, a year later, a tenure track position opened; again Iain encouraged me to apply, and to my disbelief I was chosen for the position. Without his encouragement I may not have considered academia, but he made it exciting, laudable, and important.

After twenty-five years of working alongside Iain, I now realize that caring is the characteristic that best defines him. In meetings, his quiet, pensive manner may lead you to think he is lost in his own thoughts. He is not, or, rather, often he is not. After long periods of silent listening, he enters the discourse with a pithy comment. It becomes clear that Iain had been contemplating the conversation deeply. He was dissecting it from multiple viewpoints, and inevitably brought his own unique, and spot-on perspective into the conversation. While Iain appears quiet—he is by his own admission rather shy—below his quiet reserve lie a bubbling passion, drive, curiosity, and humor. He is no shrinking violet. His powerful voice takes on the uncomfortable challenges that many avoid, never mincing his words, nor bending to a safer, less consequential position. I genuinely admire Iain's deep sense of morality, his fearlessness to stand up for unpopular positions, explain his point of view, and convince others with eloquence, conviction, and evidence.

The contrarian in Iain is not cultivated for the sake of being contrary, but rather encourages others to re-see their challenges and goals in a different light. He encourages those around him to consider other viewpoints, to become comfortable in different skins, and to see the world with fresh eyes. That is revolutionary; that is how change comes about. It's how we grow, mature, and evolve, and Iain, better than most educators, understands that this as an essential foundation for learning and growth. Personally, I witnessed Iain speak up in academic settings, when others wouldn't, and take on people who used bullying tactics to further their own agenda. Guided by his moral compass, Iain questioned their position and power, and thus prevented an injustice. He spoke while others remained silent.

At the University of Washington, Iain was widely admired for his plant and horticultural expertise. At the same time he developed a passionate concern about how we are educating our students. As chair of the landscape architecture department, he was the first, and, for many years, the only university administrator who supported efforts to establish an exploratory building model within the department. He, more than anyone else, understood the benefits of experiential learning and community service and the visceral clarity that implementing one's design brought into the students' consciousness. He would often show up and get his hands into the earth, experiencing the process to better understand the challenges and benefits of this specific learning model. I now realize this was Iain's natural curiosity to explore alternative teaching and learning methods emerging in the design education field. Coinciding with these efforts, he was also forming partnerships and collaborations with faculty in the education department and inviting them to a variety of alternative classrooms to witness and observe the teaching and learning processes. The origins of this book extend back to these deep roots from decades ago. Iain continually ponders, adjusts, explores, tests, retests, and reflects upon innovation and continually reevaluates contemporary design education. He developed his own courses to explore and refine the exercises presented in this book. He later traveled to China and Norway to test his theories within different cultural contexts. This volume contains his findings from these extensive explorations that he readily admits are just starting points from which the reader can build and adapt. Iain's profound belief in the transformative power of creativity and his unwavering commitment to making it accessible foster the necessary design intelligence to address the critical and tenacious issues we now face as designers and global citizens.

I hope the ideas in this book will result in much needed awakening of our educational potential and help students realize their full and astounding capabilities. I believe that others across many disciplines will appreciate the visionary and revolutionary thinking Iain has communicated through this extraordinary book.

—Daniel Winterbottom, FASLA
  Seattle, April 2021

ACKNOWLEDGMENTS

Cultivating Creativity has developed from deep roots with wide influences. Its origins lie in University of Washington (UW) design studio classes, and I thank Julie Johnson, Luanne Smith, John Koepke, Liz Browning, Brooke Sullivan, and Bob Buchanan for all that I learned from you while co-teaching landscape design studios. Among many wonderful colleagues at UW, three, Cathy Beyer, Julie Villegas, and Ken Yocom, deserve particular mention for keeping the faith and working with me long after reasonable individuals would have pressed the ejector seat button.

I am particularly indebted to colleagues with whom I have taught creativity classes, Leslie Rupert Herrenkohl, Professor, Educational Studies and the Combined Program in Education and Psychology, University of Michigan, Tammy Tasker, Postdoctoral Research Fellow, Educational Studies Department, University of Michigan, Sally Milnor Zyfers, M.Ed. in Educational Psychology, Juanjuan Liu, Associate Professor and Vice Chair of Landscape Architecture Department, School of Landscape Architecture and Horticulture Sciences, Southwest Forestry University, and Sun Jing, Associate Professor, Hubei University of Technology. I am also grateful to Bao Feng Li, Professor, Huazhong University of Science and Technology for his support to travel to China to conduct classes at Huazhong University of Science and Technology and to Christine Ingebritsen at the University of Washington–Bergen University exchange program for support to travel to Bergen to teach there. I also wish to thank the irrepressibly positive and supportive Dr. Rolf Reber, Professor of Psychology, University of Oslo and University of Bergen for sponsoring my visit to the University of Bergen.

My grateful thanks to my editors, Lynne Elizabeth and Ignacio Choi, who took a manuscript that was a bourach and treated it like a fankle, unraveling its convoluted text and images. Most of all, however, I wish to thank from the bottom of my heart all of the students with whom I have worked over decades of teaching at the University of Washington and in particular those who are the heroes of the classes I describe here. You will never know just how much your enthusiastic and thoughtful explorations, and your willingness to surprise yourself weekly, have meant to me. Thank you so much for your support.

Having "completed" the project, I discovered that there was yet another lap to run, and I am grateful to have had Hady with me. I wish to acknowledge the following, without whom we would not have been able to cross the finish line: the people at New Village Press for their perseverance and belief in the project during this period of personal and global adversity; Jeff Hou for connecting us with New Village Press; Daniel Winterbottom for his unfailing faith; Elizabeth A. Umbanhower and Ellie Lang for their scintillating contributions; and, finally, Kristi M. Park, so simpatico with the heart of this project, for all her spirited efforts and dedication.

WHERE
GO
THE
BOATS

Dark brown is the river.
Golden is the sand.

The journey to examine creativity began when I started asking students to create designs that would evoke specific emotional responses in an introduction to university-level planting-design class. I had been teaching design studios for years and knew that conventional imperatives, such as "design a beautiful backyard," would precipitate a deluge of toe-curling clichés. Alternatively, asking students to create designs to evoke specific emotional responses, I discovered, cut the Gordian knot, as such questions lacked precedent answers to adopt. There was nowhere to turn to for authoritative advice; there was no "correct" answer.

The absence of a definitive answer pulled the carpet of education as provider of correctness out from under their feet. Students had to rely on their own experience for guidance and inspiration to create designs. As an example, when I asked students to create designs that evoked "delight" or "despair," the students' designs were exciting and novel. They exhibited personal and heartfelt explorations rather than bland mouthings of "right" answers. Pedagogically, it seemed, we were onto something. Students made direct connections between design manipulations and presumed human responses: "If I do this to the space, plants, and

circulation, then users are likely to respond in this way." Thinking about design manipulations in this way generated empathy and understanding. Lacking textbooks to follow, students had to rely on themselves for answers, a textbook case of the limits of texts and books. Unmistakably, products belonged to each designer.

Following another pedagogical hunch, I directed students away from drawn two-dimensional designs and toward three-dimensional model making. Most students had been told, while navigating their education, that they didn't know how to draw. However, the educational system had forgotten to tell them that they didn't know how to make models! Freed from the past lessons learned earlier in their education, students moved forward with fewer inhibitions when asked to create three-dimensional designs in shoe boxes to evoke emotional responses. Freed from sentiments of "I can't," many exciting explorations followed. Like one shoe size, one answer does not fit all emotions. Models were generated in a myriad of shapes, sizes, materials, and combinations of utility and style. Shoe box designs provided students with the freedom to explore uninhibited by constraints, letting go of the idea that there was "the right thing to do." Tangible boundaries around problems encourage focused explorations. Boxes' unambiguous physical limits to explorations liberated students to think outside the box.

It flows along for ever,
With trees on either hand.

Green leaves a-floating,
Castles of the foam,

This book's ideas and conclusions derive from years of teaching design studios in university settings, but its impetus came from outside the design world. I became starkly aware of how different and idiosyncratic the processes and assumptions of design thinking were when I began to interact with faculty from other disciplines. I discovered that universities embody parallel universes and that the premises and products of design thinking were, in the university context, unusual, not to say aberrant.

Nevertheless, I came to believe that design thinking was key to thinking creatively. I began to ask myself how a designer might adapt design pedagogy to make its insights useful for other disciplines. That question was rummaging around in the back of my mind when I introduced myself to the University of Washington (UW) Honors Program some years ago. I said, "I'd like to teach a class on creativity." I expected my course proposal to be provided with the requisite forms for consideration by a shadowy committee over months or years. I assumed the Honors Program would include a question such as "What exactly did you say your credentials are for doing this?" To my surprise, the response was instantaneous, "When can you start?"

Fortunately, I had prepared myself for a quick start, as the response induced the exact feeling that initiates most design explorations where the unknown presses in and one's ideas seem to lack candlepower to disperse the darkness. So began my classes on creativity for UW Honors students, in which I experimented with questions and exercises while participants experimented with answers. We were all in the same boat, though they didn't realize that the captain lacked charts and a pilot star, much less an astrolabe, with which to plot a course.

For five years, under the guise of teaching, I experimented in Cultivating Creativity seminars at the University of Washington. In the roundabout ways so typical of design explorations, we made progress. I co-taught the first UW Honors Program seminar described in this book with Dr. Tammy Tasker in 2011. The next year provided an opportunity to take a great leap eastward from Seattle to Huazhong University of Science and Technology. In collaboration with Chinese colleagues, Professors Juanjuan Liu and Sun Jing, we conducted a similar class with design students. Following that experience, under Dr. Rolf Reber's sponsorship, I led a parallel course with graduate psychology students at the University of Bergen, Norway. This book describes the work of the diverse students in these classes.

Although I call these classes "experiments," they were, first and foremost, classes—educational explorations conducted in conjunction with students, not experiments conducted on students. Together, we experimented with ideas. As we all are at all times, the students and I were our own guinea pigs in the experiment called life. Some exercises remained the same from one class to another, others adapted to the changing needs of contexts and students, and a few bit the dust.

Cultivating Creativity reports on an ongoing exploration of how to cultivate the creative potential in participants from diverse disciplines by using exercises developed from design studio pedagogy. It is emphatically NOT an infallible manual full of precise definitions and prescriptions, nor is it a cookbook with recipes followed step by step to mouthwatering results. Rather, it's a dance card inviting you to step forward with your own explorations. More than anything else, I hope it captures the unfolding excitement of participants' explorations and the wonder of creativity. There is something marvelous in discovering that our innate creativity, so often stifled and suffocated by education, still burns.

Boats of mine a-boating—
Where will all come home?

Not surprisingly, the environments in which design thinking flourishes differ from classrooms designed for didactic teaching forms. Although explorations occur in all classrooms, conventional teaching is focused on analytics, while design studios integrate and synthesize ideas. One needs but a glance at the messiness of studio desks and pedagogy to understand that a broader range of influences is at work. Studios create synthesis processes that stand in contrast to commonly encountered tidy, orderly, and impersonal classrooms. It's not entirely coincidental that design studios resemble kindergarten rooms rather than classrooms. Studios constitute times and places where the childlike question of "why?" still permeates the air.

In addition to nontraditional classroom spaces, we also need different materials. When teaching, I noticed that if the classrooms used for explorations didn't contain the material stuff of creative explorations, we had to bring materials into the place of learning. Bags of stuff were carried back and forth across the UW campus, and a suitcase of worthless treasures was transported halfway around the world from Wuhan to Bergen. These materials were essential to thinking outside the classroom box. Creativity felt stifled in traditional venues. By alternating the space we were in and bringing in new, nontraditional materials, our Cultivating Creativity seminars broke new ground, already plowed and furrowed by daily life. Also important, on occasion, we escaped the classroom for creative field trips.

that prolonged confusion. Participation in exercises had two objectives: It put students in situations that encouraged them to find, develop, and express their innate creativity. It also helped cultivate creative attitudes of mind through trial and error. Exercise methods, such as try first, then test one's results later, are rooted in studio design pedagogy, which is, in many ways, a country cousin to the more sophisticated koans of Zen training. Exercises' ancestry may also be traced to the mentorship typical of medieval craft guilds, but, it must be confessed, the flavor of the delivery in the classes described here is personal and idiosyncratic. Classes consisted of doing exercises followed (never preceded!) by discussion and reflection. This required a bedrock of trust, faith, and confidence from both instructors and participants. Faith that, given encouragement to rediscover and develop their creativity, participants will learn to do what is right for exercises. In futures and situations we can't predict, they will act creatively. Although we don't know where they're going, the instructor's job is to help them on their way.

On goes the river
And out past the mill,

A confession: One can't teach creativity, any more than one can pull plants from seeds or fruits from flowers. However, we can create conditions conducive for creativity to flourish. Once done, we must wait patiently, attentively, and expectantly. The potential is in the seed, the students. The instructor's job is to be a thoughtful gardener, avoiding stepping on plants while weeding. Creativity is not something that can be taught in narrowly orthodox definitions of teaching. In a very real sense, we teach ourselves and one another, as individuals and as a community, to be creative.

If one can't teach creativity, and if we didn't study and discuss creativity as an academic subject, what, exactly, did we do in our creativity classes? First and foremost, we acted and reacted. Students' exercises accompanied obligingly opaque and nebulous instructions. The students were expected to engage in the act of doing the exercises in our creative courses. Doing consisted of model making, drawing, arranging materials, holding debates, making mistakes, and, at times, visiting coffee shops. Some activities were short, over by the time participants got started. Others were longer take-home projects

Away down the valley,
Away down the hill.

Another explanatory thread requires incorporation into this introductory knot. Years ago, in an open house at my daughter's school, her "improv" teacher said something that caused an audible click in my brain: "The mind cannot not be creative." Exactly! There it was, in a nutshell, a succinct summary of the creative mind. It can't but help itself to be creative! Creative thought patterns are an inevitable emergent phenomenon of the human mind, which is to say, creativity is how the mind works. Contrary to popular opinion, creativity is not an abstruse quality possessed by gifted minds, confined to unusual people whom we label as "geniuses," nor a mental operation that takes place only on favored occasions. On the contrary, human minds are predisposed to be creative. This assumption underlies all of our cultivating creativity activities and explorations. Without admitting it to myself or to the participants, my goal was to demonstrate how each of us

may live a more creative life. Such lives are not to be confused with inventing better mousetraps, cheaper widgets, or the Next Big Thing, which, according to Moore's Law of technological progress, will succeed, paradoxically, because it is smaller than the last big thing. Of course, there are degrees of creativity; the invention of the Internet is orders of magnitude more creative than recounting a good joke, but similar mental connecting processes operate in each case. To suggest that creative attitudes of mind enrich daily life is not to diminish the pantheon of greats who occupy Olympian and Nobel heights.

Accepting the metaphor that creativity is an attitude of mind and stance toward the world can also be described as "fluid thought patterns." When leading teams or students, we must either cultivate or suppress fluid thought. Exercises should avoid channelization by not prescribing routes to goals or even delineating the goals themselves. This book, like the exercises contained herein, emphasizes process over products. Products may be delightful and beautiful, but they are less significant than engagement processes with the explorations as individuals and learning communities. As with all true education, the real product is unseen and unknown. By my future results, ye shall know me.

Currently, educational orthodoxy embraces standardized testing. It seems pertinent to step aside from that vast enterprise and attest to teaching methods that explore possibilities and broaden the diversity of the definition of education. We chip away at the edifice of "education as testing" and add to, but not supplant, it with "education as exploration." Education from the skin inward and the imagination outward. However, the question of how we might make cultivating creative attitudes of mind a central part of all education lies beyond my wit, wisdom, and patience. I hope the descriptions of the participants' wonderful work will be sufficient to trigger chain reactions in readers' minds, blowing open possibilities for reigniting a sense of wonder and delight in education. Another belief that guides creative pedagogy: If we ask students open-ended questions about topics of interest to them in environments that encourage exploration, we will, invariably, be surprised and delighted by the responses. We can restate the purpose of *Cultivating Creativity* classes and this book as rekindling a sense of wonder. No wonder, no education. And the key to wonder is curiosity.

Words such as exploration, discovery, delight, and wonder are commonly encountered in descriptions of kindergarten curricula, not in higher education. Equally absent in the vocabulary of academia: play. Together, these words circumscribe WHY we want to learn and HOW to do so successfully. They deserve more space in our consciousness, curricula, and classrooms. Higher education, in its headlong rush to transform itself into "hire education," has done a thorough job of removing play, wonder, and delight from the classroom, along with curiosity, the impetus for all exploration and discovery. The tax of testing seems intent upon excising all this from education. As a result, students are bored, disengaged, disinterested, and we wonder why. The fault, dear Brutus, is not in our stars but in our curricula that are training underlings.

Away down the river, A hundred miles or more,

The explorations of creativity are motivated by an even more considerable concern: We live in a world that is exploding; a world beset by a litany of problems that include climate change, population increase, resource depletion, ecosystem collapse, and social and cultural disruptions more significant than those experienced at any time in human history. Our generations, as teachers, bequeath these dilemmas to the generations we teach. Are we preparing them for this future? Personally, and insistently, I ask myself what I can do to be relevant and help prepare this generation to address problems that my generation has so patently failed to acknowledge, much less resolve. Today's student has access to more information on an already overbrimming plate. Our current education model contributes

little to its resolution. An alternative approach is necessary to prepare students for an unimaginable future.

In 1973, Professors, Horst Rittel and Melvin Webber, introduced the concept of "wicked-problems" in their scholarly article "Dilemmas in a General Theory of Planning." In sum, a '"wicked problem"' is a design, environmental, and/or a societal challenge without a definitive answer. As educators, we must prepare students to nurture their creativity to resolve "wicked problems." I observed creativity was a topic most academics held at arm's length, treated as toxic, regarded as a contagious disease, and thus was conspicuously absent from most education. I chose to embrace it and, therefore, this book came to be.

However, this isn't a book about despair; rather, it's about repair. It proposes ideas that might help mend educational curricula by restoring creativity as a focus.

If I have omitted to say it before, let me say it now: I stand in awe of the hope, intelligence, determination, and brilliance of the students whose work I document in this book. Students appear under aliases, but they know who they are. I hope each of you accepts my heartfelt thanks for all that you attempted and accomplished in these classes—thank you all. Your work restored my faith and warmed the cockles of my heart. Your voices are inextricably woven into this text, so that to use only my name as the author is a misnomer; this is the work of a joint venture company of explorers.

The world I grew up in is as incomprehensible to contemporary students as their future is to me. Although we inhabit the same classrooms, we live in different worlds. Is the education we provide students today relevant to their lives and their futures? Our creativity exercises attempt to bridge the gulf between generations and between daily life and education and reinforce the idea "This is your education; it belongs to you. Take charge of it, think carefully, be generous, work hard."

Other little children
Shall bring my boats ashore.
—ROBERT LOUIS STEVENSON, "WHERE GO THE BOATS?",
A CHILD'S GARDEN OF VERSES

Finally, this introduction concludes with the paradox of ambiguity. We are incessantly told that knowledge is increasing exponentially, popping up around us like weeds in a vacant lot. We are also told that we are blessed to live in an "information age," in which our fingertips drip with more information than was possessed by any society in history; a sweet land, indeed, flowing with ink and money. Nevertheless, the more we "know," the more unpredictable the real world seems to become. Our future is increasingly uncertain, so our times might more accurately be described as the age of ambiguity. This book's tone is appropriate for such an age; the messages between its lines are often more important than the letters dutifully arranged and deranged along its lines. To apply the methods and ideas of this book verbatim is to miss the point and subvert its purpose. Between the lines "Quips and cranks, and wanton wiles, Nods and becks, and wreathèd smiles" dance, cavort, hint, jest, and suggest. Pay attention! Seek inspiration in its insinuating sinews to change, to reinvent, and to come full circle—which is to say revolutionize—how we think about education. A complete revolution, paradoxically, turns us head over heels but leaves us standing, irremediably changed, on our feet.

Similar to design thinking processes, this book does not provide step-by-step instructions. Let this book fall open at any page to discover open-ended explorations that suggest how we might encourage, foster, or cultivate creativity or, more to the point, help others cultivate their own creativity. By their very nature, explorations don't follow predetermined routes; they cross trackless landscapes in search of verdant oases, promising rivers, and lofty mountaintops. My guiding compass for explorations is derived from my years of design and creativity studios. They affirmed my belief that if one asks students genuinely open-ended questions in environments that don't punish mistakes but, instead, encourage risks, and if we are genuinely interested in students' processes and products, we will be rewarded with responses beyond our wildest imagination. Of course, this doesn't happen universally, but it happens again and again. The educational juggernaut is apt to lose sight of the fact that students do, in fact, want to learn and do derive pleasure from doing so.

In his book The Act of Creation, Arthur Koestler differentiates three creative types: the Sage, the Artist, and the Jester. My comfort zone lies with the third designation. This book may be read as a chronicle of a fool who rushed in where academics fear to tread and lived to sell the tale. If attended to with generosity of heart and openness of mind, this work should prove an interesting diversion, a not entirely inauspicious activity in which to while away a few hours—so long as you enjoy where it takes you and don't expect to get to where you had expected to arrive. I hope the journey will be enjoyable and educational in equal measure. I hope that it will legitimize the idea that play may be the most effective educational method evolved by the representative of the species that is doing this reading—I mean you, gentle reader. A playful mind is the best state of affairs for being creative. Creativity is child's play. Unless ye become as little children …

AS A GENERAL
RULE
GENERALIZATIONS
RULE

IT'S ON MY
TO DON'T DO
LIST

TOO OFTEN
EDUCATION!
CONFLATES
DETENTION
WITH
ATTENTION

CREATIVITY IS NOT AN END RUN AROUND EFFORT

IF YOUR HEAD'S SPINNING TURN WOOLLY THINKING INTO A YARN

EDUCATION IS ABOUT QUESTIONS NOT ANSWERS. NO?

a
journey
across
a
rock

"A Journey Across a Rock" is a self-explanatory exercise, so let me explain. Participants begin by selecting a rock from an extensive collection and imagine themselves as tiny people journeying across the stone's surfaces. One could imagine the rocks expanding into islands, continents, asteroids, and planets, transforming the surfaces so that tiny pits become yawning caverns, cracks become ravines, and roughnesses become mountain ranges. In drawings and words, participants describe their journeys across these alien worlds—imaginary journeys influenced by the specific shapes and surface characteristics of each rock. Rocks are prompts, but the purpose and tenor of journeys come from their chroniclers: tragedy, comedy, drama, thriller, sci-fi mystery, or an epic saga? Advise participants not to become overreliant on words to tell their stories. Although powerful—you read it here first—words frequently commandeer the imagination. Drawings, by contrast, enable us to imagine more freely. The students document journeys in annotated drawings or paintings. The story begins.

Rock journeys are a great start to cultivating creativity. When inspected closely, the rocks in our hands offer inspirational cues. Begin by encouraging participants to inspect their rocks, so that they can closely mine inspiration from distinctive characteristics. Encourage participants to engage all their senses to interrogate their rocks—feeling their roughness or smoothness, assessing their weight. Ask "What is my rock telling me? Is it smooth or rough? Why? Uniform or varied? Why? Is it rounded or broken? Why? Does it have a top and bottom? How large is it in comparison to its promontories and depressions? How easy would it be to traverse its surface?" Suck the rocks dry for inspiration. Rocks provided to students should be varied in size and shape but should not be too small. We are not—yet—channeling William Blake and attempting to see the world in a grain of sand. Rocks with distinctive features allow participants to select one they find appealing. Choosing a rock is important and it should be exciting! Not insignificantly, choice encourages buy-in. It's not a rock; it's my rock. Participants practice the inestimable art of close observation; rocks reciprocate and provide inspiration that stimulates the imagination. Although we start our creative explorations with ordinary and familiar materials, it's essential that we ask participants to do something unusual with them. Equating creativity with artistic skills would suggest that beautiful drawings are our goal, but no, products are incidental—it's the journey—imagining the journey—that matters. In all exercises, it's the process, not the matter, that matters.

How do participants respond? Exuberant participants glance at the assignment and jump right in, making drawings that sweep across their large sheets of paper. Hesitant participants might start with small drawings in corners. Those with cautious or reflective dispositions may begin by studying their rocks intently—eking out clues and ideas from their forms and characteristics. The studious may read and reread the assignment, hoping to find a glint of a hint of a possible direction amid its verbal convolutions and sometimes provocative literary quotes. The timid wait to see what others do.

Extracting blood from a stone is problematic, but it is incredible what can be drawn out of closely observed rocks. They spark imagination, which may smolder or become a conflagration. How participants start doesn't matter so long as they do start and, once started, forge their own routes. The imagination is always feeling its way forward into new terrain, so each exploration breaks new ground; there are no beaten tracks to retrace. Journeys may be expressed in annotated paintings, cartoons, drawings, or models. Don't try to fit processes and products into predetermined formats. Listen closely; tentative sketches may conceal magnificent stories; the strength of the imagination and the ability to express ideas artistically are not the same.

Provide opportunities for participants who are comfortable working together at a large table. In contrast, others may seek contemplative spots away from the muddling crowd, but discourage too much "sit down quietly and do your own work in isolation" behavior. Encourage competition AND cooperation by inviting participants to walk around to see what others are doing and offer comments or borrow good ideas. Borrowing ideas is not plagiarism, so long as we adjust and improve upon them and acknowledge them as precedents. To build a cohesive community of explorers, leave ample time for all to recount their travels. Discussing one another's journeys is a vital step in building a durable, supportive community of learners.

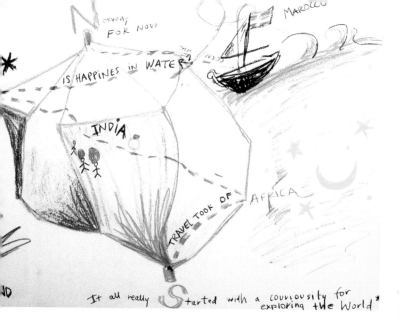

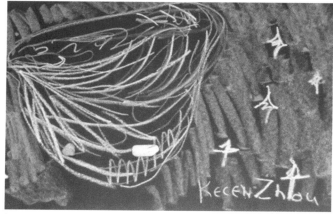

What do the products and reflections reveal? Every cohort of explorers develops its personality in response to many formative factors, from what we had for breakfast to whether the bus was on time. These affect our momentary predispositions—the enveloping cultural embraces that consciously and unconsciously mold us.

Some Journeys, Some Stories

Participants' imaginative journeys illustrate how rocks and individual lives are inextricably connected. An example, Lottie, took a Linguistic Anthropology exam in English at a Norwegian university before beginning her rock journey. She chose a white quartz pebble, the smoothest, smallest, most uniform stone available. Like her exam, it was "impenetrable" and had a shape that made it "hard to grab onto anything." The wavy quartz lines running through the dark gray slate reminded her of the rocks at home. This resulted in a rock journey that connected her home, through water, to Bergen. Lottie let her day and life influence her ideas; she practiced the mantra (which I shall repeat repeatedly throughout this book): Act first, think later.

ANNA B: *The ROCK VOYAGE included a fast working pace, making up a fearful and exciting adventure. My starting point included making a treasure card by using the rock's form as the globe's shape with a path. Thoughts of traveling came up, as these are the moments of my life, by now, where I have felt most adventurous and fearful, and it seemed natural to use it. I wanted the "rock globe" to be the treasure map... an adventure is an ongoing process. I liked the fact that we were running out of time and didn't have any time to consider back and forth how to solve it, just starting and following the first-coming ideas.*

SIG: *I really liked the "rock journey" exercise. At the beginning, I was a bit nervous that I did not really understand the assignment, and I was worried about talking about it or presenting it to the class after it was finished. But then something strange happened (or at least strange for me). It wasn't really that scary. It wasn't scary when I realized that it wasn't a correct way of interpreting the exercise. And it was very nice (and different) to produce something on my own without support from a theoretical framework or something like that (which is always the case when I produce a text or a case study or whatever).*

Adjustments to written and verbal instructions—sometimes intentional, sometimes fortuitous—can redirect responses. While conducting classes, observe how such changes alter the feeling, tone, and thrust of exercises. Play it by ear, and note responses. As with any endeavor, there's an interplay among tools, material, and minds. Unlike typical sheets of paper, long strips suggest directionality and movement, resulting in different expressions of journeys. Nothing is irrelevant—materials and our tools affect our thoughts and actions.

What Did Participants Think as They Began These Explorations?

A class composed of exercises such as these performs a delicate dance of deconstruction and reconstruction, a choreography of breaking down tired, dysfunctional educational practices and establishing fresh methods and goals. For both participants and instructors, education must extend beyond comfort zones; we must take risks. Together, we must grow accustomed to and comfortable with ambiguity. We must be willing to scrap plans, suspend judgment and try strange, perplexing things. Activities that initially seem like digressions may turn out to be central to education. We must be willing to explore creativity, not learn about or study it. Greater educational risk resides in not taking risks. Although not guaranteed, we often reap the rewards from risks. To be creative, we must take risks and accept failure.

CORRIE M: *The activity.... was interesting in a different way. It was somewhat difficult for me to transition out of regular class mode at first. With the first activity, I could feel myself getting frustrated and comparing my own work with other people's. When we paired off for the second activity, I was able to let go of that and be creative without overthinking. It was a good reminder on where my brain needs to be to be creative.*

BRENDA S: *I've decided that creativity is determined by one's willingness to take risks in the midst of creation. For example, I noticed that a lot of my classmates did not really follow the so-called "rules" of the assignment ... something I would call a risk. They didn't describe a "journey," at all and that bugged me at first. But their work was all wonderfully inspirational and beautiful. More important, I suspect that they felt quite creative as they worked. How strange! And yet the same seems to be true about my own work thus far. As I take risks, I find myself being figuratively jolted awake by my own creative thoughts.*

TOM P: *When we had our first ... activity with rocks, I have to say that I was a little taken aback. I wasn't really sure what I suppose to do at first when we were trying to express an adventure we had on the rock. Of course I took this literally and imagined myself having an adventure on my rock (a rock I really did like because of its color), but I found it interesting how some of my peers saw the rock as an entity itself, such as the rock as a symbolic brain. While these different interpretations of our adventures were intriguing, I was at the same time asking myself, "Why didn't I see it like that?"*

This journey exercise introduces a different way of addressing problems—integrative and synthetic thinking—rather than more familiar analytical approaches. Another turning point is reached when participants compare themselves to others in helpful ways rather than debilitating ones. Participants must have faith that they will reap benefits by applying these processes to other contexts.

Don't expect universal success with every exercise. Some work for some and not for others. When we are in the mood to explore, some work and others fall flat when we're out of step. Offering different kinds of explorations helps us hit the mark some of the time. Don't rush the process and shortchange reflection, the keystones of creative arches. Time for leisurely presentations and reflection is always time well spent.

Expansions and Additions

Participants' life journeys are diverse, so the variety of their rock journeys should not be surprising—marvelous drawings and stories; fearsome, exciting, and heartwarming journeys! Trust that if we pose interesting, open-ended explorations, engage participants honestly, and keep out of their way, they will

generate fascinating responses whose wonder and variety one couldn't imagine in a million years. No matter how beguilingly beautiful products are, it's the journey, the process of discovery, that's most important.

Leave no rock unturned and untraveled. Learning to observe closely is key to success; it increases awareness and prompts creative thought. Of course, when closely observing a rock, there has to be something inside both rock and viewer. Close, thoughtful, empathetic observation is the "open sesame" for imagination. There is ALWAYS something inside each of us that is accessible if we knock loudly and persistently enough or tap the right code. Exercises employ a variety of keys, codes, apps, and rhythms. (Re)discovering that if we open our eyes, the world will provide inspiration for the imagination and enhance creativity. So we should develop the habit of observing everything closely everywhere and all the time—an impossible goal but a valid aspiration. Introductory exercises succeed even if they do no more than this. Despite occupying center stage in our description, rocks are not the prima donnas of this exercise; they are merely vehicles over which creative imagination can travel. Alter materials by substituting concrete or bricks and explore materials adventurously! How might participants respond to patches of fabric—from sheeny silk to shag carpet? Avoid paper; it comes loaded with too many preconceptions.

Exercises are NOT set in stone. Expand and adapt them to suit needs and circumstances. Expansions and additions suggest how they might be modified and offer insights on the responses that changes might provoke. Changing the wording of instructions and the materials are simple changes. How would participants respond if they were invited to "dance"—waltz, fox-trot, break, mambo, tap, boogie, or roll across their rock? Substitute the words march, crawl, or proceed, and the exercise is again transformed—suggestion and insinuation point participants in different directions.

Try various working groups from individuals, pairs, and teams to see what happens. What might occur if participants were asked to supply their own rocks? How might responses change if we asked participants to draw and write blindfolded instead of emphasizing sight? Expansions into contractions open doors: Gulliver visited Lilliput and Brobdingnag. Can we also change our size and imagine journeys across silicon chips or grains of sand?

PARADISE ISLANDS

I can love a stone, Govinda, and a tree or a piece of bark. These are things and one can love things. But one cannot love words. Therefore teachings are of no use to me; they have no hardness, no softness, no colors, no corners, no smell, no taste— they have nothing but words. Perhaps that is what prevents you from finding peace, perhaps there are too many words, for even salvation and virtue.

—HERMAN HESSE, *SIDDHARTHA*

Some exercises are materially spartan, but this one is a sensory feast that reconnects our senses and education to physical reality. Participants use samples of natural materials—rocks, soil, metals, water, plants—to construct "paradise islands." The exercise encourages a "language" of material reality by cutting out language—that meddlesome middleman between experience and thought. Accordingly, our senses can speak the language of materiality. The wide range of physical qualities of the materials stimulates the senses and frees the imagination.

An assortment of tins, jars, and boxes contains the material reality from which participants can make paradise islands. Each container reveals a different natural wonder; the profusion delights and the various surprises. The sense of revelation encourages participants to revel in material reality through touch, smell, and sight—an entire material world is at our fingertips. Participants select four materials, favoring sensory experience over mental comprehension, thereby relieving overworked and weary minds. The exercise gently reminds us of something we frequently forget—the power of the "language of materiality." If we permit it, materiality is a potent source of creative inspiration. Paradoxically, heightened material perception is the antithesis of grubby materialism. Attending to material qualities is not the same as using and discarding large quantities of matter. Participants are invited to make paradise islands, though it's the making that matters, not the matter that's made. Decades of education condition us to read more into this straightforward exercise than simply experiencing the material world. Keep it simple. Discourage participants from turning it into an intellectual exercise rather than a sensory exploration. Don't impose displays of dazzling intelligence upon the materials. Experience and respond through the language of material reality. Pantheists may work in teams; monotheists may work alone.

The exercise is an antidote to our culture's tendency to substitute vicarious, mediated experience for the real, substantive thing because cutting ourselves off from material reality eliminates innumerable opportunities for inspiration. Through feeling, playing with, and manipulating material reality directly, we dispense with intermediary words and uncover fresh ways of thinking.

All my forebears on my mother's side were peasants—bent over the soil, glued to the soil, their hands, feet, and minds filled with soil. They loved the land and placed all their hopes in it; over the generations they and it had become one. In times of drought they grew sickly black from thirst along with it. When the first autumn rains began to rage, their bones creaked and swelled like reeds.

—NIKOS KAZANTZAKIS, *REPORT TO GRECO*

Having extolled the importance of materiality, it may sound strange to say that the choice of specific materials to work with—pebbles, seashells, paper wasps' nests, seeds, nuts, et cetera—is immaterial. What matters for deep sensory engagement is an abundance of choices and a variety of sensory qualities. To avoid sensory overload and ensure thoughtful explorations, it is equally important to limit the number of materials that each participant works with, because material constraints discipline sensory perception and focus the mind. Omitting religious or mythological associations or cultural metaphors from the exercise introduction avoids intellectual distractions—it's about listening to material qualities, not imposing extraneous meaning on the matter. This exercise typically evokes delight, pure and simple—we derive sensory pleasure from manipulating the material world. The participants' reflections speak eloquently of the value of getting in touch with material reality.

ELLA T: *Building utopia was so amazing. It's crazy because [we] … just started playing around with the materials … and when we realized we were making paradise, things only took off. It was just so much fun how things flowed, and I don't even know how to explain the thought process because there really wasn't much to it, which, I think, is how it should be.*

DESMOND C: *I found the activity of "creating our own paradise" to be very relaxing, rewarding, and revealing of the creative potential in all of us. You brought in a box containing say thirty-five different items, and each of us selected three…. From those three, we were able to effortlessly create a vision of paradise. However, had we selected three different elements from the box, we would have been equally able to create a paradise out of it. This, to me, shows the enormity of creativity that we have available to us…. I would argue that given the same materials, we would be capable of producing a multitude of paradises…. [This] is an expression of the versatility of creativity.*

Another thing that struck me about the exercise was how naturally and easily creating the paradise came to me. It was truly effortless … as though there was some subconscious part of my brain that was guiding the entire process. I had no design that I was following, but, rather, every little bit that I added to my paradise seemed to show me what the next bit I added should be. At the end, when I sat back and examined my paradise, it seemed to be exactly what I wanted it to be. I found the connection to nature through the natural elements that we used very rewarding.

WILMA T: *At first, I was really confused by our activity … I had no idea how to create "Paradise" out of some rocks and seeds. I didn't even know what kind of paradise I was being asked to create. Eden? An ideal land? Without a real* *plan, I ended up forming my selection of rocks and coral into a circle, like sitting stones around a fire, symbolizing community. I was surprised that my interpretation of paradise was one of community and sharing rather than a bountiful land. I always consider myself to be a more introverted person … but here I found that I actually valued community more than I'd previously thought.*

BEN C: *I don't consider myself particularly "artsy," so to speak. I'm not much for painting, drawing, etc. But this project gave me a chance to be artistic and to really sculpt something without needing the fine motor skills. It was like a mix between playing with dirt as a kid and really trying to design something artful. So thank you for reminding me that I can find art in my own ways!*

FREYA Z: *This project was sort of odd. Mainly because it was a mix of limiting … yet extremely open and maybe even vague. Sort of like, "You're going to make something with only four materials, but you can make whatever you like." (Because what does an "earthly paradise really even mean? I'm sure there's no definitive answer, since it's really up to the interpretation of the creator). Huh. I don't even know what I would do now, even though I had already done that project! … The materials given to us manipulated and drove our thought process. Our "earthly paradise" became the necessities of life. And for many, a barren yet magical, wasteland…. What I gained for this activity wasn't based on any of my own doing. My favorite part was seeing what everyone else had created. No one had anything remotely similar to one another's…. And that's a great thing.*

What's the Matter?

From early childhood explorations, we discover the material world's qualities. It's not too large a metaphorical leap to think of material reality as a language that we speak. Indeed, it's an ever-present and all-pervasive language, full of meaning and self-expression. We live in a paradoxical age of modern Western cultures reviled for being overly materialistic, yet our lives are often deprived of sensory experiences. We may possess wealth beyond Croesus's wildest dreams, yet suffer from what Robert M. Pyle calls the "extinction of experience." Alienation from the material world impoverishes our imagination and diminishes our creative potential. Money alone can't ensure authentic contact with the material world. By enticing us to work directly with materials, this exercise reminds us we speak the language of material reality. Our senses are doors through which creativity may enter our minds. I feel, therefore I think.

This exercise's premise that sensory stimulation from direct contact with the material world encourages creative attitudes of mind runs at a right angle to contemporary education, which is increasingly reliant on digital technologies. These provide almost magical opportunities for mental stimulation and understanding—we can delve into cells and observe living processes; we can fly through virtual models of real or imagined cities. But, magical though these experiences are, our brains remain embodied; we live in a real world, in which our senses are emissaries connecting brain and body to the external reality. We need the stimulus of the material world.

The human mind is not some otherworldly essence that comes to house itself inside our physiology. Rather, it is instilled and provoked by the sensorial field itself, induced by the tensions and participations between the human body and the animate earth. The invisible shapes of smells, rhythms of cricketsong, and the movement of shadows all, in a sense, provide the subtle body of our thoughts.

—DAVID ABRAM, *IN THE SPELL OF THE SENSUOUS*

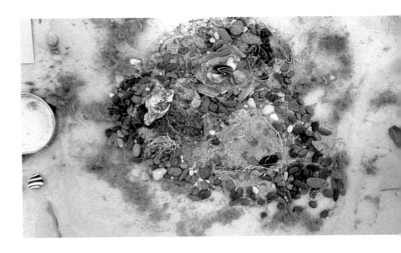

Expansions and Additions

Through years of traditional education, many participants have learned that they are not artsy. This is often due to equating art with creativity. Accordingly, if students do not consider themselves artful, they don't feel creative. Academic success often reinforces this perception. Participation is short-circuited because of the belief that one is not artistically able. Use these exercises to break out of that belief, allowing creativity to transcend learned barriers.

This exercise also goes against digital worldviews and transgresses education that is exclusively abstract and cerebral. It goes against losing touch with physical reality in day-to-day existence and affirms the senses as sources of inspiration and materiality as a touchstone for understanding. By encouraging sensory wonder, it reminds us that sensory reality is a potent source of inspiration forever at our fingertips, to be dipped into whenever our minds need refreshment and restoration. Participants, we find, are hungry and thirsty for sensory stimulation. Even boxes, tins, and jars of material trivia evoke powerful responses. How else might restoring a sense of wonder to education ignite creative attitudes of mind? Do I think, therefore I wonder, or do I wonder, therefore I think?

Paradise is not a neutral word; it is loaded with associations, most of which are positive, but not always. Association may open up fresh vistas for exploration or confine us to preconceived notions. I've used the term Garden of Eden in this exercise and found its cultural associations truncate explorations. Instructions must be rich enough to get the saliva flowing but avoid directing participants into narrow interpretations. Whether descriptions are perceived as open-ended, subtly directed, or focused will depend upon the context and the participants' biases and experiences. If we get the balance wrong initially, we can recover through midstream corrections. There's an art to making useful suggestions as creative explorations progress without becoming meddlesome. The word Islands in the exercise title seems to provide a happy focus while opening horizons of possibilities. In contrast, alternatives like beaches, mountains, or valleys seem too suggestive of "correct" responses. Islands circumscribe explorations while tickling the imagination.

The physical qualities and associations of material evoke distinct responses, so a wide variety is desirable. I've favored natural materials, but man-made materials or objects may work, though they tend to be less neutral. Try materials with different qualities and provide them in various combinations. Experiment!

As with many exercises, allowing participants to choose which materials to play with is desirable because it's a first step in buying into the exploratory process. Each material possesses unique sensory possibilities, so our choices make implicit commitments that direct explorations. Make the choosing process exciting! Emphasize the delight of discovery in opening containers—cans, boxes, jars. This is not extraneous theatrics; it sets the stage for playful engagement. Paradise island delights should inveigle all the senses but use no more than four or five materials. A groaning board from which to select is excellent, but restraint avoids overweight islands. Gluttony and creativity are immiscible.

Other exercise variables include modulating the cadence and moods of explorations. Exercises should not proceed in sterile, intimidating silence. Rules may be broken if doing so seems appropriate. As paradise islands develop, participants may be offered additional materials.

Offer suggestions, critiques, and praise but do so obliquely and suggestively rather than didactically. The goal is not to teach participants, but to encourage them to think. Anything that induces thought is legitimate. This sage advice leaves a bitter taste in my mouth, as I have ruined many excellent explorations by intrusive meddling. Experience helps us differentiate helpful suggestions from disruptive intrusions. A universal guideline: Knowing when to keep one's mouth shut is far more important than knowing when to speak. Use comments to challenge some and encourage others, but always trust participants to understand what they want to do and why they are doing it.

Exercises are infinitely malleable. Descriptions are merely starting points— the first word, not the last word in what to do. Add toppings to taste to these vanilla-flavored descriptions. Journeys may lead across rocks, but instructions are not inscribed in stone; paradise islands are not theocratically determined. The book of creativity is voluminous. It accommodates paradise archipelagoes.

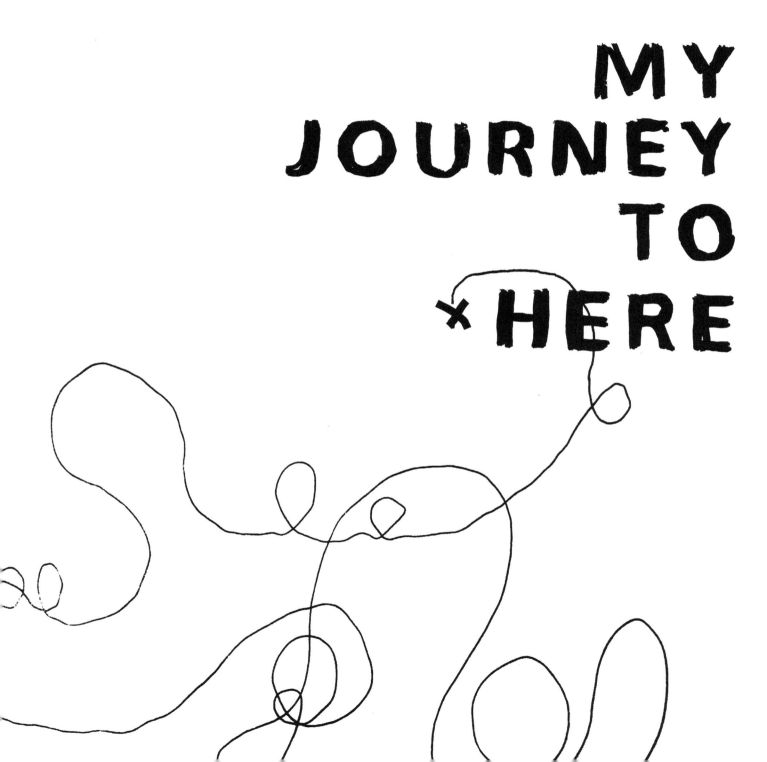

This exercise, often introduced early in a studio or course, begins with the question "How did we get here?" Answers, as we shall see, are surprisingly intriguing and revealing—the hallmarks of creative explorations. But the "how" question has corollaries: "Why have I chosen to be here?" and "How will we operate on our journey together?" We are like Chaucer's sundry band of pilgrims.

At nyght was come into that hostelrye
Wel nyne and twenty in a compaignye,
Of sondry folk, by aventure yfalle
In felaweshipe, and pilgrimes were they
alle …

We are about to embark in fellowship, on a pilgrimage; in our case, the destination is creative attitudes of mind rather than Canterbury. What better way to begin our journey than to consider how we came to be here?

Redy to wenden on my pilgrymage
To Caunterbury with ful devout corage …
That toward Caunterbury wolden ryde.

—GEOFFREY CHAUCER, *THE CANTERBURY TALES*

No doubt we assemble for our adventure with "devout courage."
Here's the project that initiates our explorations.

STUDENT INSTRUCTIONS: Project 1: Journey to Here and Now and Points Beyond

You are embarked upon a lifelong journey, education being merely a part, not apart of it—though we educators like to think of it as the vitally important booster- rocket stage, with graduation launching you into orbit. Those with creative minds see their life and work in perspective and context—AND in the immediate moment! HOW did we get here? How did I get myself into this suitable SEATUATION (or is that a seatable situation)? WHERE'S it all heading? What am I DOING here? And now? Are we here yet?

Relax. You have a stereoscopic, 3-D window seat for your journey and even some control about the terrain you pass through and the route you take—but not, perhaps, a round-trip ticket.

Avoid speeding tickets. Put your best reflection forward.

For this project, using the paper provided (or not), construct a map, chart, graph, or some sort of diagram of your journey to here. Embellish and elaborate upon the journey as an enthusiastic tour guide might do (add youphemisms as you see fit). Speculate, predict, reflect upon, and continue the diagram, describing subsequent stages of the journey. . . . Surprise yourself.

But astonishing things happen if one gives oneself over to the process of seeing again and again: aspect after aspect of the picture seems to surface, what is salient and what incidental alter bewilderingly from day to day, the larger order of the depiction breaks up, recrystallizes, fragments again, persists like an afterimage.

— T. J. CLARK, *THE SIGHT OF DEATH: AN EXPERIMENT IN ART WRITING*

Presenting ourselves to others encourages self-reflection and fosters the development of a learning community. Engagingly documenting how we came to be here begins to build participants' confidence in their creative abilities. Although commonly forgotten, there is improbable serendipity to every encounter: Here we are, "sundry folk," "fallen together" by a concatenation of choices and chances. The unlikelihood of our assembly is every bit as startling, and pregnant with possibilities, as was that of Chaucer's pilgrims assembled at Southwark's Tabard Inn.

Although the project asks participants to document how they came to be here, this assignment pointedly omits prescribing how to make these documents. Answers provide insight into where each individual came from, who we are, and where we hope to go, establishing an appropriate frame of mind for explorations of that elusive goal, our innate creativity. Individual processes and products introduce us to our fellow pilgrims and initiate us into a fellowship that will interweave competition and cooperation in ways that will, individually and collectively, strengthen our creative attitudes of mind. We will be amazed and intrigued by our stories just as, I suspect, Chaucer's pilgrims were on hearing one another's tales.

The cock crows. It's time to rise and set out, pilgrims on the road to discovery ["And made forward erly for to ryse,/ To take oure wey ther as I yow devyse "], but where, precisely, are we meant to go, and what are we meant to do? Our first pothole is the assignment, which is anything but an explicit road map. Like all exercise descriptions, it is intentionally imprecise; it hints at appropriate content, alludes to what products might be, but fails, spectacularly, to provide specific, practical guidance or conventional requirements. Unlike academia's precise and prescriptive requirements, including the specified number of pages, citations, reading requirements, report formats, et cetera, these exercises mirror the real world. They are maddeningly inexplicit. Even our subject—one's life journey to here and now and points beyond—is metaphorical rather than literal. Open-ended assignments are not prescriptions for what to do; they invite exploration and encourage personal interpretation. The assignment description requires participants to practice a foundational creative skill, the art of reading between the lines and understanding that products should be exciting, intriguing, and personally revelatory—in a word, interesting to produce and present.

What Next?

When pilgrims—sorry, participants—are smiling and animated as they present their work, you know things are going well. And why not? Exercise products are fascinating and provide insights that are unlikely to surface through conventional essays. Participants embraced the invitation wholeheartedly;

their products were diverse, inventive, imaginative, interesting, extraordinary, and individual. "Why didn't I think of that? It's SO YOU." Regardless of their brilliance and beauty, it's the process of exploration and discovery, rather than the product, that's important. Presentations, as well as products, must be imaginative and creative. As soon as participants received the assignment, ideas began to sprout, initiating irrepressible growth. Their minds had been activated and wouldn't rest until the subject had been addressed. The more interesting the assignment, the more difficult it is to put it aside for later attention. Such assignments, like Rittel and Webber's "wicked problems," "have no stopping rule." Products and participants' reflections speak for themselves .

Many reflections describe the self-doubts that projects such as this generate, but because the problem is intrinsically interesting, considerations also explain how they elicit determination to overcome individual perceived failings. Despite some reflections expressing self-deprecation, all the participants found ways to overcome self-doubt. The conclusion is clear: Invitations to develop creative attitudes of mind are irresistible when presented honestly and intriguingly. Students exhalt in the freedom that they have given themselves to explore.

Although I shall frequently suggest that creative explorations be playful, that doesn't mean the process is easy. As with all exercises, try first, reflect later. Not quite leap before you look, but leap anyway. And some find, yes indeed, developing creative attitudes of mind can be "somewhat addicting!"

WILMA L: *I'm very excited about this map project. I actually ended up accidentally skipping my next class because I holed myself up in [the library] to immediately get started on my map and lost track of time. I started thinking about what to draw as soon as the project was assigned, before I even got my sheet of paper. I was struck by the idea of a garden, with different schools representing different seasons of abundance in my life, eventually leading to the blossoming of an intelligent and self-assured young woman. [My friend] thought I should make my map in frosting on top of a cake, but I was unfortunately too busy . . . to do that. I hope to be able to do something to that effect later.*

TALYA S: *As soon as it was assigned, my mind started racing with ideas, which is something that is rare for me because I am, admittedly, a person lacking creativity. As of now I am planning to show you my journey of life through a fortune-teller. . . . I'm looking forward to beginning the Here and Now project. I have a picture in my head, but no words to go with the picture, so I need to work on that.*

ELLIE H: *I'm looking forward to creating my map . . . and challenging myself not to constrain it with the usual logic I view the world with—no geography, no chronology, maybe not even any sort of unifying theme or format.*

BRENDA S: *Typically, I function as a perfectionist, but something about this class and something about being a fifth-year senior have really opened me up to having fun and doing whatever I want with my work for this class. Don't get me wrong; every time I sat down to work on the first project, I had to fight off the temptation to fret about what my classmates or my professors would think about how my product looked. But when I let myself enjoy the process instead of focusing on the product and when I take the time to think deeply (about symbolism and metaphor especially), I surprise myself with the ideas that pop into my head. It's somewhat addicting!*

EVA K: *I wanted to wait until now to do this reflection because I was curious how I would feel after completing [it]. The idea of constructing a map of my journey to here was one that I had been asked to explore in the past, but never with the freedom of letting my imagination wander and determine the exact constructs of it all. I spent the entire week trying to figure out the format of my journey's map. The journey itself has always been the same, but this time the way I was looking at it changed. I stopped viewing it as a linear path where events simply occurred, and started to see my life's journey as an exploration and series of choices and decisions. The path I chose, I discovered and forged, opening doors as I went and leaving others unopened and unexplored…*

Seeing it all laid out in the end was striking because it cemented the belief I've always had that so many moments were pivotal in my life and without them (or had they gone differently) I would not have become the person I am today. The choices and decisions I've made and had made for me, as well as the experiences I've involuntarily encountered, have shaped and molded me into exactly who I am. That being said, my current and future experiences will determine how I change and grow and who I will become.

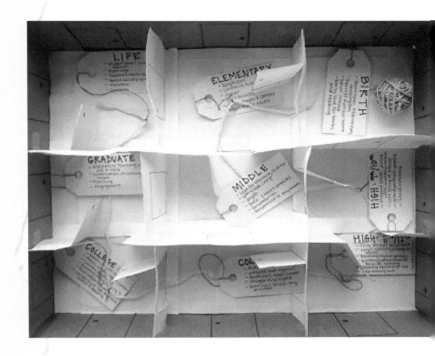

Expansions and Additions

Do we get our education from others, or do we give ourselves an education? Our explorations opt for the latter. In a murky, inexplicit way, this project description reveals our modus operandi: Our creative explorations lack conventional academic boundaries, guidelines, or paths; our journeys lack sign-posted routes, specified travel modes, and prescribed destinations. Ambiguity requires interpretation. Cultivating creativity is a risky business. Journeys extend beyond comfort zones. We are thrown back on our own resources. The work is exhilarating and addictive and anneals participants into a community of learners. Products shed light on the question of whether participants think they get or give themselves an education—they get it that they give it. In creative explorations, the instructor's function is not to convey information, and certainly NOT to give answers, but to provide space where participants may comfortably take risks, ask questions, and develop salient answers. Too often we

Our purpose isn't to learn to be creative; it's to cultivate our innate creativity; it's a drawing out, not a putting in.

doubt that IF we pose interesting and relevant questions TO intelligent students AND provide genuine latitude AND freedom to think, PLUS places conducive to explorations, THEN results will rarely disappoint us. Easier said than done, but true. Reflecting on one's life may seem unrelated to our course's purported purpose—developing creative attitudes of mind—but that's a misconception. Our purpose isn't to learn to be creative; it's to cultivate our innate creativity; it's a drawing out, not a putting in. Understanding our lives is a foundation of self-knowledge.

Time is always breathing down our necks during in-class exercises—there's no time to second-guess answers. With projects that extend over several days, time is more kindly expansive and flexible. Participants invest time, effort, and thought in projects. It is essential to provide adequate presentation time. Presentations are as crucial as products—indeed, they are often the product—so honor the time invested by participants by giving ample time to listen. The learning cycle is not complete without presentations, discussions, and individual reflections—these are central, not peripheral, to learning.

We delude ourselves if we think we can interpret products simply by looking at them. Presentations reveal wrinkles and distinctions that provide deeper insights into how participants came to be here. The richness of products' meanings requires authors' explanations. Allow participants to explain themselves and their products without interruption. Don't interpret for them; allow their voices to express their work. Unless there are good reasons to do so, don't constrain what exercises and projects can do or how participants can depict and express their explorations. How might vapid pedagogical instructions have curtailed the magnificent range of explorations shown here? It takes courage and trust for instructors to pose genuinely open-ended questions AND to accept the varied responses they evoke. Questions are open-ended only if acceptance of answers is open-ended. Avoid models of education that impose crippling restraints on explorations and thus on thought. Resist the temptation to omit reflection time and charge ahead with new explorations.

What might result if we were to invite participants to present their journeys to here in the form of narrative, poetry, dialogue, cartoons, photographs, video, blogs, maps, songs, plays, dance, mime? There's no telling what will result until participants create answers. Boundless possibilities abound. How did YOU, gentle reader, get here to this book? How does your answer hint at where your head might be heading? What pilgrimage are you on?

A final rule of thumb: When options become more open, constraints should become more rigorous, balance restraining structure and unconstraining freedom.

DIGITAL
IS AS EASY AS
FALLING OFF
ANALOG

Foreign Parts, to undertake greater Things,
oſt of his invincible Father ; At that Time
ons were making for the Exe   of theſe
          uddenly ſeized with a malignant Kind of
Small-Pox, which raging with a Violence that exceeded
human Skill, carried him off in a very few Days, to the
extream Regret of all who knew him, but more eſpecially
of his illuſtrious Parents.

AFTER his Death, his Father's Honours and Eſtates,
were, by Act of Parliament, paſſed the 21ſt of December,
1706, entailed upon his four Siſters; firſt upon their Male
iſſue, and

'Tis HE muſt draw my Sword:

HE,

Conf
of

IF I KNEW
WHAT WAS
AHEAD OF ME
I'D SCRATCH
IT.

Death
l. per
f Marlboroug   , and upon
the Death of her Grace, Henrietta, Junior Ducheſs of
Marlbo-

logy of
John L
BY Her Grace, the Ducheſs Dowager of Marlborough,
who is yet living, his Grace, John Duke of Marlborough,
had Iſſue, that

I. JOHN, Marquis of BLANDFORD, born 13 Jan.
1685-6.   (as I have already ſaid,
pag. 216. of the firſt Volume,)   the 20th of Feb. 1702-3,
univerſally lamented,

On   in King's
College Chappel,   Latin Inſcription, which
informs us, that he was born on the 13th of Jan. 1686.
and that, tho' he was amongſt the firſt in Degree
high Honours of his Parents, he was no leſs c

xvi

POETRY IS THE
ULTIMATE
ALGORITHM
YOU MISUNDERSTOOD
IT
HERE FIRST.

'Gainſt Pope
That good Cauſe, would
Had made deplorable and wretched;

of December, in the firſt yea
Reign. in Conſideration of

GRADING
IS WHERE
THE RUBRIC
MEETS THE
ROAD.

him
whe
Great Se
ſecond D

xxxii
Marlb. (D. of) com

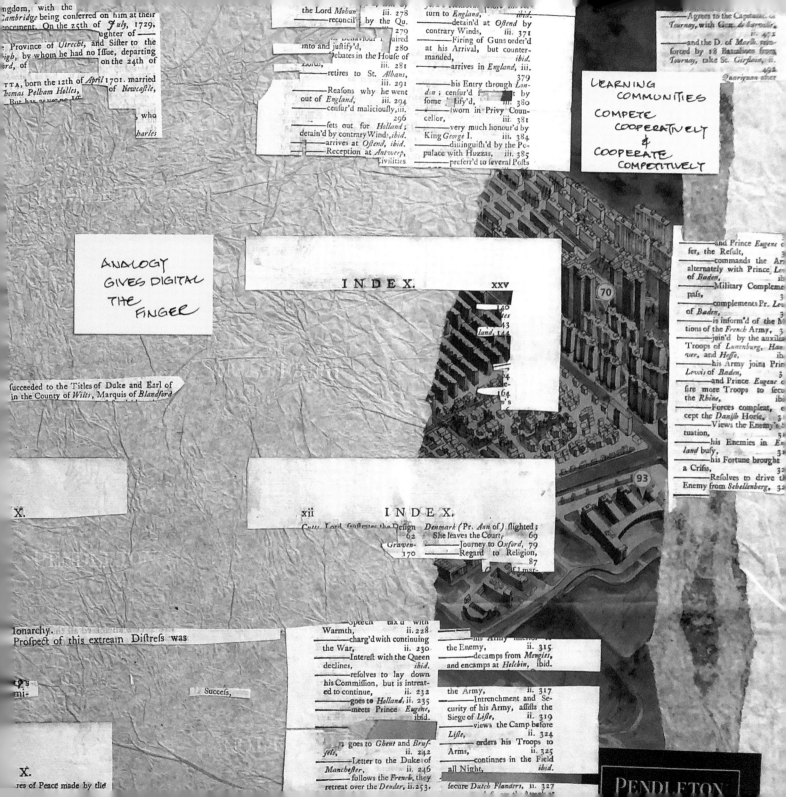

The Goal: Developing Fluid Minds

Enterprises that cannot state their goals explicitly are adrift, or so runs conventional wisdom. But perhaps the destinations, and thus the goals, of exploratory creative ventures remain necessarily elusive until discovered. Answers to open-ended questions are, by definition, unknowable when posed; they require minds that accept ambiguity to address them. Creative exercises aim to cultivate or inculcate creative attitudes of mind—a reassuringly precise but maddeningly evasive statement. In pursuit of this mirage, exercise descriptions are richly suggestive but open-ended. Ambiguity, a theme that permeates exercise methods, is a fact of life. Education should not pretend that it doesn't exist. Attempting to evade ambiguity plays into its hand.

So this discussion of methods and goals doesn't offer efficient routes to prescribed results. Quite simply, creative explorations don't take those forms. Exercises necessarily include false starts, misdirections, many beatings about the bush, and floundering in sloughs of despond. These qualities are precisely the sorts of activities and confusions that streamlined education attempts to eradicate by smoothing away inefficiencies, avoiding confusion, and burnishing efficiency so that it may transmit information competently and economically. But, just as channeling rivers destroys their underlying purposes and processes, seeking only efficient communication of information discards education's defining spirit—exploration. Supposedly efficient education is inadequate preparation for the world. The world exists beyond the ivory tower's bulwarks and battlements. The real world is a good deal more unsettling and ambiguous, and its problems are, more often than not, what Rittel and Webber called "wicked"—that is, problems that lack clear definition, prescribed methods, and correct answers. Educational "inefficiencies," characteristic of our creative explorations, are integral rather than superfluous to real education.

As unsettling as it is to traditional education models, we cannot prescribe "correct" goals and methods or chart royal roads to creative success. Exercise descriptions resemble the pronouncements of the Delphic oracle, which can be read in many ways. Why, though we lack eyes at the back of our heads, is it easier to see where we've come from than where we're going? Definitions of creativity and descriptions of goals are metaphorically explicit but literally murky. We may describe creative thought patterns as "fluid" and creative attitudes as "expansively integrative." However, like all descriptions of minds—even precise neurological ones—they are metaphorical, potently helpful, but frustratingly inexplicit.

Rigid Versus Fluid Attitudes of Mind

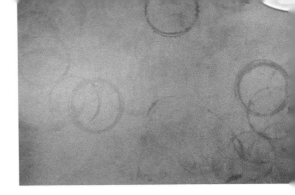

If metaphors have opposites, then the opposite of a fluid mind is, presumably, a rigid one. The latter adheres strictly to prescribed ways of thinking and won't deviate from "correct" thought patterns by assuming there is a correct answer to every question. Rigid minds despair over open-ended questions, with their inevitable logical knots and attached strings. Rigid minds, predisposed to seek "correct" answers, cannot embrace "wicked problems" that may lack answers of any sort. By contrast, what we call fluid minds or fluid mind-sets move with facility among conflicting ideas. These minds find or manufacture connections, see potentially useful patterns, look at questions from diverse and novel perspectives. They can think both metaphorically and literally. Fluid thinking is characterized by synthetic or integrative thinking. In *Designing Our Way to a Better World*, Thomas Fisher describes philosopher C. S. Peirce's distinction between deductive and inductive reasoning—methods typical of what I am calling rigid minds—and abductive reasoning, which is the method typical of fluid minds. Abductive reasoning allows us to address wicked problems creatively. We need fluid minds to develop creative solutions to combat a myriad of "wicked problems" that are affecting the planet and global populations now and will for years to come.

Those with rigid minds respond to the suggestion of fluid thinking by becoming flustered, proclaiming loudly, "This is crazy; you are destroying rationality!" Not in the least. Creative minds need to partner rigid and fluid thinking in a dance of understanding. Fluid mindsets must build on what Pasteur, in his brilliant aphorism, called a "prepared mind: "Fortune favors the prepared mind." Without preparation, fluid minds are dissolute and undisciplined. Creative explorations succeed when participants have well-trained, orderly, knowledgeable minds. Synthesis grows from solid analytical foundations. When analytical reasoning hits a brick wall and cannot proceed, thought must become fluid to integrate and synthesize. Fluid minds must know the rules and when and how to break them. Abductive reasoning synthesizes solutions. It leaps to conclusions inaccessible to deductive and inductive reasoning. Addressing dilemmas, fluid attitudes of mind don't search for the "right" solution, but may devise or invent reasonable solutions.

Developing fluid minds differs from training minds to be structured and analytic. Indeed, fluid thinking cannot be taught didactically. It can, however, be drawn out, cultivated, fostered, and encouraged. Its methods are less explicit but no less logical and disciplined. Rather than suggesting there is a correct way to teach creativity, these exercises provide a medley of methods to modify, adapt, transform, or discard ideas as circumstances and predilections suggest. Do not follow them literally and apply them slavishly. Generate environments conducive to exploration, and fluidity of mind will flourish. To make participants physically, mentally, and socially comfortable, foster communities of learners. Contemporary higher education focuses on developing rational, logical, analytic thought patterns at the expense of other forms of understanding. Too often it forgets creativity's fluid dance partner—metaphoric, integrative, and synthetic thinking that utilizes abductive reasoning and is adept at imagining, inventing, and leaping to viable solutions.

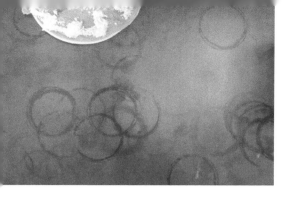

The Play's the Thing King

Are you sitting comfortably? Then I'll begin. The attitudes of mind and ways of thinking that we characterize as creative, fluid, and synthetic are best acquired through exploratory play, and only when we are comfortable can we play. In terms of fostering creativity, the question is, how can we effectively set the stage for play? Let's think of synthesis as a flowering of analytic thought and creative thinking as an emergent property of prepared minds. We imagine teaching and learning approaches that differ from those used to teach analytical thinking. Our creativity exercises aspire to loosen minds and encourage them to be more fluid. Thus they pose questions in ways that preclude—as far as possible—adopting logical ways of thinking to solve them. Paradox, ambiguity, and metaphor are our allies; puns, double entendres, and allusions litter our communication; physical activities and materials supplant the primacy of language and mental thought. These methods attempt to create playful conditions that foster synthesis, which may be described, metaphorically, as a flash of insight, a leap to understanding, a eureka moment.

Methods remain exploratory; they are not fully developed techniques, nor are they described in an order dictated by an overarching conceptual model. Instead, these exercises exhibit an assortment of ideas and possibilities, groping their way toward clarity, coherence, meaning, and understanding. Like life, they are a work in progress. It must be confessed that, during their development, ideas for activities typically preceded a clear understanding of purposes. What to do preceded "Why do it?" or "What's it for?" Ideas percolated up over the years and were pieced together and adjusted in "Let's try this" or "I wonder what would happen if" processes. None of our methods arose, like Venus from the foam, pure and perfectly formed; ideas were generated using abductive reasoning.

The Shape of Creative Attitudes of Mind

To rational minds, these descriptions of our goals and methods for exploring and cultivating creativity seem like smoke and mirrors, vain hand waving with concomitant looseness of words and thoughts, but that is precisely the point. Creative explorations must loosen the viselike grip of thoughts. Perhaps, in these explorations, replicate what happens at that moment we pass from consciousness to sleep, succumb to the influence of chemicals on the brain, lose ourselves in meditation, exhaust ourselves physically, or daydream? We rest the conscious mind and allow that incomprehensible tangle of neural circuits to do their sorting and unsorting work unmolested by conscious directives. Is this original? Not at all. It's the same old innovation all over again. Poets have been rhyming it. Songwriters have crooned it; authors have rolled it out in angst-ridden or delight-filled prose, while artists have dabbed it in pigments.

Meanwhile, educators have been laying out innovation in rubrics (alas, poor rubric, I knew hymn well), while mystics have expressed it loudly in the silence. In other venues, psychologists have been mouthing it in the gluts of a polysyllabic polyglot. New on the scene, neuroscientists with powerful tools to plot and attempt to explain fluid, creative, and innovative thinking have captured it on MRI scans. If we may call them such, our methods are but play and exploration peppered with a pinch of mental confusion to knock rational thinking off its perch at the mind's controls. It's surprising where we arrive if we allow a fluid mind to occupy the driver's seat, even if only momentarily—creativity undermines rationality.

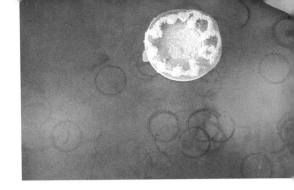

What should education's priorities be in the information age? More of the same, but faster? Further additions to the glut of information that swamps our thinking? Perhaps there's an alternative; might we focus on integrating understanding, using abduction to encourage synthetic thinking to blossom, and perfume education as the night-blooming cereus does the midnight air? Might we seek ways to cultivate creativity in individuals, social groups, and throughout society? Might education aspire to generate a more creative culture? Might education allow our minds more latitude to play, to extemporize, to explore, and to do so in expansive, unconstrained freedom unsandwiched between top-down, bottom-line thinking? Doing so, I believe, we shall be surprised by the connections that prepared minds will make and the results of those connections. We might, with profit—but without an eye to the bottom line—loosen up and allow our minds to become more free and fluid. Focusing exclusively on the bottom line employs the same old innovation all over a gain.

What Is Education For?

There's more for education to hope and strive for—to aspire to—than adding more information to already encumbered minds in the hope that more knowledge will make us more productive workers in a more efficient economy. Creative explorations don't aspire to supplant rigorous thinking and knowledge generation; they have a broader goal: to allow creative attitudes of mind to flower on top of these substrates. Education doesn't exist in a vacuum, nor do creative explorations. Participants have been thoroughly socialized, deeply acculturated, and highly educated. With hope, like Dante, they find themselves lost in the woods; students may have other resources from which to draw than a single GPS program depicting only the straight and narrow. Creativity exercises are shortcuts around linear thinking; they oppose reductionist thinking's fragmentation of knowledge—fragments increasingly isolated in the physical and curricular

structures of institutions of higher learning. Such activities seek emergent understanding to complement rather than supplant rational thinking, to take the reins when those modes of thinking reach dead ends. They try to connect the hitherto unconnected. Induce synthetic thinking to punch wholes in rational mind-sets. These goals may sound peculiar, irrational, and silly—possibly even self-defeating. As routes to education, they may appear circuitous or tangential rather than focused, logical, and direct. But, of necessity, the methods for creative explorations are evasive, allusive, and suggestive—hints, not directives. Like abduction, their explanations follow rather than precede conclusions. In time, solutions get around to justifying their genesis. The goal is to reach, develop, or cultivate mental states that are open, fluid, curious, and creative.

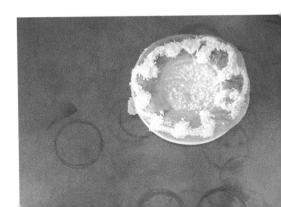

OUT, OUT
DAMNED
EXTRA

iPod
nano

AIRPORT LIMO (M) SDN. BHD.
www.almcabs.com
1 300 88 8989
PLEASE PROCEED TO DOOR 5
RM 85.50
PREMIER (Midnight surcharge not included)
Cash   From KLIA to ZONE 407
Single
              PUCHONG PRIMA
DATE PURCHASED: 54009757018
27-Jan-13 18:10
Midnight surcharge if applicable = RM41
VALID TILL:27-Feb-13   2799
PRINTED BY:AZIZAH

NA
GALLER

P
&
B

 nationalgalleries.org

GET 1 TRITE

CITY GRIND
Food & coffee from
local businesses.
in Henry Art Gallery

FREE!

EDINBURGH
CASTLE

www.edinburghcastle.scot

F
S
S
M
P

PAL

ka

Kinloch Anderson
SCOTLAND

Kinloch Anderson
SCOTLAND
Foremost experts in Highland Dress since 1868

EDUCATION =
INTENTION
IN
TENSION

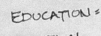

Your Receipt

SEP 2012

RT

urgh

by Tate Britain

1.20

By appointment to
Her Majesty The Queen
Tailors and Kiltmakers
Kinloch Anderson Ltd

By appointment to
H.R.H. The Duke of Edinburgh
Tailors and Kiltmakers
Kinloch Anderson Ltd

By appointment to
H.R.H. The Prince of Wales
Tailors and Kiltmakers
Kinloch Anderson Ltd

Kinloch Anderson
SCOTLAND

IT CAN BE AN
UPHILL
STRUGGEL
TO GET THE
BALL ROLLING

- Plays music and photo slideshows
- Up to 14 hours of music playback with rechargeable lithium-ion battery*
- Includes iPod nano, earphones, USB 2.0 cable, and iTunes for Mac and Windows
- Requires Mac or PC with USB port (USB 2.0 recommended); Mac OS X v10.3.4 or later, Windows 2000 (SP4), or Windows XP Home or Professional (SP2); and iTunes 4.9 or later

*1GB=1 billion bytes; actual formatted capacity less. Capacity based on 4 minutes per song and 128-Kbps AAC encoding. *Rechargeable batteries have a limited number of charge cycles and may eventually need to be replaced. Battery life and number of charge cycles vary by use and settings. See www.apple.com/batteries. Use is subject to acceptance of included software license.

MA107LL/A   iPod nano 4GB
Designed by Apple in California
Assembled in China   Model No. A111
(S)Serial No. YM552CCFTK3
(1P)Part No. MA107LL/A

626-7327-A

Commercial Street/Dock Street, Leith, Edinburgh, EH6 6EY, Scotland
Office: Tel: +44(0)131 555 1355 Fax: +44(0)131 555 1392, e-mail: enquiries@kinlochanderson.com
Shop: Tel: +44(0)131 555 1390 Fax: +44(0)131 555 1392, e-mail: theshop@kinlochanderson.com
www.kinlochanderson.com

Scottish Character

VAT No. G   23423062

urgh Airport
here Scotland meets the world

The Edinburgh Airport
App has arrived!

SM62GYT

1/1024   8952/055519301/002707
17:04   06/07/18   SS ENTRY 4
          Terminal Parking

0% 2.42
0 114
/18 20:03   ← 007702

mobile then follow the prompts to get started
and find out how many minutes, TXTs and how
much data you get in this pack.

Your Prepay Smart25 Add-On is now active.

3. Get an extra credit of $10 when you register
    online and complete your online profile for the
    first time at vodafone.co.nz/myaccount

Your Prepay Smart25 Add-On lasts one calendar month and will automatically
renew each month. Just make sure you have enough credit on the date when your
Prepay Smart25 Add-On is due to renew.

You can manage your Prepay Smart25 Add-On at any time through
vodafone.co.nz/myaccount

To use other services that are not included in Prepay Smart25 (eg. voicemail and
international TXT) you will need to top up.

For more information and support see vodafone.co.nz/prepay

PREPAY
SMART 25

Your Add-On
includes minu
TXTs and d

A

We're   if you need us:
Online   afone.co.nz
Mobile   777 from your vodafone mobile or call 0800 800 021 from your landline.
Instore

For stan   repay terms & conditions, see vodafone.co.nz/about/legal-stuff

CIRCULAR
LOGIC =
BOXED IN BY
MY BOX

proud to be associated with these
communities, helping to sustain their
livelihoods and grow their future

ed Gourmet Estate Teas are freshly
ed from boutique farms in the tiny,
ue isle of Sri Lanka. Farms that have
prospered from the labours of local farmers for
generations, it is in their dedication,
commitment and knowledge that brings
out the best in the leaf

The Gourmet Estate Tea
ETHICALLY RESPONSIBLE TEA

Royal
Ceylon Tea

PAY
INTENTION

3 Drinks

Aprisecco
2cl apricot liqueur
over ice-cubes
top up with sparkling wine

Apriziro
3cl apricot liqueur
3cl lemon juice
3cl orange juice
over ice-cubes, stir

Apritron
4cl apricot liqueur
2cl lime juice
over ice-cubes
top up with lemonade

YOU CAN'T LEARN
from
EXPERIENCE
if
YOU DON'T TRY
FIRST

University
Book Store

4326 University Way NE
Seattle, WA 98105
206.634.3400

www.ubookstore.com

WS 57 Opr 54850
9/06/2018 03:02:43 PM   #115

Now Playing
3 of 14
Just Feel Better
Santana
All That I Am
3:30   -0:55

iPod
nano

MENU

Place a bunch of stuff in front of a pair of hands—in the dust, on a table, or on a computer screen. It doesn't matter where stuff is placed. Add a mind with time on its hands and observe the result. The temptation to sort, arrange, or organize things proves irresistible. Humans sort, so this exercise explores sorting. It's an activity, a habit of mind—and hands—so pervasive that it underpins all thinking, all communication, all behavior. Do I think, therefore I sort, or do I sort, therefore I think? Like many exercises, sorting favors physical action over abstract thinking, a sleight of hand that cuts creative thought loose from the domineering mind while engaging in a seemingly trivial activity. Physical sorting may help us sort ideas in our heads.

This exercise uses diverse collections of objects and a bland invitation: "Sort the stuff," but the instructions' omissions are as significant as what they include. They don't prescribe how to sort, nor do they offer criteria for sorting or for judging results. They simply provide collections of objects and leave participants to sort them as they see fit, or as they fit, see? Although instructions don't explain the whys, hows, or what ways objects should be sorted, participants rarely need further prompts.

The sorting propensity pervades thoughts and actions. Indeed, whether we are aware of it or not, our minds are busy sorting throughout our waking hours and possibly in our sleep. Sorting underpins the processes we use to navigate and make sense of the world. What does this all mean?

We sort for many reasons: to seek order, to impose neatness, and to create or draw out meaning. Sorting arranges and connects us to the world around us and imparts a semblance of control over it. Sorting is allied with the habit of finding, or making, patterns. It's a habit that may be employed to foster creative thought. This exercise prompts us to become conscious of our sorting and classifying habits on the assumption that the more aware we are of how our minds work, the more able we are to use our minds creatively.

To prevent sorties into sorting from becoming ponderous, provide engaging collections of objects, and encourage playful attitudes of mind. Offer a wide range of items; materials should be abundant and varied. Collections of stuff should be diverse, so that each one engages us differently. They may

Sorting is allied with the habit of finding, or making, patterns. It's a habit that may be employed to foster creative thought.

include many or few objects, but not too many or too few. Items in some collections may be similar; in others, diverse. Some objects may be common, everyday things; others, obscure arcana. They may range from interesting to banal, from valuable to junk. Collections may include natural and human-made objects. Fundamentally, they should defy easy or "correct" answers and engage the mind in different ways. Like all of our exercises—and life—sorting is an exploration. Scrupulously avoid suggesting right and wrong ways to sort. Scant instructions encourage unencumbered and unscripted inquiries; let the materials provide the prompts.

Collections should evoke intrigue, excitement, and interest. Styrofoam packaging pellets, even in vast quantities, are unsuitable. Why so sure? Been there, done that. Easy manipulability is desirable, but there is a world of difference between exercises that work with malleable materials, like modeling clay, and this exercise, which promotes the sorting of discrete, unchanging objects.

If possible, place each collection on its own table and allow participants to move freely from one to another as their interests dictate. Foster student intrigue by placing boxes, tins, jars, et cetera, with the collections hidden from view on tables. This invites participants to open them to reveal their contents. Sorting quickly becomes playful, an effective learning method for creative activities, and a crucial attitude of mind for creative thought. The exercise is a Trojan horse, not for teaching Greek, but for introducing play into austerely abstract academies or buttoned-down business bureaus.

The exercise's product is its process; we reach its goal along the way, not at its end. Our purpose is to explore the sorting habit, not to produce final arrangements of objects. Discussions are crucial to success; arrange furniture to encourage movement from one collection to another to increase casual interactions and to provoke incidental conversation. Interactions can happen even at large tables, but they require more significant mental effort than bumping into fellow participants. If in doubt, consult party planners or casino operators about how room layouts may prompt social interactions.

As the exercise progresses, it, like life, acquires new wrinkles. Instead of a box or a pile of objects, participants encounter prior arrangements, patterns, orderings to consider. Should

SAM C: *Why do we sort things? Many people did this when we opened the boxes of random objects . . . but the answer to this question was never really sorted out. The activity reminded me of when I was much younger. I used to become engrossed in sorting my stuffed animals or toy car collections for long periods of time, and it never occurred to me why I did this. If it's been with me for that long (at least since I was four or five years old), it doesn't seem like it's something I've obtained through education. It seems like the brain just loves to make connections, and I probably subconsciously sort many other things that I experience every day. This also makes me think of computer science, which is largely composed of sorting objects into data structures. I wonder what kind of sorting model is wired into our brains for us to make such abstract connections.*

MAN RAY: *I personally really like the taxonomical exercise of sorting and resorting the objects, not so much because it tested me or made me feel creative, but, rather, because sorting and categorizing things is something I do to calm myself. With that in mind, it did allow me to think about my sorting practices at a different level. When I approached most tables, the objects had been sorted in one way or another. First, I looked at them and tried to decode the rules by which they were sorted. Then I sorted them based on my personal preferences, and how I thought they "should" be sorted. It was interesting to see the different approaches to the sets of objects and how they were treated by myself and others. It would have been interesting to compare how I sorted the*

objects and my background as a person to other people in the class, rather than simply looking at the sorted piles as manifestations of anonymous classmates' sorting techniques.

JULIANA Y: *The "sorting" exercise was maybe an exercise in classifying objects, but don't we do the same with people, as well? For example, despite all of the superficial differences in the box of shells, they were all seashells, serving the same purpose. Despite the initial similarity of the rocks in the next box, upon looking closer you could see that they weren't identical at all; in fact, they all had idiosyncrasies of their own and no two were the same. It's up to us either to look closer or stop looking so closely. We are all distinct, yet strikingly similar. It's a beautifully ambiguous duality that can help us manage the world around us, but at the same time cause irreparable harm. Classification, for this reason, may not be a very good reflex at all—the constant need to separate and to divide groups of people, to amplify and to even arbitrarily fabricate differences among us—it does nothing but separate us from our commonality as human beings. . . . It's bitterly saddening how many laws, at their core, are based solely on the superficial differences of skin color, of gender, of race. Our Constitution is much more aspirational than it is an actual portrayal of reality; rather, it's up to society to step away from this unforgiving need to classify everyone around us. But I digress.*

we keep, modify, or sweep past arrangements away without a moment's thought or regret? Whether to reformulate or not reformulate? Aye, that is the question. Arrangements are ephemeral. One hand plays the role of Brahma, the creator; the other, Shiva, the destroyer.

Not surprisingly, the more intrinsically exciting and diverse the objects are, the longer they hold our attention and the more different possibilities they offer. Huge collections of postage stamps or coins may retain our interest for an hour—or a lifetime—but a collection of similar leaves will be dismissed after a brief visit. Once plastic cutlery has been arranged in conventional place settings, it provides little food for thought. We invest more time and thought in sorting intrinsically valuable objects than cheap, throwaway plastic objects. How do values influence how we sort?

After a time, sorting ceases to be interesting and becomes drudgery. If you reach that point, you've gone too far—shorten the exercise time. Sorting frequently devolves into play, which may or may not enhance sorting explorations. Purposeful play? Dilatory play? Evasive play? Instructors must judge when the exercise ceases to be useful.

What did participants think of sorting exercises, and what kinds of connections did they make? The answers are as varied as

the participants. Cultural biases and perspectives also affect how we see and sort. Different approaches to sorting vividly and intriguingly illustrate how a simple sorting exercise may be performed in a myriad of ways. Perhaps only graduate psychology students would think of using a collection of coins to conduct a psychological experiment, exploring the effect on the perception of moving one coin out of place in a series of relative shininess.

We are always inventing classification systems to cope with the situations we confront in our lives. Many are ambiguous or ill-defined, and to live orderly lives, we must control them mentally and physically.

What does sorting mean? It seems to be an innate human habit that enables us to understand, order, control, and engage with the world. We sort material objects and, by extension, we sort ideas, knowledge, and information. Our desire to discover nature's laws, write elegant code, create the orderly layout of cities, and develop social and legal rules of conduct manifest this habit. Sorting and classifying go hand in the brain with thinking. Although this exercise is simple to conduct, its consequences may be profound. This exercise makes us more conscious of our tendencies to sort; it may open up possibilities for cultivating creative patterns of thought and action.

Expansions and Additions

The exercise is infinitely adaptable. We can change the materials and the numbers of objects in collections and the number of collections. We can change the familiarity, variety, intrinsic interest, and value of items. We can alter the commonalities and randomness of objects. Materials may be tailored to suit different audiences. Easily transported collections may consist of small, lightweight, and mobile items. The only unbreakable rule: Objects must be real. Resist the temptation to use items with words on them. Materiality matters; words warp.

We may also change instructions and the pace of the exercise. Following an initial round of sorting, we might invite participants to sort by using criteria such as scientific classification, hierarchy, metaphor, storytelling, or characteristic features. Each prompt warps our mental playing field differently. Suggesting that sorting should, for example, focus on similarities and differences will evoke very different responses than suggesting objects be

We are always inventing classification systems to cope with the situations we confront in our lives.

sorted to tell a story. Subtle or overt differences in the exercises can significantly affect responses. What might happen if, instead of providing a generic sorting instruction, we ask some participants to sort literally and others metaphorically? Might the results facilitate discussions of scientific classification systems and Lakoff and Johnson's proposition that all language—and thus all thought—is metaphorical? When scientists play with the data, they tease out understanding from facts by using different sorts of sorting.

Learning
Communities

Effective Learning Communities

The pedagogy and psychology of learning communities, in many educational attributes and contexts, is well documented. This chapter summarizes the power of learning communities to cultivate creative explorations. This community-focused environment is essential to the exercises described in this book, as many activities occur in groups. Learning groups appear to be most successful when participants are members of close-knit, mutually supportive groups, or communities of learners. Supportive learning communities create strong foundational social dynamics to cultivate creativity.

The trope of the "lone genius" springs up perennially in descriptions of creative discoveries. It contains an element of truth, but an iceberg is a better metaphor when considering an individual's brilliance. Less than 10 percent of an iceberg's mass is visible above water; its bulk lies in a communal ocean. All of us, as well as being creative individuals, are products of culture and society. Those who claim to be self-made" are, more often than not, ignorant, forgetful, or duplicitous.

To foster innovative thinking at its highest potential, how do we develop supportive learning communities for creative explorations? How do we generate environments where participants interact comfortably—sometimes cooperatively, sometimes competitively, but always in mutually supportive ways? How do we work together in pursuit of that elusive goal, creativity?

Based on my experiences teaching creative courses, a solid foundation to build learning communities relies on mutual trust. Thriving communities possess a dynamic tension that allows groups to flourish individually and collectively based on mutual trust. Trust is built among students by providing an unwavering belief that they, and their peers, can undoubtedly be creatively brilliant.

Size Matters and the Matter of Size

How large should learning communities be? Experience suggests that ten participants are too small, twenty-five too large, while from twelve to eighteen seems ideal. Lest these numbers sound firmly authoritative, let me garnish their qualifications. Many other factors than size are influential, including each participant's quality and commitment, developing shared experiences or mutual familiarity, contextual support, and time. Successful communities are sustained by positive interactions over time. One cannot be definitive about what size is best. The number of instructors also affects the size of effective communities. Two instructors can be more effective by providing alternate perspectives and experiences than one. However, three instructors may provide too many competing voices. Two instructors might increase the size of effective groups to between eighteen and twenty-four.

Although creative explorations are usually—though not always—enhanced by participation in groups, the group's size is less significant than the quality of interactions. Supportive interactions tend to be competitively collaborative and collaboratively competitive—a dynamic balance that is simultaneously supportive and challenging. It's difficult, and perhaps futile, to be definitive about appropriate or successful classroom/learning contexts. Community interactions, pedagogic methods, and education goals are inextricably connected—parts of an integrated whole. Too much differentiation may disintegrate understanding.

Do We Think to Do or Do to Think?

Your education belongs to you. Participants in thriving learning communities feel comfortable asking questions, questioning answers, and questioning questions—that is, challenging the presumptions and premises of exercise questions. Here's the conundrum: To engage successfully in creativity exercises, participants must have creative attitudes of mind and interact in a creative spirit. Asking which comes first is to misunderstand that each cultivates the other in positive feedback loops. To generate creative attitudes of mind in well-educated participants, a good deal of deconstructivist dismantling and constructivist building must occur.

The sound of hammering, both taking apart and putting together, reverberates metaphorically throughout creative classrooms. Learning environments should produce the sound of unintimidated and unmediated staccato music. Participants should be encouraged to voice their opinions freely and question one another's—and the instructor's—arguments. These are the noises of participants actively engaged in the craft of creative explorations. These pedagogical techniques come from

design studio explorations that encourage doing and active engagement, a modus operandi.

Generate contexts conducive to open, fluid, and searching interactions and explorations. Create places where participants feel unconstrained and can work freely together with materials, with ideas, with contexts, indeed with their minds. Each participant in a thriving learning community invests sweat equity and expects the same from the other participants. They trust themselves, one another, and their instructors. Students are comfortable playing different roles exploring leadership, being a team member, and, on occasion, being the outsider.

Participants in engaged learning communities recognize that their education belongs to them. They are responsible for obtaining, rather than receiving, an education. This responsibility determines how they interact with one another. We must strive to empower active participants rather than passive recipients.

Stage Set and Match

Setting the stage and developing creative learning communities requires a delicate balance under the best of conditions. It is rendered even more challenging because we don't want to reveal too many details of what we will be doing. An element of surprise is a crucial attribute of creative explorations. There's little authenticity in familiar territory. A delicate balance should be sought in creating openness, generating trust, secrecy, and ensuring that investigations are fresh and unpremeditated. Painting "No Admittance" on the class gate, or syllabus, is unprofitable. Still, some sort of cautionary welcome is necessary to ensure that those who pass the gate are alerted that they are expected to behave, think, and act differently from the way they would in "normal" classrooms. These cautions are neither "trigger warnings" nor "spoiler alerts," two odious contemporary clichéd euphemisms. Considerable unlearning and undoing of the doings and learnings of prior passive education is required. On the instructor's part, unlearning entails having greater faith in participants. Such are the foundations of active, engaged, collaborative learning communities.

Education, therefore, is a process of living and not a preparation for future living.

—JOHN DEWEY

Box Talks

One can't take more than a couple of creative inhalations without coughing up the phrase "think outside the box." The box—in which each of us resides comfortably boxed in—is our comfort zone. Creative learning communities have to become comfortable, trusting groups of explorers so that participants can, with trust, if not comfort, step outside their comfort zones. The same applies to instructors. In creative explorations, all comfort zones are on the chopping block. Thinking and doing outside comfort zones is challenging. Activities during the first few days of building successful learning communities should help participants become comfortable extending tentacles beyond their comfort zones. This requires some finesse. How does one make participants comfortable with uncertainty, ambiguity, and confusion? How can the start be a positive ferment rather than a disorienting frustration? And how can instructors become comfortable with not being fully in control?

Lulled by Syllabi

The syllabi of well-ordered courses set unequivocal and specific expectations for what participants will do and learn, when they will learn it, and why it's essential. These syllabi are also clear about how participants will be tested; they aim to minimize doubts and avoid misinterpretations. Creative explorations

are not like that. Creativity explorations don't predict the destination of learning objectives. Creative explorations follow different patterns and end up where they do, not where they are told to go by a syllabus. Students should start with fuzzy course descriptions and goals that require more trust, faith, hope—and charity—than conventional courses do. Of necessity, creative explorations are risky business. Surprisingly, over time understanding creeps in and silently transforms participants. Realizations arrive without participants' realizing it. Despite the ambiguity, creative explorations do not lack goals and learning objectives. Out of necessity, these grow out of learning subjectives, not objectives. Effective syllabi convincingly croon, "I'll get to that later; be patient, and you'll catch the cure." They also hedge their bets, whispering, "For further obfuscatory explanations, reread the course syllabus."

Environments Conducive to Conversation

Field trips are education's equivalent of Monopoly's Get Out of Jail Free cards. They impart freedom and enormous opportunities for cultivating creativity. They are sanctioned excuses to leave classrooms and promise—or at least hint at—possibilities for fresh and inspiring experiences. They may take us to times and places where opportunities that bypass classrooms come knocking. Even the prospect of a field trip induces thoughts of freedom. They may be touch papers that ignite creativity. Field trips don't replace other academic activities; they are contrasts that complement classroom explorations. Advocating for field trips is not a paean to truancy; rather, it recognizes the necessity of periodically disrupting routines, getting off track so that we might get back on track. Trips outside of the classroom acknowledge the value of breaking routines to give the mind a longe leash, provide white space, and survey larger horizons.

Field trips are breaks that complement and often complete the work of educational routines. They are the necessary get-away-from-it-all breaks that allow our unencumbered minds to sort it all out. They provide venues for synthesis that no amount of analytical footwork in classrooms can provide. Field trips

recognize the necessity of working hard and then taking breaks. Field trips are hardly a new idea; they are a commonplace idea that we readily advocate for others but, more often than not, chose to ignore in our own lives. Field trips are a medicine we mean to take as soon as we feel up to it. We most need the restorative benefits of field trips precisely when we don't have time for them.

Field trips must be real and physical; virtual reality is no substitute. Senses can stimulate creative thoughts and ideas that are inaccessible to mental stimulation alone. For minds and senses that crave big data, take a field trip outside to encounter an array of physical, perceptual, and psychological experiences that may induce creative attitudes of mind. Getting out of the classroom promotes lifelong learning, which means everywhere learning. It need not wait until we graduate to begin.

Unsure if field trips are necessary to cultivate creativity? Don't take my word for it; here's what students said (following page).

MAN RAY: *Sitting in Trabant discussing everything from worldly travels to siblings and hometowns, I was at ease. Our conversation flowed freely, drifting from topic to topic without any worry of becoming too engrossed with our discussion and ignoring the task at hand—perhaps because the task at hand was to become engrossed in our discussion. It reminded me, in a way, of the discussions we had in class. At first, class discussions always feel a little rigid, but once the momentum picks up, the conversation is unstoppable. At the coffee shop, the conversation started down a steep slope, growing faster and faster, naturally flowing between topics and keeping me constantly engaged. In retrospect, rereading my brief notes of [words] such as conversational and sibling, they ignite a fire in my mind, reminding me of the many topics and ideas we discussed. I feel like, after [the visit], I grew so much closer to my three peers in a way that the classroom, with its rigid rules, didn't allow. Thank you for allowing us this opportunity.*

SAVANNA G: *I honestly thought two hours was going to be way too long to talk without the long, awkward pauses, but in reality our time at the coffee shop flew by. Free-flowing conversations like the one we were able to have are all about creativity, taking topics and connecting them together through common stories, experiences, ideas, thoughts. It's great when you can look back on conversations and go back through all the different topics that got you to where you ended up. I do think it's necessary to have some level of common interests or views for these types of random connections to be made, but it's crazy how small those levels sometimes need to be...*

This type of conversation doesn't happen all the time, but relaxing at a coffee shop with classmates is definitely conducive to it. Now the question is, what about that particular situation makes us be able to let go of what's right and just chat? For me, it's the fact that there are no expectations to try to live up to. There is no right or wrong in a coffee shop. No one is watching and expecting laughter or tears or mind-blowing intellect. Classrooms, on the other hand, are slightly different. Although classrooms don't stop the flow of any possible creative conversation, they do certainly make them feel slightly more difficult. Classrooms mean something very particular to everyone who has made their way to college. We have all spent enough hours glued to our chairs to know what's generally expected of us when we are let loose to converse. If we follow these expectations or not is another matter, but their presence creates an obstacle the mind has to puncture before truly allowing for the full range of creative flow. It's really hard to undo what we have been taught for all of our lives, and therefore when we sit in the classroom, we are students, and in general, we will be making some sort of effort to follow what we think is right.

COFFEE CUP-SLEEVE ADVERTISING

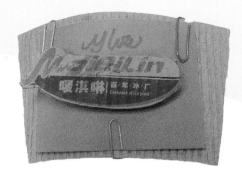

If there were a rule for judging the effectiveness of creativity exercises—which, of course, there isn't—it would be "the simpler, the better." Simple materials, simple instructions, simple ambiguities. And if this nonrule were to be applied to exercises, then the coffee cup–sleeve advertising exercise would excel. It's simple, straightforward, and generates appealing products. An added bonus, it uses common, cheap, everyday materials—coffee-cup sleeves—products whose ubiquity and utility ensure our obliviousness. The exercise involves taking sleeves, tearing them open at their seams, turning them inside out, and using revealed surfaces as places to advertise oneself. What better topic to promote than ourselves? The exercise is a continuation of introducing ourselves to learning community members and, by extension, to the broader world. This is me! I'm here! Pay attention!

Advertising on coffee-cup sleeves is hardly an original idea; indeed, it's hard to find sleeves without advertising emblazoned across their surfaces. Our innovation is to turn the concept inside out. Tweaking a commonplace idea to serve a modified end is a gambit common to creative thinking. Fresh work surfaces present participants with a perennial question: How do I wish to portray myself to others? Such projections torque the ancient Greek admonition "Know thyself."

Providing choice is always an encouraging starting point. Invite participants to select sleeves from a diverse collection. Tearing the sleeves open to reveal fresh surfaces uncovers questions: What IS this exercise about? What AM I meant to be doing? What is the "right" answer or approach? Pens, markers, knives, and scissors are readily available to encourage modification of

Quick first passes at the challenge acclimate participants to activities and reveal problems.

the sleeves. Work typically begins slowly; self-promotion is an alien and confusing idea. Confidence grows as participants chat. Do I chat, therefore I think, or do I think, therefore I chat?

A good strategy for maintaining excitement is to stop before participants finish, so they can inspect one another's work and draw ideas and inspiration from their peers. As mentioned, it's okay to copy an idea, so long as one improves it!

Quick first passes at the challenge acclimate participants to activities and reveal problems. The first sleeves made it apparent that markers and pencils were ineffective on dark brown dimpled surfaces. Accordingly, students substituted colored card stock and continued. The second round proceeded more slowly and deliberately, but having reviewed one another's work bolstered confidence, and participants explored ideas more freely.

One participant capitalized on the sleeve's circular continuity by wrapping her figure around it, upraised hands catching falling feet: "I am falling, am I?" Another student's sleeve contained punch-out pieces to be assembled into a building. Inserting a cup into a green sleeve precipitated a contrasting red fringe—a functional action activating its message. A sleeve, made by a woman with small hands, responded to how sleeves are held. A small hand, with finger extensions for larger hands, gripped

the sleeve: "Small size, big power." One participant's second sleeve completed his first iteration of a face, with a tree added overhead: "I read in the forest. My mind is flying." By ignoring practical constraints, participants can generate an enormous diversity of approaches. The possibilities are limitless when creative minds are unleashed. The grim reaper of practicality will, in time, cull excessive and unrealistic approaches.

Minds released from constraints are free to make innovative breakthroughs and ridiculous mistakes. Creative explorations are risky business, but mistakes made early in the process can lead to fresh approaches and insights. Silicon Valley's mantra, "Fail fast, fail often," applies to this line of thinking. Downplaying traditional sleeve functions resulted in a flowering of creative interpretations.

ANON: *In my eyes, this course is really interesting and incredible, and I never took a course like this before. In this course, I tried something that I'd never done. The tasks you assigned every time made me confused at first, but I could work it out in the end by using my own idea. So I find that there's no "right" answer for every question. What you need is your own answer and exploring your own mind. What's more, by watching others' presentations, I see the flames on others' minds. And being questioned by others, I learn to express my idea to them. Little by little, I learn that if you want to be creative, you need to be unique and stick to your own idea at first.*

Results ranged from inspiring to inappropriate; the line between brilliance and ridiculousness is slender and mutable. Whether products are practical or not isn't the point of the exercise. What matters is learning to look at situations in ways that encourage creative expression—acquiring the skill of approaching things in a novel way. The ability, knowledge, or tool of being deliberately ignorant frees the mind to think creatively. We must learn to be knowingly naïve. We must know when to let our minds out of, and when to put them back in, the box.

Minds released from constraints are free to make innovative breakthroughs and ridiculous mistakes.

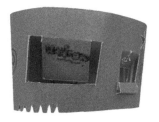

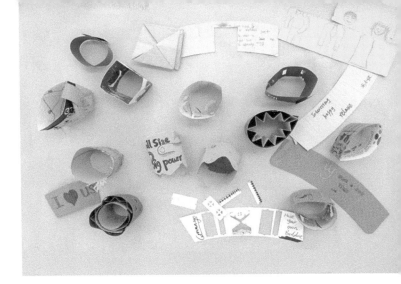

Expansions and Additions

This exercise uses ubiquitous but ignored objects, cardboard coffee-cup sleeves, the unheeded stuff of everyday life. In the United States, sleeves are reassuringly familiar. They are everyday objects that we pick up, use, and discard unthinkingly. Since they possess little intrinsic value, we pay no attention to them; thus, they offer a subtle and invisible entrée into our daily lives. Noticing, in fresh and novel ways, things we had hitherto taken for granted opens our eyes to creative possibilities—sleeves can become something else. Recalibrating our attention to notice the stuff of daily existence may provide creative insights in familiar and unfamiliar contexts. This exercise invites participants, using their understanding of how advertising works, to see sleeves afresh, thereby altering their relationship not just to the sleeves but to their own self-images. Such changes make us more observant and more self-reflective, qualities that foster creative attitudes of mind.

What other everyday objects might we use? Consider cultural context when selecting products with little intrinsic value. Objects that are commonly abundant have the potential for use in creativity exercises. Materials on which we can write, draw, or paint present opportunities. Easily manipulated materials offer different possibilities than rigid materials—the more common, familiar, and unnoticed, the better. 'Misusing' materials encourages us to inspect their potentials. Seeing our familiar everyday world in fresh ways is the essence of creative perception. Devise exercises that help develop this form of perception. Does it matter if the products work? Not in the least. We are not inventing new widgets; we are inventing new ways to see.

Noticing, in fresh and novel ways, things we had hitherto taken for granted opens our eyes to creative possibilities

POSTHASTE:
ART FROM ANYTHING

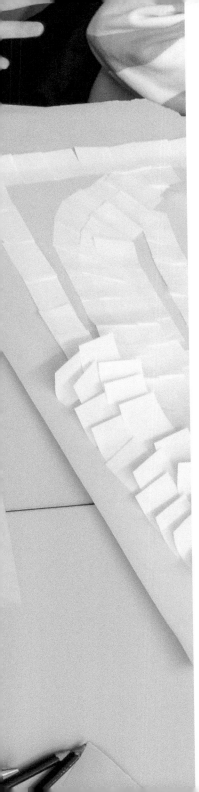

Act first, think later! Provide space for a dozen or so participants around a large table, each supplied with a pad of small sticky notes and a large sheet of paper. Invite them to look to their left and, using the sticky notes, create a profile of their neighbor. NO drawing. NO tearing or cutting. Just stick the notes on the sheet. Don't understand? Consult a Cubist. When done, share. Laugh with delight then, eyes directed to the right; repeat. Commitment is low, explorations entail little risk, and mistakes are easily unstuck. The taboo against staring is broken, so profiling is undertaken in a free and convivial environment, the tone light and cheerful. Participants walk around and comment on one another's creations and may profile instructors.

Exercises vary in length; this one is short, in order to prevent participants from becoming stressed about their presumed lack of artistic ability. Just do it! Unsure about what to do? Steal a furtive glance at your neighbor. Ah, we're all in the same boat, you think. As long as one is doing something—whatever that is—one is doing the right thing. There's no one right way to do it. Brevity prevents the overthinking that leads to paralysis. Act first, then reflect on results. Without action, there is no reflection. No reflection means no learning. It's surprising how frequently we can surprise ourselves when we jump in and try. Products break creativity blocks. Sticking helps us become unstuck.

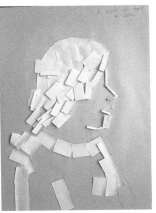

Participants discovered a loophole, in that the exercise instructions forgot to prohibit folding, twisting, or bending the sticky notes. Like weeds poking through sidewalk cracks, human ingenuity cheerfully defies lesson-plan paving. Illicit products reveal that bent paper, like bent rules, can generate breakthroughs. "I can't draw" is a common refrain during many exercises. Still, it's surprising how many participants are surprised by their ability to create a recognizable likeness of their neighbor by sticking to it.

Brevity prevents the overthinking that leads to paralysis. Act first, then reflect on results. Without action, there is no reflection.

But what does it all mean? Short exercises are fast-paced; they keep us on our toes and get the blood flowing. If participants can anticipate what's coming, it's time to change direction. A rule for exercises: Keep participants engaged; keep them guessing. Vary time from long and convoluted exercises to short and sweet ones. Vary materials and activities. Engagement is key. Introduce surprises. Short exercises may fill gaps between more extended exercises or serve as limbering-up exercises. Avoid developing a regular cadence—anathema to fluid thinking. As a general rule, exercises should confuse the overconfident, surprise the rote learner, delight the engaged, inspire the hopeful, tickle the sensitive, reward the observant, and leave everyone with a peculiar aftertaste in their minds.

At the risk of stirring up trouble, exercises should also infuriate the smugly powerful. Substituting sticky notes for pencils does an end run around self-imposed "I am not an artist" constraints and frees participants to engage in a supposedly artistic venture unencumbered by self-doubts. The assignment's unexpectedness is essential to its success. It relies on the fact that we have never learned that we don't know how to peel and paste sticky notes. Finding ways to circumvent self-imposed mental constraints provides routes to creativity and fluid thinking. Ray Bradbury's admonition "When they give you lined paper, write the other way" is always excellent advice.

BILLIE L: *Today's production of the silhouette of our neighbor was the single best thing I have produced in this class so far. I feel that the essence of C. was captured in the Post-it character, and I must say I am quite proud of myself. I had no idea I could actually produce something that would be realistic. It was a very enjoyable exercise.*

RAVEN R: The last two exercise is "making a profile" and "writing a response letter which is although too late."

We made the profile in a relatively complex way: We teared the papers into different shapes to form the hair, the eyes . . . compared to the works by American students, which were all just made of the shape of square, we were really making too complex.

Do we Chinese prefer to use complex things? Or are we always making things complex?

Whether it's true is still uncertain. We do own something "pure and simple"—the painting by Qi Baishi is much simpler than [a] da Vinci, I think. But anyway, Western minds are considered to be more "straightforward."

To me, to be straightforward is an efficient character; and using simple things to express an idea clearly is harder than using complex things. So less is more? I'm not sure, but at least sometimes it's true. That's why when we tried to use only squares to make the profile, I heard the complaint "Oh it's much harder!"

Finding ways to circumvent self-imposed mental constraints provides routes to creativity and fluid thinking. Ray Bradbury's admonition "When they give you lined paper, write the other way" is always excellent advice.

Expansions and Additions

As mentioned previously, in the early years of education, many of us have been taught, unintentionally but effectively, that we don't know how to draw. This learned inhibition forecloses on possibilities inherent in graphic explorations. This exercise capitalizes on the fact that we were incompletely trained in many ways but allows room for other visual communication skills not commonly taught. Free from prior-learned artistic inhibitions, participants can undertake various activities; examples include model making and collages of paper or bricolage, and many more! This particular exercise opens doors to quick and easy representation. Becoming aware of self-imposed prohibitions is an essential mental leap. How to do so—or should we say "be so"?—is the question.

Any material, from toothpicks to lima beans, may be considered. What other materials that are at hand, kicking about, easily procured, worthless, or leftover can we find—in profusion—for creativity exercises? What might we do with them? Anything has potential, except, please, paper clips; this item's virtues have been too widely extolled. Excellent places to hunt for materials include dumpsters, office supply cabinets, and recycle bins. We might also frequent trinket shops, dollar stores, thrift shops, and party-supply establishments. We are not confined to man-made materials. Nature provides abundance—so look outside, too! I have used bud sheaths from giant timber bamboo instead of bottles in the language of form exercise. The idea that we need unique locations, artfully contrived circumstances, and ingeniously manufactured cues to be creative is ridiculous. Creative attitudes of mind ARE human nature. It can't be said enough: The mind cannot not be creative. All we need is a log to fall off, to trip our minds over. Serendipity remains coy. We must learn to meet her halfway and embrace her wholeheartedly.

The message is clear: We can be creative anywhere at any time with anything and anybody. The ball is in your court. Any questions?

CONNECT

Creativity connects; it's mental glue! Making connections is a highly prized ability and is, perhaps, the attribute most commonly associated with creative minds. Is the process of making connections an ability, a skill, a practice, a habit, an attitude of mind, or a gift? The question remains open, but regardless of how we characterize it, making connections is fundamental to creative thought and action. We live and think by making connections—catching the morning bus, coming to an understanding around the watercooler, or seeing how connecting two seemingly unrelated ideas may reveal larger truths.

Connections are, however, not created equal, most prized are eureka moments. I was blind, but now I see! To integrate seemingly unrelated facts into coherent, connected wholes requires synthetic thinking. How might creativity exercises foster this ability? We may practice making connections anywhere and at any time by asking ourselves how things in our vicinity are connected. Provide participants with a box of shoes, ships, sealing wax, cabbages, and kings and ask them to make connections among them. The goal is to make participants conscious of this remarkable ability, which we take for granted and often employ unconsciously. The following connection-making exercises are clumsy efforts to make us aware of this amazing ability. Connect and improve them.

We practice this seemingly serendipitous experience by combining discussions of unrelated objects and physical activity. Provide participants with a medley of unrelated objects. For example, participants can buy magazines, discuss their contents, and then draw diagrams showing connections among the magazines. Provide ample time for discussions, but only ten minutes is available to diagram connections on a whiteboard. It's essential to leave too little time for the last step. Belaboring it will cause the activity to freeze up. Providing too much time can also create the temptation to develop a "perfect" diagram, which, of course, is impossible. Everyone should wield a marker

IONS

and participate, pell-mell, in a pandemonium scrimmage of creative connecting. Excuse me while I push you out of the way to draw a connection.

Not only are connections not created equal; neither are connection-making processes. Nevertheless, both exercises demonstrate our brains' commonplace—but astounding—ability to connect in revealing ways. Using explorations in Seattle, Washington, as an example, the process is simple.

Furthermore…

The results of hurried diagrams connecting magazines are chaotic and messy. Whether they resemble a spilled spaghetti dinner or a bad hair day is irrelevant, it's the dramatic revelation of our ability to make connections that matters. Messy diagrams can be swept from whiteboards, but the seeds of understanding our remarkable connection-making propensity are planted in fertile minds. Will they take root? How might they flower? Time will tell.

ELLA T: *As we talked… my first group had a difficult time coming up with connections between magazines. We, in short, were thinking too hard and being too narrow-minded. Things got crazy on the board, though, and I absolutely loved the visual representation of connections. Tangents are never tangents to me anymore; they're connections. I'm not sure how much my other instructors in other classes classes are going to like me for that, but I suppose that just means it's time for them to learn that lesson, as well.*

MAN RAY: *To be completely honest, I don't know how much I appreciated the magazine connection exercises… I don't feel successfully creative unless I feel uncomfortable or unsure of my decisions. The same goes for being challenged academically—unless I feel awkward, uncertain, or question myself, I feel like something is too easy. While it was perfectly interesting to discuss the different magazines and find connections between them, I didn't feel challenged or creative. I do understand, though, that expecting that of every activity is unreasonable.*

Connections Via Magazines

Only connect! That was the whole of her sermon. Only connect the prose and the passion, and both will be exalted, and human love will be seen at its height. Live in fragments no longer. Only connect, and the beast and the monk, robbed of the isolation that is life to either, will die.

—M. FORSTER, *HOWARD'S END*

It's all about connections, isn't it.

Creativity, I mean.

Creativity and connections, that is.

(Those are?)

Connections and creativity.

Proceed, posthaste or otherwise, to Bulldog News or another newsstand and buy a magazine you've never read before but find interesting or intriguing.

Read it. (Look at pictures?)

Create a simple diagram of its contents.

Come to class prepared to discuss your magazine

first in small groups, then as a whole class,

following which we shall (de)scribe an "inter-connective knowledge network"

(term copyright of the CC seminar)

on the whiteboard

The following exercise is more straightforward and direct but has the same goal: to reveal to participants our astounding ability to make connections by practicing the art of doing so. Participants selected an object from a collection of papers, studied and discussed them, placed them on a sheet of paper, and drew annotated arrows describing connections. Although these methods are forced and arbitrary, they nevertheless demonstrate to participants Homo sapiens' remarkable ability to connect things that may lack any obvious, logical, functional, or other apparent relationships. The only surprise is the lack of surprise evinced by participants in exercising our surprising ability to connect.

Con—nect—ion—s

We get too certain of ourselves traveling backwards and forwards along the tramlines of empirical fact. Occasionally one gets hit softly on the head by a stray brick which has been launched from some other region.

—LAWRENCE DURRELL, *CLEA*

Creative minds find connections between things, objects, events, ideas (etc.) that others fail to see. Their minds become dense webs of connections and they become adept at finding connections. Today, we shall practice the art (or is it a science?) of finding or making connections. This will be in—ter—est—ing!

Select one item from the file of papers and study it carefully. Through individual discussions with each person in the class, find connections between your paper and those of every other person.

Then . . .

If you are born of the artist tribe, it is a waste of time to try and function as a priest. You have to be faithful to your angle of vision, and at the same time fully recognise its partiality. There is a kind of perfection to be achieved in matching oneself to one's capacities—at every level. This must, I imagine, do away with striving, and with illusions too.

—LAWRENCE DURRELL, CLEA

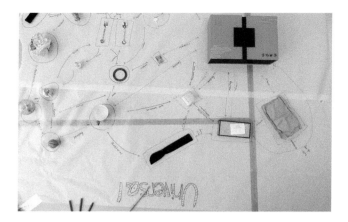

From a teaching perspective, drama frequently enhances exercises; vide the moment of stunned silence when, with minutes remaining, participants are asked to diagram magazine connections on a whiteboard. What? How can one possibly create such a complex diagram in such a short time? There are too many questions: Should we document the relative importance of connections? Should we start by identifying patterns? What connections are significant? Time dictates a jump into the fray feetfirst. Not knowing where we're heading, we must nevertheless act decisively. We can progress by adjusting something once it's there. Partial diagrams talk back in ways that blank boards don't. Try. Adapt. Adjust. Participants' frenetic jostling to get topics and connections on the board are a potent metaphor for how our brains develop neural networks. Education is the process of making up your mind.

To make meaningful connections, we must know what we are connecting, so participants examined the medley of papers with interest. A lengthy discussion about what they were and what they meant preceded a discussion of how to connect them. Do we find or invent connections? Are connections intrinsic to objects or do observers generate them?

DANA B: *Then we made connections among things. The task was to connect different objects that we all had, and again it was a bit funny to see that long talks about political issues and other stuff were drifting the attention away from the task. There sure is a lot of knowledge among us, but we could rather spend some of our energy on solving the connection task. Personally, I don't think I can judge my work properly just by talking about it, but I rather have to try out and see it and then change and rearrange after seeing it in reality.*

I found this task rather amusing, actually—I would say it was a lot of fun for me, in finding out with each person how to connect to their item. Because even objects that didn't seem alike at all suddenly made our fantasy start working, and we found an equal definition of the objects that made a common link.

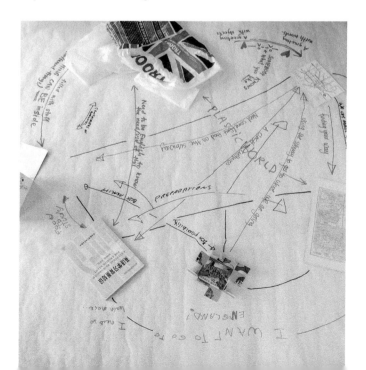

finding your way

using the subway to get to

A class of cultures

Need some fast food on the subway

PLASTIC

Through experience teaching this exercise in various cultures, it was clear deeply ingrained cultural norms influence how participants engage in such exercises. Allow creativity exercises to adjust themselves to cultural contexts—to provide a degree of comfort, but not too much.

As in most exercises, the richness resides in the process, not the products, but this doesn't mean that products are trivial. Quite the contrary, engaging products celebrate participants' splendid, but transient, discussions. A culturally influenced tidy diagram derives from using a single definition of connection. Its weakness is that it ignores other types of connections: materials, colors, words, cultural creations, size and shape, human-man creations. What it loses in variety of connecting criteria, it gains in clarity. Is one approach better than another in exposing participants to the connection-making process? Does the consensus-building process stifle or promote connection making? Does it enhance or diminish creativity? Those predisposed to believe that creative individuals tend to be "lone geniuses" may respond differently to these questions than those who believe that creative individuals are the products of their communities. Students always provide an interesting insight into this inquiry.

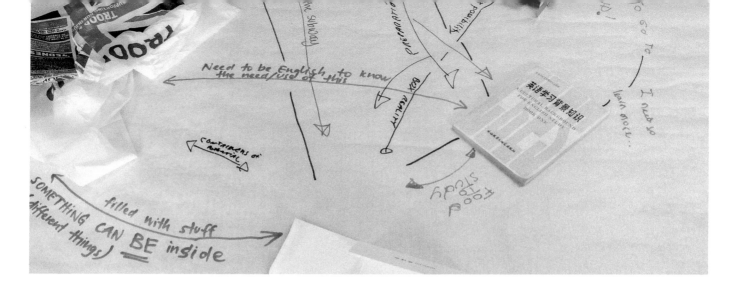

Expansions and Additions

The ability to make novel connections among objects, activities, or ideas may be a signature characteristic of creative minds. But connections are not all created equal—some are trivial, others momentous.

Making mental and physical connections is so fundamental to how we think and act that, for the most part, we take it for granted. Surprisingly, we rarely try to cultivate the ability explicitly. Creative insights frequently take the form of seeing or making useful or interesting connections that others hadn't noticed. Well, of course! Why didn't I think of that? The exercises focus on demonstrating to participants our ability to make physically explicit connections and do so playfully and without judgment.

How else might we hone this skill? The possibilities are boundless: We might make connections among objects, among activities and behaviors, and among words and images. We might practice the art expansively and generally or narrowly and precisely. We might do so in sociocultural settings or natural environments. There is no limit; making connections is an attitude of mind through which we view and interact with the world and live our lives. If I propose that making connections is a defining trait of creative thought and action, then we might cultivate this ability, which deserves closer attention.

Here's a medley of ideas for developing a connective attitude of mind:

· Spend a day making a particular kind of connection.

· Generate many kinds of connections among objects such as material, color, form, value, familiarity, purpose, meaning, etc.

· Make multiple connections to build complex, interrelated connection networks.

· Make spatial, temporal, and behavioral connections.

· List connections that define the essence of our culture.

· Put this book down and, without moving, make a list of one hundred connections among the things you see around you. On second thought, don't bother; that sort of instruction turns an exciting adventure into a pedantic chore. Find ways to make connection-making playful.

Making connections may lead to seeing patterns and thinking in systems, which opens additional doors for exploration. Becoming conscious of how we think is essential to cultivating creativity

EDUCATION
WE HAVE
MET A COGNITION
AND
IT IS US.

CREATIVITY
IS BUSINESS
AS UNUSUAL

EDUCATION CONFLATES DETENTION WITH ATTENTION.

MOST DEFINITIONS of CREATIVITY SHOULD BE PUT BACK INSIDE THE BOX.

ALL THE WORLD'S A STAGE YOU ARE GOING THROUGH

PAY ATTENTION AND ATTENTION REPAYS WITH INTEREST

Contexts Conducive to Creativity

There are no particular places or times that are ideally conducive to encouraging creativity. Rather, we should think of creativity as an attitude of mind that we can engage in wherever we happen to be, whenever we happen to be there, and with, or without, whomever we happen to be with. However, places conducive to creative explorations tend to be comfortable, engaging, and flexible. Sometimes it helps to have time on our hands; sometimes it's good to feel time slipping through our fingers. This chapter offers a few broad suggestions for physical conditions and psychological contexts conducive to cultivating creativity.

Physical Types of Classrooms

Much creative exploration occurs in educational settings, so a word or two about the physical qualities and psychological associations of classrooms is in order. What moods do classrooms commonly induce, and what are appropriate degrees of orderliness or disorderliness? In general, custom-built places that are beautifully fitted out tend to be unsuitable for creative activities. The fresher the paint, the less blemished the walls, and the more expensive the furniture, the more inhibiting and thus unsuitable they become. As muddy paths welcome exploration in well-worn shoes but discourage movement in precious new shoes, so, too, well-worn environments tend to be comfortable for creative explorations, while perfect environments inhibit physical and mental freedom. Made-to-order places are often made to order users around. Places that are worn in to the point of being worn-out permit fluid thinking and encourage minds to be highly charged but at ease. Orderly places inhibit rather than encourage fluid, creative explorations; we hesitate to mess, damage, misalign, or use them. On the other hand, messy, uncared for, shoddy, and chaotic places also inhibit creativity in different ways. Between these extremes are comfortable environments that are open invitations to exploration.

Such places, and times, possess a latitude of physical freedom, physical and psychological comfort, and some material facilities to prompt and liberate minds from prescribed mental paths. Conducive places are informal and casual, comfortable, and inviting.

They provide facilities to explore, try things out and make mistakes without concern about irreparably messing things up. "Should I be doing this here?" is a question that should not arise.

Setting Up the Stage or Upsetting the Stage

Spaces adapted for use as creative venues are frequently, and particularly, successful because creative explorations are comfortable in easily altered places. At a moment's notice, for example, furniture can be rearranged to accommodate changing needs. It's surprising how mind-altering the act of altering furniture can be. Predictable furniture arrangements prompt predictable outcomes. Unpredictable setups upset. Walls have ears. Tables and chairs have tongues. Furniture arrangements send messages. If rooms used for creative explorations are neat and orderly, one can, at least, elbow aside implicit hierarchies by rearranging tables at discordant angles to walls to create conditions that encourage participants to try out fresh ways of interacting. Rearranging furniture for each session can keep expectations off balance, inducing interest and encouraging thoughts to stray from normal routes and routines. Do such changes really aid creative explorations? Testing this claim would require "rats in a maze" experiments, with obligatory control groups. Life's too short. Shove tables out of alignment, experiment, and see what happens! Apply Melville's prescription: "There are some enterprises in which a careful disorderliness is the true method."

Creating Atomspheres in Which Creative Thoughts and Actions May Flourish

Classrooms frequently come with excess baggage. The more orderly and uniform they are and the more nailed down their furniture, the heavier the baggage. Excess baggage charges for education can take a lifetime to pay off. Desks set in uniform, fixed rows are tailored to train orderly, compliant, and complicit cogs. Wordlessly, they prescribe the right ways to behave. They are the box. Their silent prescriptions and proscriptions—obey authority figures—are antithetical to creative attitudes of mind.

By contrast, places conducive to creative explorations don't scream authority, don't prescribe actions narrowly. They don't tell us precisely how to behave in them. Accordingly, they subversively challenge participants' behavior patterns. Be sure to arrange classroom furniture in ways that overtly or covertly challenge social hierarchies and common spatial expectations: Balance order and chaos. Consider further possibilities with—and without—furniture.

Of course, creative attitudes of mind are not manipulated as easily as furniture. Creating what we believe will be a conducive physical environment does not guarantee creative responses. Simple manipulations of physical environments help, but think creatively to support free-ranging thoughts and risk-taking acts. Be bold. Just do it and see what happens.

I WAS JUST THINKING THAT ...

HOW ABOUT ...

BEAR WITH ME FOR A MINUTE WHILE ...

HOW OLD IS IT?

OUR PLACE
IN THE
FLOW OF
TIME

This exercise begins with scraps of nine-and-a-half-inch-wide wood siding of odd lengths, leftovers from a house remodel. It also starts with a question rather than instructions: "How old is it?" Together, objects and questions may seem unpropitious, but they exemplify a recurring theme: The question I'm asking is not the question I'm asking. As in many creativity explorations, overt instructions conceal more substantive underlying questions. In this way, questions are similar to Rittel and Webber's "wicked problems," in which "[e]very wicked problem is a symptom of another, 'higher level' problem." This wicked question—"How old is it?"—invites participants to chew on meatier questions: What is the meaning of time, and what is our place in it? To be effective, creative thought and action must understand, and be comfortable with, their place in time. The exercise's most grandiose goal is to place participants on a solid footing in time. Why is this desirable for cultivating creativity?

The topic of time is wickedly tricky. Much of contemporary life is displaced in time. We experience time as fractured and fragmented and are beholden to beeping devices and demanding apps. We exist in states of perpetual disturbance and distraction. These platitudes are, of course, du jour commonplaces, so what to do? Can we develop meaningful relationships with time? What does this question mean? This exercise aspires to bring time to life, stretch temporal perceptions beyond immediate insistencies, and place us comfortably in long stretches of time— fluid thinking in the river of time.

Initially, participants draw inspiration from the materials themselves. Careful inspection of the scraps of siding reveals that they embody centuries of time in their material substance. They are old-growth western red cedar harvested around the turn of the millennium. Close examination reveals huge numbers of tightly spaced lines running the boards' lengths—annular rings that reveal that the boards were cut from massive tree trunks. Each light line between dark ones physically records one year's growth. Counting lines reveals that the trees were centuries old. We begin to ask ourselves what our seemingly innocuous question—"How old is it?"—really means.

Is the question about the boards as objects, the age of the wood itself, or are we being asked to consider the age of the trees from which they came? The more we look, and think, the more ambiguous the question becomes. Our goal is not a definitive answer, but a consideration of the meaning of time itself and our place in the flow of time. We count the lines. Losing track, we start again—lines are hairsbreadth apart. The edge of one board reveals that it is some 250 to 300 years older than another board we examine. Human generations are encapsulated across the life spans of these boards. Tangible materiality provides timely inspiration.

As in many creativity explorations, overt instructions conceal more substantive underlying questions.

ANON *The other day we took class at the O2 café, which made me think Wow, a class can be so relaxing and enjoyable like this! At that class, I fell in love with the smell of a piece of cedar tree. And we count the annual rings of the tree. Feel us so tiny in front of the thousand-years old tree.*

PENNY S: *This . . . activity let us think about our place in time. I thought that the exercise . . . was very interesting. It got me thinking about how strange it is to define what age is. Should we be defining the tree based on when the very inside of the trunk was "born," or is age a measure of how old the tree has been the way we see it? It might have started growing thousands of years ago, and the history of this past is still on the very inside of the tree. But the whole history as it stands, with all the marks representing years, is still new when considered as a compilation of time. And then you can also get into the question of whether we are talking about the age of the tree or the age of the piece of wood before us. Should the piece of wood only be as old as how long it was in that cut-up state? That made me think how strange it is that we so simply and reflexively define our own age as the time since we were expelled from the womb. If we've been growing and changing since then, can we really say that our place in time is defined by that one event so long ago (our birth)? Couldn't age be how long we've been the way we currently are? Or are we ever even actually static for long enough to count? I also started thinking about people's use of their own time. If someone is able to have much more meaningful experiences and accomplishments in a year, was time more meaningful for him? Somehow larger or more pronounced, the way that some fruitful years are represented by larger distances between marks on the tree trunk? In the end, I can't say a have a good way to answer any of my own questions. The more I think about finding an answer to any one of them, the more I just come up with four or five more questions. This is probably why poets can seem to go on forever in their descriptions of time's elusiveness.*

How are creative minds conscious of time? Might different relationships induce different creative responses? How might we be situated in, and attuned to, the flow of our own time? Might we gain insights by stepping out of the river and consider time from its banks? Metaphors aside, the point is, creative individuals should be conscious of their relationship to time: how we are rooted in the current time, where these ties have sprung from, how time's course has evolved, and where our own time is headed, or persuaded to go by our actions. The topic is slippery and elusive, but creativity exercises must pay attention to time. Time cannot be put in a box to be inspected and pondered. Accordingly, this exercise is more speculative than most—it's an invitation to think about how we might think about time. What can we learn from how participants responded to these scraps of wood?

Cultural influences were evident in this exercise, as noted in the student's reflections.

Did participants' perception of time expand beyond the confines of the present imperious moment and individual life spans? Do our imaginations grow if we locate ourselves in more prolonged periods than we usually contemplate? Does examining the old wooden boards enhance reflection and make us more creative? The impossibility of answering such questions should not discourage explorations of the effects of time on creative attitudes of mind. Furthermore, the close reading required for this speculative exercise underscores the importance of attentive observation. While casual glances lack traction, creative understanding grows from careful observation. The exercise also reminds us that, when viewed with wonder, the natural world may be a never-ending source of inspiration. Creative minds are wonder-full.

MARY H: *On the topic of time: I sometimes feel that I overly concentrate on the future. My goals and dreams drive my everyday life and tasks, what I choose to focus on, and how what I value will "ultimately" determine where I go. When's my next test? How much should I actually study for it? Will it make a difference to what I want to be in the future? Et cetera, et cetera.*

It can be daunting to think of how small an individual is within the vast intricacies of this universe…

Equally as important, our situations and backgrounds influence each of us. Thus, although I find myself running my life according to what's going to happen next, I can't deny that everything that's happened to me thus far shaped the person I am at this very moment. The wood pieces definitely brought this idea to life. Each section is seemingly a "sliver" in time. It tells a story. Some pieces showed signs of fire; others showed good years of growth. Furthermore, each ring of life builds upon the other, ultimately making a robust tree. It reminds me that we are constantly in a feedback loop, considering what to do based on what we know.

VICTOR J: *Even though the length of every year is the same, the memory and mark it has on us is distinctive and special. …Every piece of cedar wood had unique markings and etching indicating how old it was and giving us a history to trace, and like pieces of cedar, each of us has memories and a sense of time that is different, showing how we came to be at this university. The pieces of cedar and our discussion of time made me realize how dynamic history, the present, and future really are; how every moment and everything we record is controlled by our perspectives and point of view. Time can be pretty exciting.*

Expansions and Additions

In the modern world, our lives are ever more hurried. Time flashes by. We rarely step back to contemplate our lives in longer time frames. To be creative, we are told, we must be "in the moment" and "ahead of the curve." But to fully understand the moment in which we live, it may be necessary to step outside time's incessant rush and locate ourselves in longer natural, sociocultural, and historical time frames. Understanding our place in time means awareness of the current moment's unique qualities and how it is similar to and different from other times.

How might we use the materials at hand—and the time available— to examine embodied time? The possibilities are endless. Might a creativity exercise explore technological time by using scraps of circuit boards culled from ancient computers? Time and again, time and a gain, we may ask, "What does it all mean?" Natural materials, particularly those generated by living processes, offer potent connections to time unavailable in nonliving and man-made materials. Wood—whose fibers encapsulate centuries of time—is particularly potent.

There are no right or wrong ways to think about time. This exercise is a speculative example, not a universal prescription. It derives its potency from inspiration embedded in the material; time is not merely embedded but also embodied in the wood. The boards provide unique invitations to think about time creatively and in ways that are inaccessible if we consider time only in the abstract or look at time expressed in nonliving materials. The lumber scraps are natural yardsticks against which we can measure and contemplate our lives. They put our lives in perspective. They allow us to calibrate time more expansively and develop broader perceptions of time. Deep time meets instant messaging.

This assertion that connectivity to time and place are essential groundings for creative thought and that temporal humility may be a useful trait for getting things in perspective remains a speculation; it requires critique and testing. The exercise is a stumbling adolescent in need of other eyes and minds to expand and refine him. This topic is an awkward attempt to address our relationship to time and its potential to enhance the creative mind. How else does time leave its imprint on our material world? In what other ways might we make elusive time physical and tangible? Plants are a particularly rich vein to mine. What possibilities lie in their diurnal and annual cycles and their growth and decay?

Our relationships with the old and the new also present possibilities. Time may add value to, or subtract it from, material reality. Sometimes we extol the new; other times, we revere the old. Why? Why does weathering make some materials more beautiful, while wear and tear destroys others' appearance and value? In the present day, why do we pay more for "distressed" clothes— jeans with holes, for example—than we do for unblemished clothes? Creative ideas may be good because they are fresh, new, and disruptive or because they reinforce time-tested truths. Our relationship to time is nothing if not perplexing. Therein lies the potential for exciting explorations, timely and timeless exercises. Will they be effective? Time will tell.

POSSIBLE

Begin by providing participants with a plain sheet of paper and an unadorned instruction: "Make the sheet of paper seem as LARGE as possible."

Sheets are a normal size and a neutral color. Nothing could be simpler—or so it would seem. Beware! No instructions this bland could be anything other than duplicitous. Break out the bland-aids!

While the size of one word in the exercise instruction calls attention to largeness, the pertinent word is seem, for the exercise is all about perception. Specifically, how do we manipulate the perception of a familiar, unassuming, innocent object? How do we make a sheet of paper seem as large as possible? We explore the art and science (or is it magic?) of an activity that permeates our lives from advertising to politics and communications: perception. Like those activities, the exercise is not what it seems at first glance. See what I mean?

The instruction catches participants off guard. It is clearly off base and requires students to use a normal sheet of paper in abnormal ways. Students almost assuredly and immediately experience the uncertainty and confusion common when confronted with a conundrum. Participants stare at their sheets of paper, which, at least initially, return blank stares. If the deer-in-the-headlights moment seems excessively protracted, a timely reminder may be in order: You are not alone. It is permissible to check what others are doing—or not doing. Suddenly, out of the blankness, ideas emerge, and participants get busy.

Products display the mind's remarkable inventiveness. Who would have thought of that? Sheets of paper expand before our eyes

We explore the art and science (or is it magic?) of an activity that permeates our lives from advertising to politics and communications: perception.

and minds. Some responses play games with the senses, while others try to trick the mind—is perception sensory or mental?

The magician's wand of the human mind transforms the sheets of paper. Approaches vary widely, including graphic metaphors, such as drawings of solar systems, manipulation of scale perception by adding a tiny human figure in a corner, perspective manipulations—tromp l'oeil effects; and a long corridor ending in a curve, suggesting an unseen continuation. Are approaches that require sophisticated explanations or complex conceptual understanding as convincing as direct manipulations? It depends. One participant resorts to allusion by writing "death" on her sheet because nothing is bigger than death. Isn't life bigger? No, she has a point; death ultimately triumphs. These approaches manipulate mental perceptions through metaphor and symbolism rather than through visual or physical manipulations, but they all leave the paper intact.

Another category of responses tears into the subject or cuts it to pieces: a snowfall of confetti; enormous uncoiling strips. Paper twists and torques. Holes open. Unleashed ingenuity confirms that we can't circumscribe the field of possibilities, no matter how hard we planet.

But that's not all. Participants build models, adding a third dimension of possibilities. Like two-dimensional solutions, some models may be understood by looking at them, while others require an explanation of underlying conceptual ideas. Does a sheet torn into thin strips and joined to make a large web that catches attention make the sheet seem larger than one that consists of a single large hole? How does a net compare with a house outlined on the floor by another participant? Would the illusory house be enhanced or destroyed if paper strips were thinner or more widely spaced? How do we judge such creations?

This approach goes straight for the jugular, or more literally, the ocular—masks eyes. What is the perceptual effect of a pair of paper glasses that covers the entire world of visual perception? More economical of effort, but perhaps less elegant, is the act of simply holding the sheet in front of our eyes—a brilliant solution or a case of hoisting the white flag of surrender? Success is measured not in products but by how much the exercise enlarges participants' thoughts and generates conversations that continue to unfold further possibilities.

Even though they all responded to the same exercise, each reflection has a different focus and personal interpretation. Unlike classes, whose goal is to have everyone learn the same information, each participant in creativity exercises embraces something different. The learning objectives promote something uniquely and individually relevant. Open-ended questions and explorations do not aspire to corral answers into tight, prescribed places.

Open-ended questions and explorations do not aspire to corral answers into tight, prescribed places.

PHOTO CREDIT: TAMMY TASKER

ADIA N: *I was really excited to be thinking about the challenge in ways other than the literal interpretation of physically manipulating the paper to its biggest perimeter, or volume (even though those interpretations require creativity as well). I thought about perspective, and to whom the paper needs to be large or small, and if I should only focus on making one aspect of the paper large, such as folding it to increase the height or…. making the paper seem infinitely large to the person wearing the glasses…*

It made me think of my college application process, and my college writing teacher telling us that writing a unique essay, just getting the admissions officer's attention, was half the battle won. In a sense, that is where true innovation comes from—thinking a little differently from those around you, and despite seeing the same things, being able to draw inspiration from the things that others wouldn't think twice about, and it makes me aware of trying to develop that skill.

MAN RAY: *The paper exercises were interesting and successful because they allowed for many different approaches. The added constraint of talking to each other and seeing a few projects around us was the most fascinating part, though, as it seemed as though people* *thought it would be "uncreative" to do something that had already been done. I decided that doing something that had already been done and doing it BETTER was what I wanted to do, as improving on an existing form is a form of experimentation, I think.*

COLLIE K: *Given a simple blank piece of paper we were each able to come up with unique and creative ways to make the paper feel both extremely big and small.... If we [had been] given this assignment at the beginning of the quarter, we would have sat in front of the piece of paper until one of us had enough courage to start the project. Over the course of the quarter I have seen a change in both myself and the rest of the class. We are able to look at something ordinary and turn it into something extraordinary within a matter of seconds.*

AVEN S: *Seeing everyone's different ways of making the piece of paper seem LARGE was great! There were so many approaches that people took, which.... once again shows the uniqueness of each person's brand of creativity. One thing that I noticed in myself, though, was a very competitive spirit. I (subconsciously) was thinking that I had to have the "most creative" way of making the paper seem big, surpassing everyone else's level of creativity in their method (as if there were a way to judge that!) ...Anyway, it got me thinking about the place of competition in creativity. Done healthily, competition can definitely spur people on to more creative approaches to problems, projects, et cetera. Where is the limit to competition's benefits to creativity, though? At some point.... a competitive environment could provide an incredible depth of solutions with limited breadth, while a lack of competition could allow for a lot more breadth than depth.... Bottom line: I'm curious about the effects of competitive spirit on creativity.*

Expansions and Additions

What other exercises can we imagine for manipulating perceptions with sheets of paper? An alternative exercise may ask participants to make a sheet of paper seem as small as possible. This will elicit different responses, but the goal of manipulating perceptions remains constant. Contrast may be used to influence the perception of size: A sheet of paper has been folded into a tight bundle and placed at the corner of a larger sheet to make it seem relatively small.

More broadly, what other perceptions might we manipulate? Consider how our desires are manipulated: Supermarkets arrange produce to seem fresher, jewelers enhance the luster of diamonds, and the fashion designer makes new clothes more essential! As our understanding of perception grows, we imagine more and more opportunities for flexing our creative minds. Will thinking about manipulating others' perceptions increase self-awareness? Will we become more conscious of the ways our

perceptions are manipulated? Will deeper reflection reveal how our preconceptions affect our perceptions? I perceive, therefore I think, and vice versa. As we become more conscious of manipulating instances in our daily lives, would this heightened awareness make us more receptive to the hints, nudges, and opportunities for creative responses?

Like many exercises, this exercise's genius resides in familiar, accessible materials to perform an unexpected task. A less obvious virtue is the surreptitious introduction to the idea that our interest is not in the manipulations themselves, but how our manipulations affect observers. We are tinkering with human perception, not paper. Overt questions conceal deeper metaquestions. Again: The question I'm asking is not the question I'm asking. Creative responses ignore superficial questions and address underlying questions. Realizing that this exercise is about perception is its essential starting point. A feat of pulling the rug out from under our minds.

Devise invigorating variations of this exercise to derail the train of stale thought processes. Introduce variations when trapped in interminable meetings in airless, windowless rooms with desultory participants. Awake and report back on what you think, do, feel, and perceive.

SERENDIPITY:
THE ABILITY TO FIND
WHAT YOU ARE NOT
LOOKING FOR
JUST WHEN YOU
NEED IT.

THERE'S A NAP
for
CREATIVITY:
SLEEP ON IT.

SATISFACTION
GUARANTEED
or
YOUR IGNORANCE
BACK.

AU PARFUM DES ROSES " BEE
des roses "BEE&Flower" un nouveau produit de l
sintals, qui date d'une longue histoire, renommé depuis lon
s clients. Offrant les anciens traits, le nouveau produit sent te pa
Nous vous proposons ce bon article de toilettes et essayez-le.
nghai, Chine

"FLOWER" JASMINE SOAP
A sparkling product of "BEE & FLOWER" BRAND
We now recommend you a new product of JASMINE
scented soap for your enjoyment. It is made of selected
materials and natural JASMINE essence, which gives
you a delightful and lasting fragrance. Just give it a try
and you'll no doubt be convinced.
SHANGHAI CHINA

"BEE & FLOWER" ROSE SOAP
Another sparkling product of "BEE & FLOWER"
scented soap for your enjoyment. It
materials and natural ROSE essence.
delightful and lasting fragrance. Just give it
you'll no doubt be convinced
MADE IN

参香皂
香皂，历有年所，久负盛
大用户所喜爱。今在保持原有
种新产品——蜂花人参香皂。该
有天然人参成份，具有保护和滋
香气醇和馥郁，用后留香特久，诚
特向您推荐，并请试之。
中国制造

蜂花百花美容
厂生产蜂花牌橙香皂，历
国内外广大用户所喜爱。
一种新产品——蜂花百花美容皂。本
有保护滋养皮肤之功，达到美容目的。末
用新型百花香精配制而成，香气芬芳馥郁，
令人心旷神怡。特向您推荐，并请试之。
中国制造

蜂花茉莉香
厂生产蜂花牌檀香皂，
地广大用户所喜爱。
中新产品——蜂花
含有天然茉莉花香，用
佳品，特向您推荐，用

"FLOWER" BOUQUET BEAUTY SOAP
Another remarkable product of
"BEE & FLOWER" BRAND
Just as every other soap bearing th
"BEE & FLOWER", this new product
selected materials and is guaranteed for
quality.
Moreover, it is well scented with "FLORAL
BOUQUET" essence with a fragrance that is so fantastic
and everlasting. Just try it, and you will see our sincere
recommendation is convincing.
MADE IN CHINA

"BEE & FLOWER" JASMINE SOAP
A sparkling product of "BEE & FLOWER" BRAND
We now recommend you a new product of JASMINE
scented soap for your enjoyment. It is made of selected
materials and natural JASMINE essence, which gives
you a delightful and lasting fragrance. Just give it a try
and you'll no doubt be convinced.
SHANGHAI CHINA

"BEE & FLOWER" BOUQUET BEAUTY SOAP
Another remarkable product
"BEE & FLOWER" BRAND
Just as every other soap bearing
"BEE & FLOWER", this new product
selected materials and is guaranteed fo
quality.
Moreover, it is well scented
BOUQUET" essence with a fragrance
and everlasting. Just try it, and
recommendation is convincing.
MAD

蜂花人参香皂
厂生产蜂花牌橙香皂，历有年所，久负盛
内外广大用户所喜爱。今在保持原有
另一种新产品——蜂花人参香皂。该
含有天然人参成份，具有保护和滋
，香气醇和馥郁，用后留香特久，诚
之功，特向您推荐，并请试之。
为盥洗佳品，特向您推荐，并请试之。
中国 上海

ENG SOAP
oduct of
BRAND
bearing the name
is made
new for its
s g
ified which will produce a
ct skin. It is well scented
with a fragrance that is
SHANGHAI CHINA

蜂花茉莉香皂，历
我厂生产蜂花牌橙香皂，排在保持原有特色
受到各地广大用户喜爱，蜂花茉莉香皂。该皂香气
广一种新产品——蜂花茉莉香皂，用后留香特久，诚为盥洗
含有天然茉莉花香，用后留香特久，诚为盥洗
佳品，特向您推荐，并请试之。
中国制造

"FLOWER" JASMINE SOAP
"FLOWER" JASMINE SOAP
"BEE & FLOWER" BRAND
product of JASMINE
of selected
a

"BEE & FLOWER" JASMINE SOAP
A sparkling product of "BEE & FLOWER" B
emend you a new
oyment
essence, which gives
Just give it a try
INA

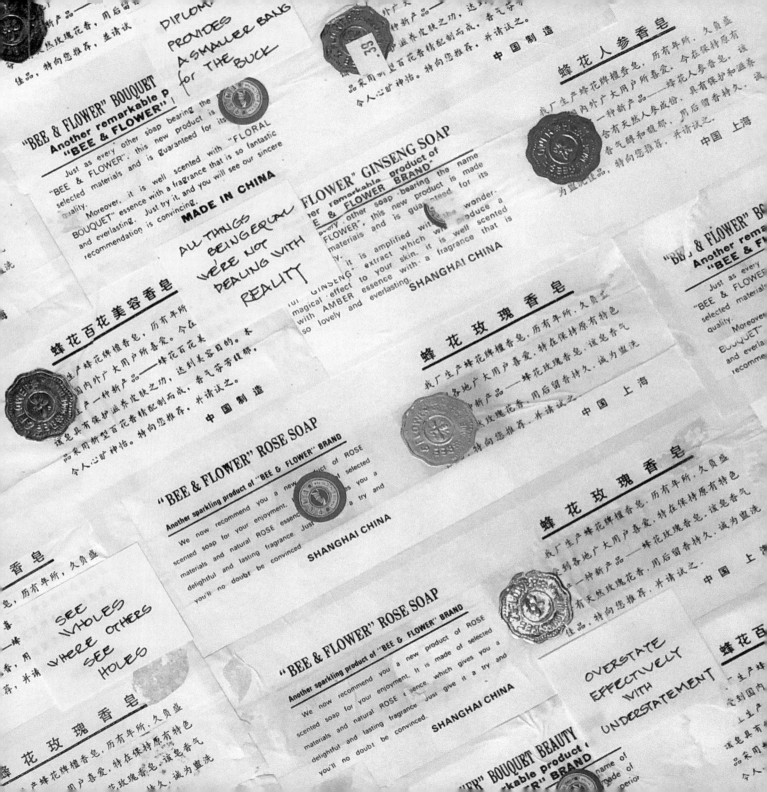

Methods and Madness

Methods and Madness

Methods for cultivating creative attitudes of mind augment rather than supplant analytical thinking, on which creative thought builds. Analysis leads us to the brink but cannot make the leap of integration and synthesis—connecting the hitherto unconnected. Integrative thinking, characteristic of creative thought, takes over when analytical modes hit brick walls. Creative thinking requires a logical, rational mental structure as its base, but it must shake and dislodge those structures when they prevent us from penetrating beyond rigid logic. Synthetic, creative insights build on analytical foundations. We should loosen the grip of analysis and our conscious minds' demands to allow our subconscious neural networks to do their work unmolested by conscious directives.

Play: Playful Thought Patterns

Creative ideas are as frequently sparked by thinking outside the brain box rather than relying exclusively on what lies within. Many of the exercises described in this book get us outside the cranium's comfy confines. Creative thought may spring from bodily senses and emotions as much as from our brains. As Lackoff and Johnson assert in Philosophy in the Flesh, the mind is embodied. Nothing frees us from mental confines better than play. Creative thinking may be encouraged by making and messing around and can be enhanced through social engagements and cultural connections and by interaction with the natural world. Play lubricates creative attitudes of mind. I play, therefore I connect. We cultivate rather than teach creativity, and our most pervasive method is play. However, playfulness may be looked down on in educational settings, where it is considered the antithesis of serious study and thought. Nevertheless, scientists play with the data, policymakers play with scenarios, and financiers—though perhaps they shouldn't—play with the numbers. Play is similarly negated in the corporate world. Yet immensely successful enterprises such as Apple, Xerox, and Bell developed fabled facilities where employees are given the freedom to think and explore, and creative play is encouraged. Play is Homo ludens' most sophisticated method of thinking. Most of the exercises described within these pages encourage different methods of play to flex the creative muscles.

Active Exploration: Journeys

A spirit of exploration aids creative thinking. Exercises encourage exploratory journeys—all roads lead to roam. Though "A Journey Across a Rock" is the most explicit of all the exercises, in one way or another, all exercises are journeys. Exploration requires cloaking exercises in ambiguity rather than clearly explaining what to do and prescribing "correct" routes to predetermined destinations. No mystery, no exploration, so how do we introduce journeys? Our creative journey participants are set loose with sketchy directives and ill-defined directions. "Quips and cracks and wanton wiles" add suggestive noise that further clouds objectives but also elucidates and inspires directives. Participants must feel their way through the resulting confusion and formulate approaches to take. They must also learn to question the questions—a characteristic trait of creative thinking. Participants receive minimal guidance on how to resolve their confusion; they must take the initiative, make connections, and see where these lead them. In this way, participants discover for themselves the magic of forging routes to self-defined destinations. It's tragic to be so destination-oriented that we forget to notice or participate in the educational journey.

These explorations' broader goal is to transcend classrooms and see life's journey as creative exploration. Setting out alone on such journeys is daunting, so we cultivate communities of learners, fellow travelers, sociable pilgrims, recounting their tales along the way to Canterbury.

Risk Taking: Mistakes and Successes

I went to the lost and found counter and asked for myself. They said they hadn't encountered me till now. Exploration entails risk taking. No risk, no reward. Creative thinking encourages risk taking and making mistakes. We learn to take risks, experience success, and failure, make mistakes, and, hallelujah, learn from them! Making mistakes—and recovering from them—is a fundamental learning method. Humility helps. Superiority is a distinctive and remarkably robust form of stupidity. Permitting ourselves to make mistakes and learn from other people's

mistakes allows us to test ideas through trial and error. Exercises requiring participants to make mistakes deliberately are obviously paradoxical—deliberate mistakes are a contradiction in terms. But they covertly suggest that mistakes are inevitable and provide valuable lessons, so we persist in the paradox. Mistake-making exercises delineate the boundaries of culturally acceptable explorations. In many contexts, sexual and political "mistakes" may be taboo topics. I'm of two minds, yes and know.

Surprise, Surprise: The Prize Is Surprise

Authentic explorations are frequently punctuated by surprise, so we require participants to surprise themselves in how they participate and what they produce. Surprising oneself is as easy as falling off a log—deliberately. Another paradox. Can we provide explicit directions for how to do this? No. Nevertheless, given time, participants learn to do so. Like many of the instructions, the requirement to surprise yourself seems ambiguous when looking forward but is surprisingly clear in the rearview mirror. Practicing behaviors and thought patterns that inculcate surprise have surprising results. Surprise is enmeshed in creative attitudes of mind and interactions. In creativity exercises, we may surprise both ourselves and others, and others' surprises may further surprise us. It should come as no surprise that surprise is a great way to learn.

Introduce exercises in ways that facilitate surprise. Instructions should appear confusing, frustrating, and thwarting to encourage open-ended exploration. Participants are well on their way to learning to surprise themselves when they begin to question the question by examining their underlying assumptions, presumptions, and preconceptions. When we look with curious minds, it's surprising how many ways we can invent surprise. It's surprisingly easy to surprise ourselves when we step outside our heads, our ruts, and our routines for an hour or two. Asking participants to surprise themselves may seem daunting until they discover that they can do so by action, by exploration, by making mistakes, and by taking risks. Surprising ourselves encourages fluid thinking.

Paying Attention, Close Observation: Making Connections

It can not be overemphasized that the art and science of careful observation are critical to creativity, but we will try. Observation leads to questioning, a form of curiosity; curiosity encourages further observation; and the positive feedback loop may lead to discoveries and answers. If you want an education, look for it. The same guidance applies to creative inspiration. Exercises encourage observation in many ways: going to new

places, engaging in unusual activities, prescribing uncommon conversation formats, and working with novel materials and objects. Observation is the hook that catches attention and makes connections. We use the world—physically, socially, culturally, and formally—to encourage observation. Discerning connections among things or ideas that others see as unrelated is the essence of creativity. Making connections—along with other most important goals—is, without doubt, most important.

Act First, Think Later: Reflection

Implicit in the goal of thinking on one's feet without getting them in one's mouth is the necessity of action—act first, think later. This medicine may cure the habits of second-guessing ourselves, overpreparing, self-criticizing, evading making decisions, and other manifestations of analysis paralysis. However, it's not universally appropriate; there are many contexts in which it is unwise to act or speak before thinking. Although quick thinking shouldn't encourage making hasty, ill-considered decisions and actions, acting first and thinking later can be a useful means to break cycles of being unable to make up one's mind or overcoming writer's block. Simply put, it forces us to do something.

The exercises described herein deliberately make the stakes for the results of hasty actions low. Acting first and thinking later is appropriate only if we do, indeed, think later and reflect on our actions' results—accordingly, frequent reflections are required from participants and are critical to this learning process. Emphasize the acting first portion initially, then emphasize the thinking later part. Learning to respond quickly makes the mind more agile. Jump to it, then step back and reflect. Thinking later emphasizes the importance of reflection in completing the cycle of exploration. All too frequently, thinking later takes the form of tests—followed by forgetting everything.

Making and Doing, Thinking with the Senses, Speaking the Languages of Form, Materiality, and Process

Thinking comes in different shapes and sizes, not all confined to the brain. Making sense is a form of thinking. We may think with our hands and bodies; we may think with our emotions and senses. Body language and behavior speak volumes wordlessly. These ways of thinking allow exercises to engage the embodied mind and multiple intelligences. They broaden the scope of exercises to include tangible activities drawing inspiration and ideas from the material world. Exercises that engage in making, doing, and tinkering may express creativity physically through craftsmanship. Thinking is enhanced and encouraged through engagement with the world. The exercises draw on external sources for inspiration and help us think materially, socially, and formally. We discover that the world is a never-ending source of inspiration, an incubator of fresh thoughts, and a generator of understanding. In educational contexts, a great deal of time is spent on verbal and numerical abstractions, forgetting the plethora of inspiring ideas and perceptions in the physical world around us. We spend too much time in our heads and not enough time in the real world.

Exercises reveal other "languages" we already speak fluently but unconsciously, our ability to read meaning in forms, materials, and space. We are so comfortable with these unconscious forms of communication that they slip effortlessly off speechless tongues. Building and making exercises flex our imagination by making us conscious of these languages. Stretching the metaphor, we also speak the "language of time." So comfortably immersed are we in our respective cultures that we navigate them masterfully without being conscious that they are a "language" we speak. We become aware of this only when those from another culture can't relate, and we misspeak—cultural cues and meanings.

Moving between spoken and unspoken languages is a powerful method for encouraging fluid and creative thinking: substituting a spatial metaphor for a linguistic phrase, translating words into

Literal and Metaphorical Thought Patterns (En)countering Deep-Seated Thought Patterns

It's no great leap from recognizing nonverbal languages to realizing that metaphor is one of the most profoundly useful and dexterous tools in our mental toolbox. Metaphors short-circuit plodding, rational thinking. One metaphor may be worth a thousand spreadsheets. But there's a time and a place for both. When used thoughtfully, metaphorical thinking may complement literal thinking by freeing the mind from the straitjacket of logical, rational thought. Metaphors make thought patterns looser, more engaging, and more connective. Fluid thinking is well versed in shifting between poetry and prose. The exercises use language in ways that encourage mental flexibility. To foster fluidity, they frequently interpret metaphors literally and literal thoughts metaphorically. We must become transcribers, ration metaphors, and meter rational thought.

materials, or substituting a picture for a thousand words. Thinking by manipulating the physical world cuts out the meddling verbal middleman. We are adept at ascribing human values to inanimate objects. We find it natural and effortless to play with materials to see what ideas and understandings emerge. Such practices loosen the icy grip of analytical thought patterns on fluid, connective, associational, and metaphorical thinking. Analogically, we use our fingers to think digitally. Nonverbal languages provide fresh perspectives and engage other intelligences. The leap to synthesis is frequently effected through them. Lean on the material world for support and inspiration.

Think with Emotions, Values, and Beliefs

We also explore the creative possibilities inherent in the treasure trove of emotions, values, and beliefs. Despite efforts to eradicate these from education—to avoid the messy inconclusiveness that inevitably accompanies them—emotions, values, and beliefs are essential to creative thinking. Arguments about right and wrong lack unambiguous black-and-whiteness and instill the spirit of reconciling contending views. We cannot sanitize education by making it "value-free." Creativity exercises embrace emotions, values, and beliefs as powerful forces that motivate, govern, and spur us onward. To ignore their power is to lose a supportive ally in our creative explorations.

But a caveat: Beliefs may influence creative endeavors positively and negatively and are only creative allies if we don't become their slaves. Overdone, they may overwhelm, and straitjacket thought. If ignored, our insipid thoughts and actions will lack conviction. Their potency for influencing how and what we think makes them essential attributes of creative attitudes of mind. They perform jobs for which placebos need not apply. Think with emotions and emote thoughtfully. Challenging individual beliefs may challenge personal being—dangerous territory, but territory that creative explorations cannot leave unexplored. Exercises that arrange materials to create paradise islands or a lineup of glass bottles in order of relative "honesty" allow explorations of values as sources of creative inspiration without treading on the tender toes of beliefs. They interpret personal and social values through physical actions and material manipulations. Arguing about the honesty of bottles rather than people defuses volatile passions while retaining our values' motivating power.

Outsiders and Insiders

Creative individuals navigate culture's cutting edge and are frequently outsiders, or are regarded as such. But, to be successful, creative people cannot reside entirely beyond the pale; they must retain a toehold in the camp. They must be facile at moving back and forth from insider to outsider status, chameleons, able to switch clothing without being turncoats. Creativity exercises put participants in varied social contexts or unusual positions, easing them from their comfort zones into more turbulent waters and, in turn, making them more comfortable in diverse social roles and relationships. The exercises dip a tentative toe in these waters, but much remains to be done with regard to exploring diverse social contexts, engaging in social games and socialization processes, finding inspiration in other cultures, and learning more about one's own culture. Those with fluid minds can't be stuck in their comfort zones. They must comprehend both the outsiders' and the insiders' viewpoints and learn when to forge ahead and when to step aside. They must walk in their own and in others' shoes. We can't be creative with a self we don't know, nor can we be creative if we know only ourselves.

Provoking Inventiveness Through Quick Thinking

Quick! Quick! What do you think right now?

Sometimes we are provoked into making creative connections by merely being required to give quick responses. When thought processes are jolted into action, normal or conventional responses may be short-circuited. Sudden changes of direction, sudden confrontations with the unexpected, suddenly finding ourselves on the spot can bring to the surface things that a decade of careful plodding won't divulge. Quick thinking may catalyze synthesis. The exercises in this book look for ways to pull the rug out from under participants without totally upsetting the applecart. Occasional stumbles may cause us to put our best foot forward.

Cooperation and Competition

Creativity: It's not all about you, nor is it all in your own head. Sometimes it's about stepping outside your head and looking around for inspiration—which frequently comes from social interactions. Being social animals, we find inspiration in interacting with others, particularly when interactions occur in conducive settings: candlelight, soft music, a fragrant breeze off a murmuring ocean. To fully inspire creative thought, we need settings that comfort AND challenge. Interactions among learning community members should balance cooperation and competition in a healthy back-and-forth manner. To everything there is a season, a time for competing, a time for cooperating. Exercises like the ones herein encourage both.

Real and Authentic Versus Simulated and Virtual

Our world is increasingly infatuated and inveigled by all things virtual. Beyond infatuation, the year 2020 brought virtual reality into reality when the physical realm was considered unsafe due to a global pandemic. However, it's time to get real, to turn the clock back to material reality. Physical reality is reassuring in ways that mental and technological constructions may not be. Materials put us in touch with solid, enduring, and responsive reality. Of course, reality may be dangerous, uncomfortable, and threatening; it's not all a bed of thornless roses. Exercises that use real materials and objects may forge useful, integrative connections between education and daily life. Reality is reassuringly authentic; a stubbed toe hurts. Virtual reality is not a placebo for the real deal.

Creative exercises require us to think on our feet, get in touch with the real world, and get busy with our hands. We tailor reality to our needs; the whole cloth can hobble imagination, particularly if exercises too closely mimic real-life activities. Separation, abstraction, and metaphor can discourage us from responding conventionally. For example, an exercise that closely replicates the context and procedures of interviews may be too similar to actual interviews prompting real interview responses.

This is appropriate if we wish to hone interview skills but ineffective if we are trying to induce fresh, creative responses. "A Journey Across a Rock" IS a journey, but of a different order from a real journey. Professional development workshops simulate real situations, and participants respond accordingly, learning to perform skillfully in those contexts. The goal of cultivating creativity is different and encourages participants to respond in interesting or exploratory ways.

Creativity exercises enter parallel universes by introducing them in ways that may appear illogical, irrational, and confusing rather than realistic. They act as wedges, beginning with thin ends that are only slightly confusing and unusual but ending, as participants acclimate to their idiosyncrasies, with deliberate ambiguity and confusion.

Embracing Ambiguity as an Ally

If there is one thing we can count on concretely, it's ambiguity. The world is ambiguous; no point pretending its knot. Learning doesn't help. The more we know, the more complex and convoluted the world's "wicked problems" become. Ambiguity can't be evaded or outsmarted. Ambiguous situations seem to remain impossible. The exercises in this book try to turn the "problem" of ambiguity inside out and think of it as creativity's outer garment; it's a coat of many colors: a shroud of invisibility, a ticket to ride. Accepting the ambiguity of situations and problems opens doors to exploration beyond rational, logical thought patterns. Ambiguity's nebulousness cannot weigh us down. By developing a fluid mind, a world of ambiguity is a world to explore, a world of opportunity. Ambiguity is another reason why exercise goals should be inconclusive, their requirements inexact, and their methods inexplicit. Hazy ground rules free participants to explore independently and creatively.

Synthesis and Integration

The road to hell is a one track mined. Would you mind if, for a moment, I speak metaphorically of the mind, or at least the brain? I suspect that our brains evolved to be what they are because they developed through engagement with the world in ways that were flexible, adaptable, and open. Our minds responded to the world's suggestions expansively and digressively rather than solely with one-track conclusions. We might even hypothesize an evolutionary advantage to brains that possess synaptic connections that remain unattached and—dare I anthropomorphize the brain?—that are inherently sociable and willing to establish new connections at a moment's notice. "Hi! I'm dopamine; I've heard all about you and am pleased to finally connect." Might we conclude that, no matter how brilliant a rigid mindset may be, it can't be creative if its synaptic connections are too orderly, tidy, and thus predictable? Creative mental circuitry needs spillover to allow it to form casual, unexpected, and seemingly random connections—hence our metaphorical goal of fluid mindsets that can create serendipity out of nothing. Of course, all synaptic connections shouldn't be chaotic and undisciplined; we must balance orderly discipline and freewheeling association.

Conclusion

Fluid mindsets can connect disparate and seemingly unrelated factors more easily than can rigid and controlled thought patterns. They foster synthetic and integrative thought patterns. To the analytic mind, synthesis remains maddeningly evasive, hard to describe, much less define. We learn to synthesize by doing, not by being taught. Nor do we teach people to be creative. Creative education isn't a taughtology, but we can encourage the development of synthetic, integrative thinking and provide settings conducive to creative explorations. The exercises herein were invented to put participants in a muddle, without a paddle, and encourage them to sort their way out of the exercise. We learn to enjoy the process of exploration through play, to pay attention to the terrain we cross and to our fellow travelers. Creative minds see wholes where others see holes. To creative minds, unrelated things are one big hapless family. No matter, we are all on track to the same destination: creative, fluid, synthetic thinking.

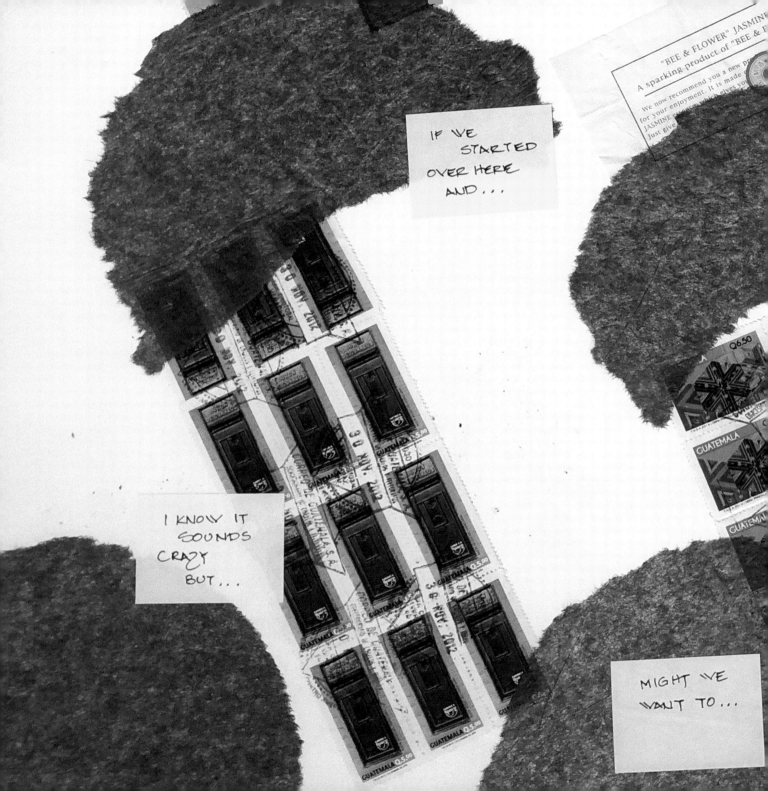

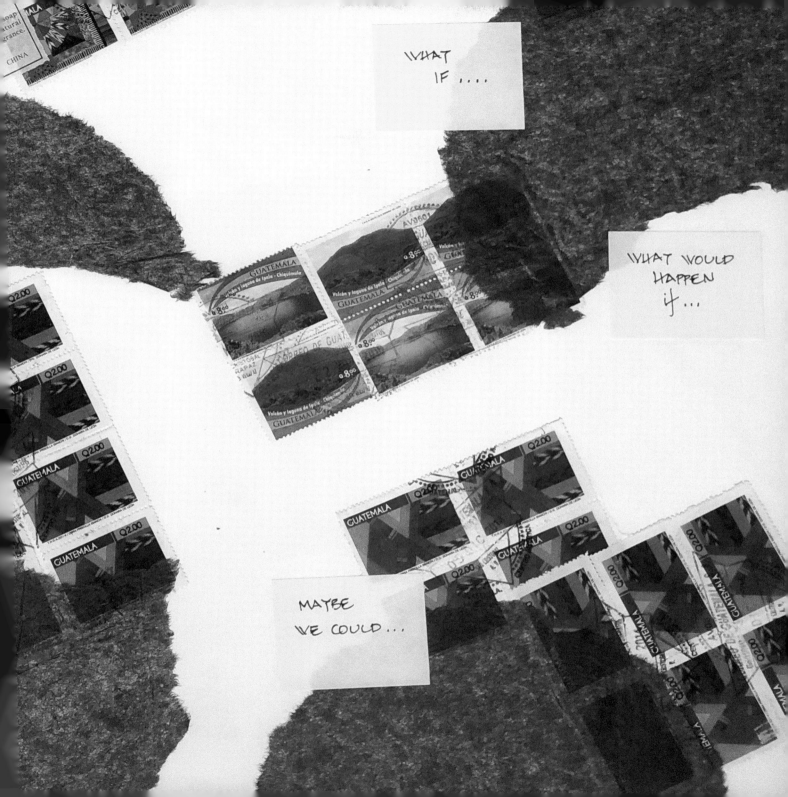

SPEAKING
the
LANGUAGE
of
FORM

The language of form is a wordless but eloquent means of communication. It is the lingua franca of professions from product design to spatial design, and it reaches deep into two- and three-dimensional arts. It is a universally understood language, fluently spoken by some, unconsciously mouthed by others. It is based on the concept that form has meaning, even though our interpretations of meanings vary, just as they do for written communications. Becoming conscious of this language opens doors for creative exploration and thought. We explore the language of form by examining common, everyday objects—in this instance, glass bottles.

Like many exercises, the process here is reassuringly simple. Participants are provided with large sheets of paper and colorful markers and asked to draw the lines and forms of a collection of glass bottles of varied shapes, sizes, and colors. To avoid overreliance on sight, participants are encouraged to run their fingers over surfaces before drawing their lines and forms—to get a direct feel for the forms rather than observe form at arm's length. After exploring the language of form by drawing lines and shapes, participants are asked to translate this language by adding written descriptions of the lines along their length. At the risk of sounding like a broken record, let me repeat: Products, though often beautiful, are less important than processes. Our goal is to reveal that we speak the language of form, not make beautiful drawings. The information age comprises more than digits. Form lies at the heart of information.

Despite its beguiling simplicity, the exercise description contains a stumbling block. Providing paper, markers, and objects implies that the task is to create beautiful and accurate drawings, which is not the goal. It is to look directly at the forms of bottles and transcribe their lines. It is difficult for participants to see beyond the bottle-drawing task to seeing the forms of bottles. Worse still, participants conclude that to demonstrate their creativity they should select novel viewpoints or generate self-expressive interpretations. They have been asked to practice their scales; they aspire to create symphonies. The goal is even simpler and broader than drawing; it is to become conscious that we see the world through the lens of form.

Live the Lines of your life; Play Tennis!

Why bottles? Why not mousetraps or paper clips, or any other everyday product? There's no reason to confine ourselves to bottles. But bottles are remarkably obliging, both as subjects and objects, for exploring the language of form. They possess clean, simple, unambiguous lines and shapes. They are comfortably familiar objects—a bottle is a bottle is a bottle, so what? However, glass bottles tailor their materials to function in exquisite, elegant, and economical forms. Bottles are functionally beautiful.

The exercise works best when participants have become comfortable with several prior exercises' idiosyncrasies and are willing to take risks and try new approaches. Innate predispositions and skills largely determine the participants' engagement. Some jump in and draw freely; some, having convinced themselves that they don't know how to draw, are hesitant. Others begin slowly and thoughtfully, observing their bottles closely or spending time running fingers over their surfaces, sometimes with eyes closed to counter sight's tendency to dominate our thought processes. Tactility encourages grounded, wordless understanding, which diminishes the debilitating tendency to draw what we perceive is there, not what we actually see. It's hard to persuade participants that this exploration of the language of form is not a drawing exercise. It's also hard for minds domineered by language to give voice to the language of form. The meaning of form is independent of words. It can be intrinsically inspirational. The exercise counters the presumption that all thought, all inspiration, must pass through the medium of language. So why add words

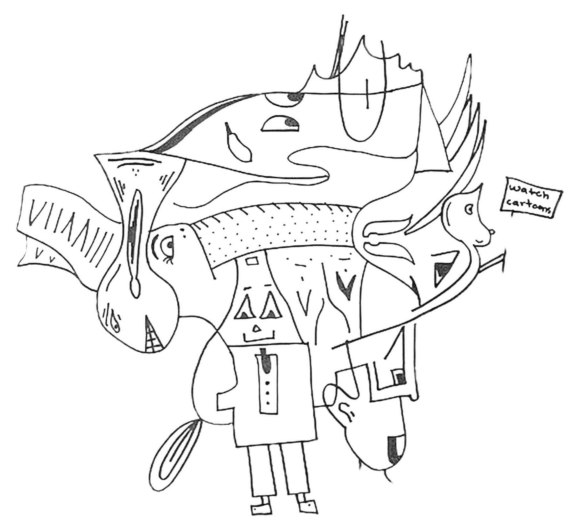

As in many creativity explorations, overt instructions conceal more substantive underlying questions.

Can you handle it? Rodeo #13. RIDE WILD.

after drawing lines? Hopefully, by translating lines into words, we may become more, not less, conscious of our facility with the language of form.

How did participants respond to the exercise and its nettlesome admonition to explore forms? The following reflections shed light on how they addressed this dilemma. Like many exercises, this one begins with trial and error to grapple with the seemingly contradictory instructions and ends with a confession that it is far easier for us to communicate through the familiar medium of words than to express our ideas in a language we are less conscious of speaking.

When we use the word language metaphorically for understanding forms, it reveals that we are all multilingual. We speak the languages of form, materiality, culture, values, power, nature, numbers, et cetera. No doubt, there are more. I grow tongue-tied. The premise of this and other language exercises is that by becoming conscious of our multilingualism, we expand our mental horizons, revealing more opportunities to think and act creatively.

Instructions are exercises' starting points, not their last word. They should be adjusted and adapted as circumstances suggest. Stay fluid. Be flexible. In the iteration that Juliana Y responded to, participants were encouraged to repeat the exercise quickly, to think of bottles as having personalities, to draw their bottles' "signatures," and to modify one another's drawings. Suggestions should encourage participants to see bottles afresh, but without biasing how they see them.

WILMA L: *I was particularly challenged by the form/bottle exercise. I could NOT figure out how to represent the bottle by drawing forms, shapes, and lines without actually drawing the bottle itself. My first draft was stilted and contrived because I attempted to bypass the restriction of not drawing the bottle. Instead, I drew separate lines on both sides of the sheet of paper... Frustrated by my output, I switched to looking for internal shapes in the bottle and proceeded to draw those on a new sheet of paper. I drew the sunken rectangles in the sides and the curved reflections on the neck. It still looked a lot like a bottle (albeit one drawn by a seven-year-old), but the process I used was one of convincing, powerful lines and drawing what I felt. I found the word... came a lot easier than the lines.*

TRICIA H: *This week's bottles exercise was especially helpful and interesting for me. I noticed that if I didn't think anything but sort of kept my mind calm and fuzzy, an idea for drawing the bottle's "signature" shape came more quickly and easily and was often more appropriate or unusual than if I'd thought about it beforehand... Overall, this discovery makes sense, because when my mind is "calm and fuzzy," it is relaxed and thus able to function creatively more effectively.*

DREW M: *I found the "language of shape" activity to be particularly difficult, in that it took me a great deal of staring and thinking (or perhaps unthinking) to get to the form of the bottle as something other than a bottle. I think I managed the idea fairly well in my initial drawing, but something seemed to pull me back to adding back more of the bottle aspect by adding the second layer. Whatever that something may have been, I guess it just goes to show that stepping beyond the bounds of one's comfort zone can be an essential step in tapping into one's deeper levels of creativity.*

VICTOR J: *In this assignment, I realize how hard it is to be creative, especially when the assignment is about drawing lines, shapes, and forms to represent a bottle. However, I also experienced how rewarding it was to make a connection between, on the surface, two unrelatable items. It was hard, really hard, but when I was able to visualize the features of my bottle as people whom I have crossed paths with, it opened a new dimension to the bottles. It was quite fun imagining each and every bottle as a person.*

MAN RAY: *I really liked the jar signature project. While circling around the table, "correcting" the signatures others created, I found myself looking at certain parts of the bottle in order to draw the signature. However, when the bottles were only accessible for seconds, I found myself freer. I hardly thought while I scribbled lines and swirls. Interestingly, these also seemed more "accurate" than my original signatures. While the thought—through signatures visually represented the bottles better, I thought the impulse signatures captured a, I don't know, "better" impression, a more "real" experience, and a "truer" reaction to the bottle in comparison to the instances where students were provided more time to think.*

JULIANA Y: *I loved the theme of "language of form"—it's a concept I've subconsciously noticed but never took the time to fully think about. I've always wondered how it is that people's signatures often mirror their personalities, but now I know that it is a common perception and observation that we all share—much like a real (whatever that word means), spoken language... [I]t was interesting seeing how people's [later] drawings varied from their initial drawing and the speed drawing. Lines were less restricted, less thought out, and more "natural." This, I believe, is a key component of the language of form—it does not lend itself to thought-out analysis, but, rather, to impulsive and instinctual action. But of course you could go the simple route and say that the bottles themselves were, indeed, quite pretty.*

Expansions and Additions

It bears repeating that exercises are neither set in stone nor glass, so consider the possibilities of plastic bottles; shampoo and detergent bottles, for example, are expressly formed to differentiate and sell products. The signature forms of many products come readily to mind. Try eliminating the forms of shampoo and detergent bottles recently implanted in your mind.

Opportunities abound for exploring how form can in-form creative attitudes of mind. We live and think not just in our heads but also in a world of forms. Whether natural or human-made, forms have meaning. Some meanings are intrinsic to the qualities of materials; some result from formative processes acting on materials over time—consider the forms of mountains and valleys sculpted by ice and eroded by millennia of rain; other meanings are extrinsic, applied, and surficial or skin-deep. Again, recall the forms of ever so familiar plastic bottles—would you like ketchup or mustard with that in-form-ation? The language of form may be unspoken, but

limiting our choices · broadening the question

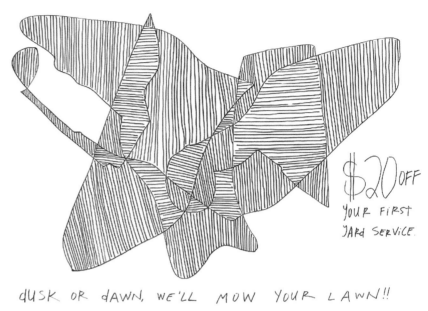

$20 OFF
YOUR FIRST
YARd SERViCE.

dUSK OR dAWN, WE'LL MOW YOUR LAWN!!

it is not unread. Form is informative and influential. Whether we are conscious of it or not, we read forms and interpret meanings. Effortlessly and unconsciously, we conclude this form is beautiful, that is not; this form is useful, that is not. Learning to read the meanings of forms opens up opportunities to understand the world in greater depth and from different perspectives. Creative minds see everything from multiple perspectives. They can shape-shift at will from one perspective reading to another.

We rely on the stability and legibility of forms; consider the uncanny effects of mutating forms, the shape-shifting abilities of mythical creatures, and the denizens of horror movies. When words fail us, we resort to thinking and communicating in forms. Diagrams, symbols, insignia, and graphic structures may convey meaning more succinctly and elegantly than recalcitrant words. What doors, what windows, what avenues, what possibilities does the language of form open to our gaze! Exercises may engage with

spatial forms or the forms of solid objects; innumerable objects could be used to explore the language of form. I have favored glass bottles, but also consider natural objects: leaves, beach pebbles. What else possesses forms that excite our understanding of the language of form and allow us to use this understanding to enrich creative attitudes of mind?

The language of form informs us of other languages to explore: space, behavior, body, materiality, culture. The world is our oyster and our language. The twin languages of form and space lie at the heart of my own discipline, landscape architecture. Although I have tried to avoid infecting all creativity exercises with my professional biases toward spatial and ecological design, this exercise comes close to home. I trust it is acceptable to revel in form, form giving, and interpretations of the meanings of forms—which span the delectable to the despicable—in at least one exercise.

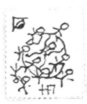

The
LANGUAGE
of FORM
REVISITED

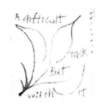

Creativity exercises are not set in stone; like creative thinking, they are fluid and can be revised and adapted for further inspiration. This brief exercise revisits the language of form exercise, replacing its large sheets of paper with small perforated sheets. Participants are asked to record their impressions of the language of form exercise on the back of postage stamps. The paucity of space is complemented by a short time frame. It's a quick, almost incidental, "interlude exercise." It has no laconic and discursive instructions, just a terse verbal prompt and a ticking clock. Blinkandyoumissedit.

Life rarely provides useful handouts for what to do: "If this had been a real emergency/exercise, you would have been told where to go and what to do… later." Surprise is a perennial pick-me-up and knock-me-over element of life, catching us off guard and disabling preconceived responses. The novelty of using the back of postage stamps invites inventive responses, one of which might be "Are we really confined to the back of the stamps?" Where expansive sheets of paper tolerate, even invite, mental lassitude, sparse real estate raises land values and focuses attention. Speed and severe constraints are a high-octane mix for inventiveness or freezing us in our tracks. The exercise's incidental, low-stakes character encourages the former. Despite the limited time, the exercise reinforces the importance of reflection and recapitulation, of returning to a question posed in a different light and seeing it afresh.

In theory, we could substitute scraps of paper for postage stamps, but this theory doesn't work in practice. Choosing a size for paper scraps is an arbitrary decision, and arbitrary constraints lack substance and tend to be ignored. Stamps have defined perimeters; thus spatial constraints stick. It may seem paradoxical to cultivate creativity with constraints, but constraints are not merely helpful but essential in all creative endeavors. They focus attention and limit the range of explorations. No constraints, no direction. Know constraints, know direction—paradox upon paradox, the more open-ended the question, the greater the need for constraints. The trick is to select and apply the right constraints. Our constraints here are time and paper. Tiny postage stamps

contrast with earlier papery expanses. Short time periods contrast with earlier temporal expansiveness. Constraints are a designer's best friend.

The intrinsic interest of stamps over paper scraps adds a hint of added value to the work and heightens the significance of the responses—a further mental constraint AND inspiration. Queen Elizabeth's image on British stamps may or may not be mentally inhibiting, but her presence adds a dimension absent from scraps of paper. Repeating the exercise with a second two-pence stamp provides a second chance. The work's intensity may not be as delicate as that of a goldsmith mounting a precious jewel or a circuit-board assembly-line worker's soldering, but is focused nevertheless. Participants get to work, heads close to the table. An air of concentration pervades the room.

In a fast-paced, instant-messaging, all-atwitter society, it would be nice to have the courage to spend more time on reiteration and reflection while emphasizing the value of exercises by slowing the pace to gather fresh responses. But, like dieting and exercise, we know we should, but we rarely take the time to do so. This exercise is a reminder that reiteration is time well spent and can provide fresh insight.

This exercise also reflects on the concepts of abundance and scarcity. When materials are scarce or precious, for whatever reason (unusual, old, peculiar, valuable), do we adopt more cautious attitudes and use resources more deliberately and carefully? With abundance, do we respond oppositely? In what ways do material resources affect attitudes of mind? Do different attitudes evoke different forms of creative expression? The main lessons: Grasp what comes to hand and use what comes to mind; enormities of opportunities lie within tiny and trivial materials; possibilities for wonder exist beneath our noses in commonplace places. Surely enough for a brief recapitulation exercise? Interlude exercises are "elevator pitches."

FREYA Z: *Our little doodles on those itty-bitty stamps, as small a project as it may have been, seemed to elicit the most creativity from me, or at least the most natural, an uninhibited creativity. In the previous projects, I started at one idea and let the idea morph around in my head before I took action. With the stamp, I let my actions morph around until I reached a final result. I started with sensuous curves to mimic the curve of the bottle, letting my pen direct me. From there, I let the lines on my stamp dictate my next move. Looking back, it's much like the process that most teens go through when they doze off in class and doodle in their notes. In both cases, I didn't have any well-thought out or rigidly structured plans. It was the form of the creative process that differed. Which is more important? Which produces the most creative outcome? Creative thought and planning, or creative action? Is it possible to have both? This is something I would like to explore further, though I'm afraid of a giant, chaotic creative overload!*

JULIANA Y: *I did very much enjoy the stamp activity. I like that you make us do most... activities twice, including this one, after seeing each other's work—it really changes the substance of the second product. We all like to think we're individuals and acting completely autonomously and creatively, but the truth is, the extent to which we're influenced by other people is substantial. And that's not necessarily a bad thing; collaborative creativity can oftentimes produce better products than individual efforts... A quote from last Wednesday stuck with me: "You must know the rules before you break them." I can't seem to explain why, but that rings so true to me.*

Expansions and Additions

By confining exercises to separate chapters, I may have inadvertently suggested that each should be done once, and then we should move on. Not so! Exercises benefit from repetition when we give them new twists that encourage fresh ways of responding. Twists may be subtle or dramatic. The quirky twist of this exercise was to restrict space and time—to stamp out inessentials. Confined space necessitated getting to the essence of what one wants to say and tossing out the fluff and extraneous ideas. Imagine kneading and folding, kneading and folding bread dough, again and again, and then again to lengthen its yeast strands. We knead to know how exercise iterations can do something analogous.

How else might we reinterpret the language of form exercise? Could we tear and interweave the earlier drawings on our large sheets of paper? Could we add more verbal descriptions along the lines? What could we do with other materials, paint, coffee, new bottles? What might happen if we thought outside the box and broke the bottles, or, horror of horrors, what if we introduced digital technology and photographed bottles and drawings with our phones? Three-dimensional printing? Retain the interest of participants. Press the "refresh" button to alter exercises so that they don't become dull and repetitiously, repetitious.

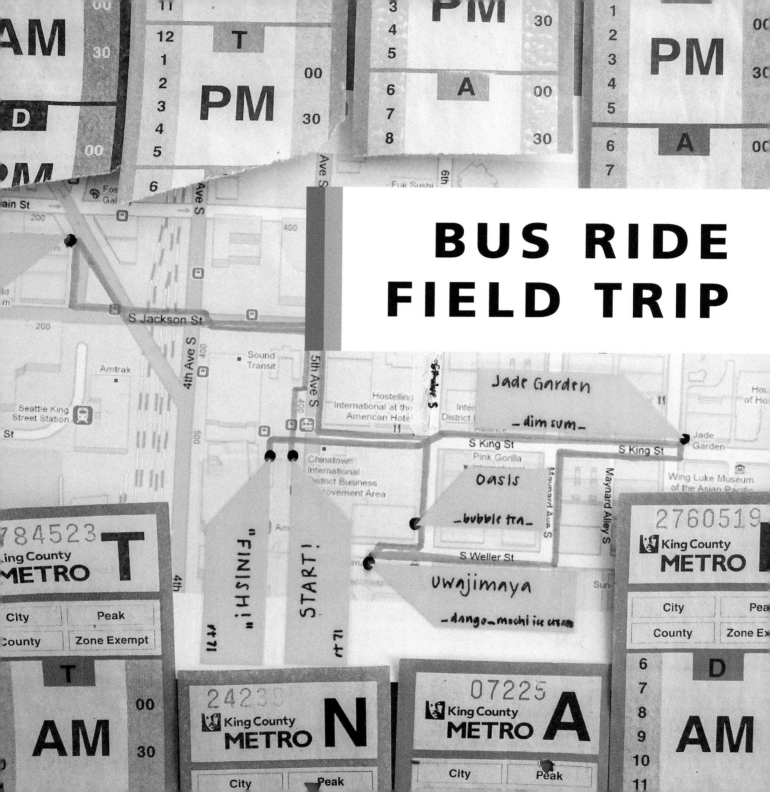

BUS RIDE FIELD TRIP

The journey of a thousand discoveries begins with one step out of a daily routine. This exercise leaves the classroom behind to seek new insights and understandings. Based on the proposition that a change is as good as a rest, participants were instructed to catch an unfamiliar bus and experience the journey, emphasizing the journey, not the destination. To make the field trip memorable, participants were also asked to record their experiences in the form of epic poems or photo essays of the experience, not necessarily the destination. Field trips can often encourage thinking about the influence of place.

In contrast, this exercise encourages students to travel beyond daily routines to influence creative frames of mind. Some trips were successful, others ill-fated. Yes, 'to travel hopefully is a better thing than to arrive," but better still to have planned the trip well. Calling the exercise a "qualified success" means it was largely a failure. We caught the bus but missed the mark. Nevertheless, such an exercise is instructive because we can learn from the instructor's mistakes while celebrating participants' indomitable courage.

The idea of using cheap public transit for a journey sounds promising and practical. The theory seems sound: Bus rides would be a simple way to take us out of our routines and allow us to experience the positive effects of travel on our mental state. Participants would observe the changing scene and consider their lives and those of their fellow travelers. The unfamiliar journey would dislodge comfortable preconceptions and attitudes of mind and encourage fresh mental associations, connections, and realizations to flourish. What could go wrong?

Well, rosy-hued theory foundered on the shoals of Seattle's cold, wet, dreary winter days and bus schedules that butted heads with tight class schedules. Finding time for open-ended bus rides in highly structured class schedules proved difficult. Published schedules were no guarantee that participants would return in time for their next class. An exercise conceived as a relaxing break turned out, in many cases, to be stressful, inducing moods antithetical to creative frames of mind. A soupçon of forethought might have anticipated these problems.

The way participants chose to conduct their field trip affected their experience. Those who traveled during class times worried about time, and their journeys were counterproductive. Those who bent the rules and made the most of fair weather to take weekend bicycle rides succeeded. Despite schedule hiccups, presentations recapitulated field trip experiences imaginatively. They included epic poems, photo essays, and a lively skit. Reflections recounted interesting stories and are particularly informative because they honestly describe rides that did and didn't work.

Why am I including an exercise that didn't appear to work? This exercise brings up the reality of students' lives—grueling schedules, midterm pressures, and bleak winter skies—that contribute little to the joy of exploration. Lest there be any misunderstanding, let me emphasize this is not how to induce creative attitudes of mind. Some exercises miss the boat; some miss the bus; some arrive in the harbor, while for others, "all the voyage of their life Is bound in shallows and in miseries." This exercise's seed is sound, but the soil in which the stressed seed was planted was stony. How could it be restructured, or completely changed, to explore better travel as a propellant for creative attitudes of mind?

Expansions and Additions

Field trips can leaven the educational loaf and make it more palatable and nutritious. Departing classrooms need not be truancy. Breaks in hectic, overscheduled daily routines offer chances for us to find ourselves. Travel's positive effects can enhance creative attitudes of mind. How can we experience the positive impact of travel within necessary constraints? Imagine the surprise of taking a bus ride to somewhere you've never been and finding yourself along the way. The value of reflective time within the maelstrom of daily life cannot be overemphasized. Reflection time is not a substitute for learning, but it is essential for our minds to connect, integrate, synthesize, and understand what we have learned. We benefit from regaining our perspective on the whole journey and where it is taking us, or where we are taking it.

Field Trip 2: Boon or Bused?

Travel As Impetus for Creativity

You cannot in my view be truly and transformatively creative in your thoughts if all you are really concerned about is making a buck off the results.

—J. V. MATSON, *BREAKTHROUGH INNOVATION: A GUIDETO BUILDING YOUR FUTURE*

I have travelled a good deal in Concord.

—HENRY DAVID THOREAU, *WALDEN*

Much as we would like to transport you to other realms, lands, shores, horizons, pastures, archipelagoes, capitals of principalities, like Valduz, et cetera, for this exercise, time constrains us and we must, perforce, be inventive in our explorations of the effects of travel on creative frames of mind. What to do? Aye, there's the rub and that's the question! Here's an idea:

Catch a Metro or CT bus or light rail—other than ones you may use on daily commutes or are "frequent fliers" on. Defy Terminus! It's time to get beyond the boundary stones demarcating comfort zones.

Go places, but don't go complacent!

Go somewhere else! Sit in a different seat! Travel with two companions! Listen! Observe fellow travelers! Look out the window! See the world anew!

Ah, but a (wo)man's reach should exceed her/his grasp / Or what's a bus rid for?

Remember

Destiny resides in the journey, not the destination.

(Does that make all that goes before you reach your destination predestination? Probably yes, if the bus sticks to its prescribed route. Traffic diversions are, however, something verse):

where the bus stops, there shop I
Here Tyeburn throttled, massed murmars march:
where the bus stops there shop I: here which ye see,
yea reste.

—JAMES JOYCE, *FINNEGANS WAKE*

Individually AND collectively, record your journey as an epic poem OR, this just in, a photo essay sent from your iPhone or other such device.

Our job, as creative individuals, is to transmute the mundane into the magical.

Catching busses and leaving the driving to others can provide contexts amenable to reflection. On this field trip, the journey itself was intended to induce free and creative attitudes of mind. In what other ways might we trick ourselves into adopting such frames of mind? Can we learn to release our minds so that they may roam more freely? Can we loosen the leash—or noose—of preconceptions that we usually keep tightly knotted around our minds? Can we surprise ourselves out of our routines and expectations? This is what field trips try to accomplish.

Bus travel aside, are there other ways to create the experience of being away from desk-time conditions? In other words, how can we generate liberating attitudes of mind that allow the unconscious to do its synthesizing work? This exercise tried, unsuccessfully, to concoct vacationlike conditions of freedom in a short time. It attempted to put participants in novel settings that might induce fresh experiences. What other ways might we do this to generate creative attitudes of mind? Could we, for example, turn annoying but necessary activities such as waiting in lines for services, walking to obligatory meetings, or commuting to work into creativity exercises? How might we use enforced inaction time in the interstice of our daily routines to promote creative mind wandering? Freedom to synthesize and enjoy the journey? That's the ticket!

TALLY A: *The most surprising part of this week was definitely yesterday's field trip. To be honest, I didn't have a very good time. I couldn't know exactly how the other members of my group felt, but their comments and the overall downcast mood suggested that most of them felt similarly. I don't know exactly what caused this brooding, glum feeling, but it wasn't simply the gray weather. Half of us had midterms... so we were on a very tight leash. Returning to campus on time, rather than experiencing the journey, became the focus of the outing. We also talked a little about how the newness of our external location seemed to distract us from our internal creativity.*

ANON: *Even though the trip itself wasn't a great experience, I'm grateful to have gone because it's left me with a lot to think about. First, having a predetermined end point to creativity (such as a scheduled midterm) can be very limiting. The creative process hinges upon a sense of boundless possibility—ideas flowering from ideas in a beautiful, infinite fractal. Everyone knows that, realistically, all journeys and ideas reach some sort of conclusion eventually, but no one wants to know exactly when and how they will end... Having no way to anticipate or control the end point enables me to appreciate the journey.*

Second, the field trip made me consider the delicate balance between the internal and external components of creativity. Creativity is an internal process that requires inspiration from external factors. Too little external stimulation produces stagnancy, but too much is overwhelming. The internal-external ratio is different for everyone, which is why some people love to travel the world, while others find meaning in walking the same path every day for forty years. I tend to live more on the internal side of things, which may be why this off-campus adventure left me feeling more anxious than inspired.

EVA K: *I got a parking ticket while we were out adventuring for Friday's field trip activity, and ever since I've been thinking about the cost of creativity. Normally, I'd dismiss the ticket as a slight bump in the road, but this one carried a hefty fine: forty right dollars for parking in Zone 6 for more than two hours without a permit. I think I had a mild heart attack when I saw the dollar amount on the ticket and realized that this had just officially become the most expensive school assignment I had ever done. Despite the damper it put on my mood that day, I've started to connect that ticket to the trip as part of it rather than a secondary, detached consequence. Perhaps I got dealt a lucky hand after all and was given the opportunity to think about the costs that accompany all great ideas. It seems silly at first to connect creativity and consequence as going hand in hand, but when you dissect some of the greatest ideas of all time, there were often negative costs that came along with them...*

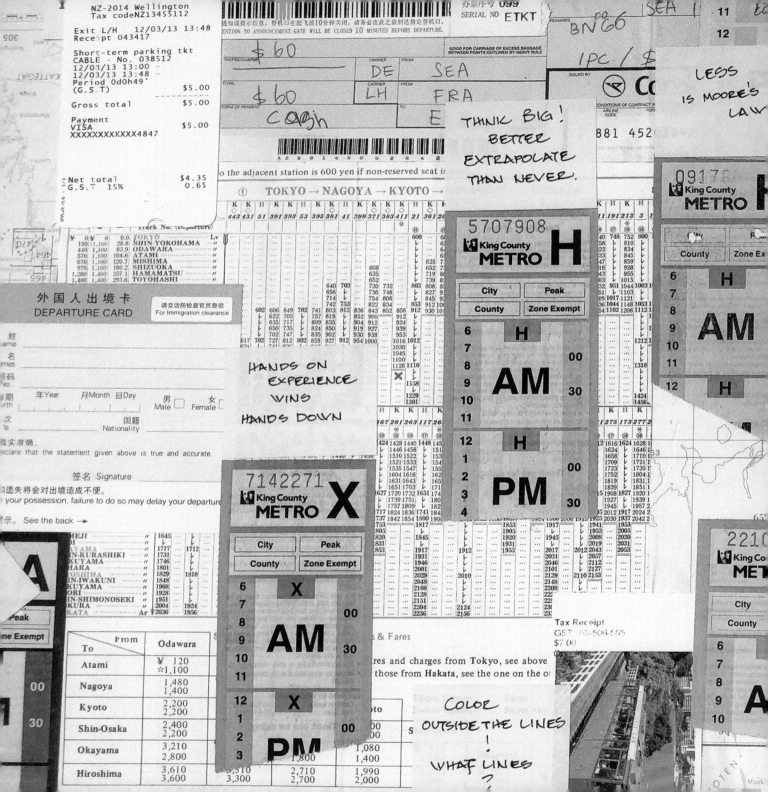

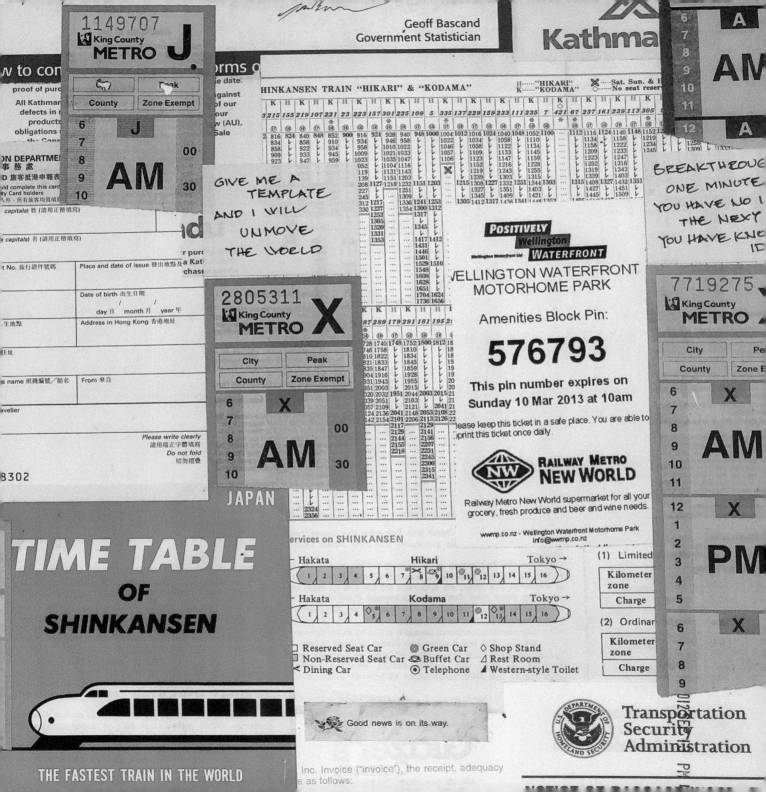

WHERE?

Crafting Instructions

Instructions for Crafting Creativity Exercises

Explicit questions such as "What's two plus two?" invite explicit responses. Definitive instructions for actions suggest correct responses. The clearer the instructions, the more precisely the circumscribed answers. In contrast, instructions for creativity exercises have different goals. Pose questions as open-ended invitations to explore rather than inviting prescribed responses. Use the power of suggestion to hint, allude, and infer what one might do rather than dictate what one should do. Thus instructions are often acutely obtuse, convoluted, suggestive, and associative rather than blandly explicit. Such questions are maddening; they conceal, rather than reveal, their intent and verge on confusion and opacity. They open doors but don't prescribe where to go. This purposely ambiguous approach encourages participants to think and develop their own directions for exploration and find their own questions and answers. In designing creative exercises, we are not particularly concerned about answers; we are more interested in the thought processes and encouragement of fluid thought patterns than in fortifying rigidities. And so, to rule out rule following, we write assignments

in ways that encourage reading between the lines, interpreting and translating assignments, and, ultimately, questioning the questions. Assignments and exercises are launchpads for curiosity.

Surely that's enough clarifying obfuscation? No, exercise instructions go further. One may add literary quotes or, occasionally, images to hint that others have traveled these ways before us, but quotes are never explicit signposts. We borrow quotes that legitimize departing from prescribed, definitional, logical thought patterns, ones that suggest that metaphorical approaches may be more helpful than literal ones. Assignment descriptions are provocations, sometimes procrastinatingly so, or when we tire of that approach, they are succinct and sharply to the point.

Beribboning instructions with extraneous clutter—allusions, suggestions, connections, and confections—offers varied starting points or hints as to how one might, if one so wished, develop an approach to the exercise. Signposts are allusions, suggestions, inferences, and obliquities. Instructions require participants to excavate questions from them.

If instructors wish answers that mimic their voices, they are better off chatting with parrots. On the other hand, we should recognize that participants' lives are often overfull and might benefit from emptiness; therefore, some instructions provide emptiness that invites exploration of open space. Such exercises cultivate creativity by providing minds with space and time to be expansive, flower, open up, or rest productively.

Elaborate exercises can surprise us, but simple and elegant prompts are often better. Brief exercise instructions may be more effective trip wires for imagination, interceding with our attention when least expected. With time, creative minds need only gentle prompts to evoke creative attitudes of mind. A falling apple or a scrap of paper may be all that a primed mind needs to kindle a conflagration. Creative thought and exploration need prompts that foster and reward fluid attitudes of mind, not just on special occasions set aside for being creative, but always and everywhere. Cultivating creativity is about cultivating a mind-set with which to live our ordinary daily lives. A set mind is not a creative mind-set. Creative thought is fluid, supple, and exploratory, insinuating itself into problems like dampness into basement walls.

The following rules for generating creativity exercises outline the pedagogical and philosophical underpinnings of the theme of cultivating creativity described in this book; they are the structure of an educational ethos. Think of these rules as components of an integrated system, not a list of unrelated ideas. But the list is tentative and incomplete, for, like all creative thought, it is a work in progress. Except for the first rule, the list is not hierarchical.

Creative attitudes of mind are not confined to education, so the rules also apply to life and lifelong learning and may help us live full and meaningful lives. If we may unearth a definition of creativity from these rules, it would probably suggest that our goal is to live full, abundant, and meaningful lives and to be engaged and connected. A life full of creativity is a far cry from a pursuit of fame and fortune, with venture capitalists beating paths to our door. Creativity is only peripherally about making better widgets or a fortune. To enhance their flavor, garnish these rules with a grain of assalt.

Even when we break out of the preconceived notion that to get an education is painful, exercises should be fun. Serious purposes are not at odds with playfulness.

Rules for Unruly Behavior

The first rule overrules all others: there are no hard-and-fast rules for developing creativity exercises.

Exercises provide guidelines, hints, nudges, winks, not strict rules to be adhered to unthinkingly.

Exercises should be real and relate to participants' lives.

Rules should span the debilitating gulf between education and life. Education does not occur exclusively within the confines of classrooms. Lifelong learners should learn from their lives. Exercises should dissolve artificial distinctions between life and education.

Exercises should not exude even the faintest whiff of academic probity, veracity, and rectitude.

This almost universal rule discourages responding to exercises academically. Exercises should disarm overachievers who have figured out how to succeed in the education mill and the affairs of life.

Exercises should engage participants playfully.

This may be a silly way to put it, but it's not stupid. Even when we break out of the preconceived notion that to get an education is painful, exercises should be fun. Serious purposes are not at odds with playfulness. Avoid heavy-handedness; encourage lighthearted, playful explorations. Play need not be trivial. Descriptions walk a fine line between seriousness and ridiculousness, between making sense and nonsense. Descriptions should be rational within their parameters, which are not necessarily the same as those of the real world.

Xrcs shld B quick 2 prvnt ovrthnkng and ovanlyzng.

Act first, think later. Try, then reflect. Short and sweet. Small is beautiful. Short exercises reduce opportunities for egos to become enamored of and defined by their products, making it easier to accept criticism.

Exercises should encourage experimentation and be mistake-friendly, so descriptions may be composed in ways that condone misunderstanding, misconception, misinterpretation.

More than just tolerating mistakes, we should encourage, delight in, and learn from them. Exercises may lead participants astray and beguile, delude, and deceive them, but they should always do so in playful ways. Descriptions should trip up familiar responses that we routinely and unthinkingly fall into.

Exercise descriptions shouldn't be explicit.

Exercises should never be specific, unambiguous, and clear. They should be suggestive and invite multiple interpretations rather than point "right this way, folks." They should leave room for interpretation. A creativity exercise should be presented deceptively, requiring participants to discern subtexts, read between the lines, uncover slumbering implications, and decode inferences, all of which may reveal a communication's true meaning and purpose. This fluidity is fundamental to a creative attitude of mind.

Exercises should be open-ended to encourage self-directed explorations.

Instructions should be vague and suggestive, hinting at avenues for exploration rather than prescribing right and wrong ways to explore. Vaguely worded assignments drive participants who are unused to loose reins to distraction—and then to thought! This approach is not without risk—participants may veer wildly off track—but all teaching and learning involve risks, and if explorations are truly open-ended, there is no one right track.

Exercises should generate environments conducive to fruitful, promising, useful activities. They should encourage participants to share their explorations and destinations.

Exercise descriptions should open doors and should be positively suggestive and encourage discussion and collaboration. Assignments will be interpreted differently by each participant, fostering peer learning. Ideally, participants learn more from one another than from instructors.

Exercises should keep participants, and instructors, guessing. Participants should not know what is expected of them—at least not with certitude.

Exercises transfer responsibility for interpretation to participants, who can't fall back on "I'm just doing what I'm told and giving you what you want." Participants must take ownership of their explorations and methods but relinquish exclusive ownership of results. The ball should be in the participants' court.

Exercises must be surprising.

Exercises must discourage standard responses. They should catch even the most en garde participants off guard and pitch curveballs for those on the straight and narrow. Participants succeed when they are surprised by their creations and understandings. "Wow! I didn't know I had it in me."

Exercises should be varied and different.

Exercises activities should explore various skills and interests, so the participant will excel in some and not in others. Different materials can also encourage fresh responses.

Exercises may get more and more peculiar as anticipants become comfortable experimenting in ambiguous situations.

Exercises are more crook books than cookbooks. Each exercise should make participants stew anew, bake awake, fry and try, grill and thrill, boil and toil. Successive activities should dig participants in deeper and deeper one step at a time rather than have them fall head over heels into a trap.

Syllabi descriptions should discourage participants from enrolling who would not appreciate the ambiguity, doubt, and confusion—perhaps frustration and anger—that successful exercises incite. At the very least, they should give fair warning that an adventurous and open mind is a prerequisite of the class.

Exercises should be personal, the distinctive creations of individual instructors.

We're not on the straight and narrow, so they should be idiosyncratic. Exercises should also be personal in order to forge authentic connections between instructors and participants, but they must not be designed to boost instructors' egos. To avoid serving up standard fare that ceases to be nutritious, exercises shouldn't be repeated ad nauseam or ad infinitum—whichever comes first.

Exercise materials should be used, and used up. This includes idiosyncratic materials that mean a lot to instructors' lives.

Everything is expendable in the pursuit of creativity. Letting go must be practiced by instructors as well as by participants. Good materials may tell stories; they should possess hidden meanings, and conceal intrigue, but should not be overly valuable, precious, or delicate. They should include natural and man-made objects. Some should be familiar, everyday objects—the sorts of things we know and ignore—others should be surprising, unusual, and intriguing. All should invite inspection, adjustment, manipulation, and play.

Exercises should have no right, and probably few wrong, answers. They may succeed even when their purpose is not immediately apparent.

The meanings of successful exercise will, like burrs under saddles, make themselves known more and more insistently for the rest of the ride. Creative seeds retain remembered half-lives even when half-forgotten.

Exercises should not try to generate common outcomes.

Typical classes have common goals and outcomes: "This is what you will learn in this class." Creativity exercises don't have a single uniform, predetermined lesson for everyone. They should invite varied interpretations and conclusions, which should be self-tailored to fit each individual's needs.

Exercises should leave time for reflection. Important learning happens after exercises are over. Descriptions should require reflections.

Learning happens through participants' discussions and reflections on what they have done. Success isn't measured by course evaluations, but by participants' self-assessment reflections. Instructors should also learn and reflect AND let participants know they are doing so! Can instructors' reflections add to participants' learning? Are instructors willing to reveal themselves through their reflections?

Exercises should experiment with methods, and instructors should constantly take risks.

Absurdly utopian? Dangerously radical? Uncontrollable? If that's what you think, drop creativity and return to the well-worn path of rote learning and retention, followed by regurgitative testing.

Alternatively, generate new exercises that avoid being instrumental and don't rely on prescribed tried-and-true teaching methods—especially those "guaranteed" to induce innovative thinking. Exercises should encourage exploration of the unknown, not beat forced marches down well-traveled paths. Experiment! If participants are expected to take risks, instructors must do so, too.

Exercise descriptions can balance meaning and nonsense. They should unstick the glue of convention, reality, and certitude.

Exercises should help participants anticipate and enter magical places and lose their bearings, but only partly. They should unbalance participants but not subject them to WWF strangleholds. Exercises should be calibrated to provide just-in-time support to help participants generate individual ideas.

Exercises should lead participants to the interface of the known and chaos.

Exercises should operate at the boundary of—or one step beyond—comfort zones. They should find places where the mind can be fertile, connective, and expressive, which are often located at the edge of chaos. Comfortably edging participants to the brink of chaos may be accomplished through humor and incompleteness.

Exercises should be posed in ways that prevent them from being addressed rationally—or irrationally.

Exercises are dilemmas that can be resolved only by cutting the Gordian knot and should be posed in unamenable ways to logical thought and analysis. They should contain elements of chaos, confusion, illogic.

Exercises should be hedged in by constraints while remaining open-ended explorations.

Constraints should provide direction and guidance without favoring specific conclusions.

Time available for exercises should be limited—just enough to finish but insufficient to do so completely.

There should never be enough time to do everything, but there must be time to present results and reflect. Time constraints require participants to make quick decisions, which precludes the blossoming of self-criticism. Short time lines encourage hurried, but not rushed, action. If participants become bored, the exercise is too long.

Exercises should vary in length, some long, some short, and some exceedingly short.

Exercises should keep participants guessing, keep them thinking, keep them on their toes. Short exercises may warm them up initially or help pick up the pace if long exercises go flat.

Finally, the second most important rule to break: Exercises should bring on the dancing metaphors.

Lakoff and Johnson explain that "[t]he essence of metaphor is understanding and experiencing one kind of thing in terms of another." Exercises add a twist to this mental cocktail. Some may interpret common metaphors literally. Others understand the literal metaphorically. Literally and metaphorically, that's about it.

Has it become apparent that a primary purpose of creativity exercises is to exorcise bad habits acquired and reinforced by education? Habits include, but are not limited to, judging success by comparing ourselves to others, wanting to give the teacher the "right" answer, being scared to voice opposing views, and wanting to be right and be praised.

There's a great deal of undoing to be done. An unnecessary repetition: These rules should be peppered with a grain of salt. They are guidelines and suggestions, not immutable laws and directives. Adapt them so that only the fittest for your circumstances survive. Test them evolutionarily. They're flexible, so fold, bend, twist, and torque them to fit needs; torque out of both sides of your mouth without getting bent out of shape. Enjoy.

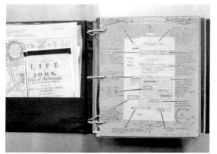

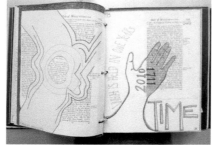

RECONSTITUTING THE BOOK

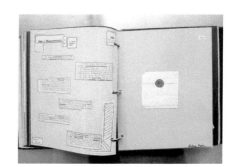

This exercise takes words that we commonly use metaphorically—deconstruction and reconstruction—and enacts them literally, deconstructing an old book and constructing a new one. We do so by cutting pages, one per participant, from an old book and having participants reconstitute their pages for inclusion into a new edition. The older the book and the more highly educated the participants, the greater the induced horror and the more effective the exercise. Deconstructed books must be valuable. Last year's phone book doesn't cut it. In this example, we cut pages from volume three of The Life of John, Duke of Marlborough, printed for J. Wilcox, against the New Church in the Strand, London, in 1736.

What? And Why?

The act of creation frequently requires destruction. Here, participants create something new—a book page—at the price of destroying something of venerable age. Creation is rarely free of costs. Destruction may be creation's shadow. To be reborn from the ashes, the phoenix must die. The success of creative acts may be judged by comparing the value of what's destroyed to that of what's created.

Page by page, participants reconstitute a sliver of the Duke of Marlborough's life, contributing a modified old page, mounted on a sheet of colored paper, to a new book, each page a unique signature. Literally cutting apart an old book conveys an unmistakable message: Destruction can be liberating, but both individuals and societies must learn to control this liberating force. In artists' hands, destruction may be generative and lead to renewal; in the arms of dictators and armies, it is something else. For some participants, the price of admission to this exercise is unpayable; they can't bring themselves to modify their venerable-through-age pages; others leap to the task and dismember pages after cursory glances. Some participants respond thoughtfully to their page's content, finding inspiration in the text, the unusual typography, or the old paper's tactile qualities. It's not over till it's overt. Instructions provide no guidelines for the "right" thing to do. To prevent the exercise from becoming an academic, historical, social, or political activity, we limit contextual information. However, some participants examine the duke's life and history on their phones during the exercise.

A theatrical introduction is desirable to enhance the initiating destructive act. Perhaps begin by passing around old leather-bound books and encouraging twenty-first-century participants—whose lives are full of facsimiles, reproductions, copies, simulations, simulacra, and virtual imagery—to handle the real thing. Draw attention to centuries-old books' physical and sensory feel—the coarse-textured brittleness of thin paper and the ghostly translucent watermarks; the creaks of sewn bindings; how pages curve and lie; the unfamiliar characteristics of old typefaces. After slaking our thirst at the well of the old, we are ready to assign our sacrificial tome to the altar of creativity. Deconstructionists worship at the alter.

Draw attention to the book's frontispiece by including a copy with the exercise instructions. Roman numerals reveal a publication date about a quarter century shy of three hundred years ago, a date older than most of our society's institutions. It is older than the United States. It predates by centuries the technologies that sustain our daily lives.

MDCCXXXVI MDCCXXXVI* MDCCXXXVI* MDCCXXXVI* MDCCXXXVI* MDCCXXXVI* MDCCXXXVI*

Re:Text Pretext

Creativity takes what we have—at hand and kicking about our minds (or culture) so to speak—and rearranges it to make something new. There is a magic to this unpredictable transformation of the familiar, the old, the dated, the known, into something new—whether it be a new form, or meaning, or understanding. Rebirth.

Culture continually renews itself—evolves—driven by incremental creative transformations, large and small, revolutionary and evolutionary. Reaction.

Today we shall participate in this process literally, as deconstructionists and reconstructionists, by reassembling an old text into a new text, each of you creating a unique one-page response to a deconstructed book, which we shall fold into a reconstructed or reconstituted book. Each of us shall knit a distinctive new creation from the old, responding to the old but putting our individual stamp on the ongoing product, just as our lives put their stamp on our culture.

Reproduce and Reflect.

MDCCXXXVI MDCCXXXVI* MDCCXXXVI* MDCCXXXVI* MDCCXXXVI* MDCCXXXVI* MDCCXXXVI*

Participants in academic settings respond with shock as we cut out pages. Disbelief may transform into consternation and anger. We are desecrating academia's holy of holies: old books. Our purposes are serious: to place our lives in the stream of cultural time, to participate in the process of extracting new meaning from old, to refresh and restore cultural understanding.

To illustrate possible responses, we may review pages created earlier but should do so briefly to avoid suggesting "typical" or "right" responses.

Although the products are appealing and revealing, they are not the main point; it's the exploratory process and the reflections that matter, not the matter itself. How did participants respond? How did this generative act feel?

The phoenix rises from the ashes. Old becomes new; we lament passing but take joy in its rebirth. There is phoenixlike magic in transforming a dated and outworn book into something fresh and new. The act regenerates, whether it be a reformation of an existing meaning, an interpolation of new meaning, or an understanding at right angles to the original text. Day by day, season by season, decade by decade, cultures transformatively renew themselves. Such changes may be incremental or massively disruptive, evolutionary or revolutionary. This exercise reenacts the never-ending cycle of creation and destruction.

VA K: *[O]nce again I felt free. I won't lie: The idea of cutting up a nearly three-hundred-year-old book made my heart stop. I think it actually did when the first slice was cut....Once I got over it, though, it felt amazing. I realized we weren't destroying; we were creating. I tried to do the page justice with my carefully constructed castle and the way I designed my page. I couldn't stop running my fingers over the paper. The texture of the paper and text printed on it seemed like they deserved a new form that would honor the old. It felt too important to compromise or ruin, so I was careful to preserve the integrity of the page even as I cut and glued it. I'm keeping the scrap... because I can't bear the thought of throwing it away. That page and paper is too good even for recycling. I know I'll repurpose every last piece in art projects that will ensure that the history of it is not forgotten.*

ELLA T: *[It was]...painful. Destroying a book that no one understood. It's kind of crazy, though, to think about. Because if we don't care about what John did hundreds of years ago, who is to say that someone hundreds of year from now is going to care about what we do?...Does it really matter if the future generations don't care? But at the same time, that's what historians are for. They love history and, for the most part, love learning about every aspect of history, including the life of John...*

Creativity exercises are playful but serious business. Serious exploration can be particularly effective when cloaked in lightheartedness—becoming affairs of the head and heart. Exercises like this challenge on many fronts; they are not exclusively "intellectual." At first glance, cutting up a symbolically valuable object seems destructive, but this action encourages us to examine deeply held beliefs and values. The destruction would have been trivial had we made confetti from yesterday's newspaper, but cutting up something important makes us ponder time, our place in the flow of time, and what we do with our lives. The exercise has physical, psychological, and symbolic dimensions. It demonstrates what legends and religious texts assert: Creation and destruction are intertwined. Its lesson is painfully clear: Creativity builds on what went before; the price of the new includes destruction of the old.

SAM C: I, along with many others...flinched when the book was cut. I've been thinking about this reaction for a while, since it doesn't seem like something logical. The book, after all, feels no pain, and it's likely not going to be used for any better purpose in the future. Perhaps it's just that I've become so accustomed to books, especially old ones, being symbols of knowledge passed down in our culture: something to be revered and looked after. Cutting out pages goes against how I have been brought up, and it made me reevaluate how I have been shaped by my upbringing.

...Why does something being antique make it so valuable, even though it will probably never be used again? Does age make an object better in some abstract way? Are we afraid of losing information, even though you can probably find the same book online? Isn't it better to just recycle it? Thinking logically, especially within the mind-set of our environmentally conscious culture, it seems like it is.

Expansions and Additions

The idea that destruction is creation's shadow is true, whether it be the creation of objects or the invention of ideas. The new cannot but destroy the old. We assimilate this by taking an abstract idea and making it concrete. Demolishing an old book that is regarded as sacred is deliberately provocative. Books preserve and transmit knowledge; they represent sacred values. The greater the perceived value of the things we destroy, the more influential the lesson.

Thoughtful participants will, of course, ask questions to clarify what is required and how they should proceed, and instructors are obliged to respond. However, since one of the lessons is to learn to navigate our ambiguous world of values and actions, answers should generate further confusion, rather than clarify, and should do so until participants realize that the more questions they ask, the more confusing the requirements become. Think of K.'s dilemma in Kafka's novel The Castle and Yossarian's predicament in Catch-22. The exercise places moral authority firmly and inescapably on participants' shoulders. You're on your own. You decide. Good luck! Don't screw up.

Consider other options. Might one ask bankers to cut up a medley of foreign banknotes or, better still, hundred-dollar bills? Yes, but those are imperfect substitutes because they possess specific monetary value rather than elusive symbolic value. What materials could we use whose symbolic value exceeds their actual value?

Footnote: The exercise had a happy ending. After more than a decade of desecration and reconsecration, our new edition of The Life of John, Duke of Marlborough, received the imprimatur of acceptance—it became a part of the University of Washington Libraries' Special Collections.

MAN RAY: [T]he book activity was one of the most interesting and challenging experiences I've faced in my university career.... I was always told to handle antiques with care, respecting the years that they have lived through and the age in the pages. To me, this was by far the most challenging task ever, "disrespecting" the sacred book. It made me think, though—is this disrespect? Or is this breathing new life into an otherwise dead text? If it is only seen but not read, not felt, and not brought to life, is it disrespecting to reverse the stoicism that has frozen the words in place? Placing the pen on the page and crossing out word after word took so much planning, and even more mental strength. After five minutes of flipping the page back and forth, I realized if I didn't stop thinking and start acting, I would never get anywhere, and my page would be just as dead as it was when I first picked it up. As soon as I jumped over that hurdle, I was free, and my hand skated across the page, doing but not thinking. This freedom is something I've struggled with—the freedom from indecision, from fear, and from being petrified of being wrong. I'd like to think that, through this exercise, I've expanded the horizons of my freedom and can begin to approach the spontaneous life I crave.

[This page intentionally left blank.]

INTENTIONALLY BLANK

INTENTIONALLY BLANK

This is a test of the Exercise Broadcast System.

If this had his been an actual emergency, the attention signal you just heard would have been followed by official information, news, or instructions.

Many exercises have employed diverse materials; this does the opposite, drawing inspiration from what's not there—drawing a blank? Let me evade. In the Tao Te Ching, Laozi reminds us: "We mold clay into a pot, / but it is the emptiness inside / that makes the vessel useful." This prompts us to ask, Might participants in creativity exercises find usefulness and inspiration in emptiness? Surely, in the right hands and minds, emptiness can be made fulfilling. Seen positively, negative space is an invitation to explore. Emptiness is everywhere; opportunities to fill in the blanks and connect the dots abound. Throughout human history, the incompleteness of emptiness has demanded attention— blank spaces on maps, the vast emptiness of our enveloping universe, the scattered islands of human understanding amid vast expanses of dark matter ignorance. All cry out for attention. How might creative attitudes of mind find emptiness fulfilling?

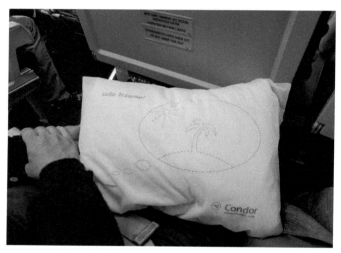

If emptiness is a happy hunting ground for creativity, how might an exercise be developed? Here's the confession: This chapter's text is an evasion of emptiness: I have yet to devise practices for cultivating creative attitudes of mind through emptiness. I have nothing to show the results of a completed emptiness exercise. Opportunities cry out for attention. The mind draws a blank. "This concludes this test of the exercise broadcast system."

Expansions and Additions

What resources might we consult for ideas? Naturally, we turn to the Internet and find it brim-full of emptiness. More or less, we should expect nothing less or more of it. "This page intentionally left blank" has its own website. Of course, there are books, but even Raymond Jones's "This Page Intentionally Left Blank: FM-101-Knuckleheads is unhelpful. Frustrating.

If at first you don't succeed, take a-right-turn and explore another possibility. Consider the intriguing emptinesses that fill dense and interminable online agreements. All of us have scrolled through endless text to check the box saying, "I have read and accept the terms and conditions." What fascinating possibilities did we miss in our impatient scroll? What is waiting to be explored and exploited, sources of existential emptiness?

On the other hand, thinking outside the Cage, how might creativity exercises be inspired by silence? There's no doubt that ways in which emptiness, blankness, and quiet exist might contribute to creative attitudes of mind. They deserve much more consideration. Creative explorations of these fields may succeed when we allow our minds to relax and wander, leaving the subconscious to do the heavy lifting. However, trying to empty the mind to create appropriate contextual moods may be self-defeating, as they are all too easily contrived rather than authentic. Frames of mind receptive to emptiness arise of their own accord and cannot be forced or manufactured in exercises. This chapter leaves the question of what to do with emptiness intentionally unanswered.

Seattle Post-Intelligencer
A HEARST NEWSPAPER | WWW.SEATTLEPI.COM
KING, SNOHOMISH, PIERCE...

EXTRA
TUESDAY, SEPTEMBER 11,

Attack

• 2 airliners destroy
World Trade Center

• Third plane slams
into Pentagon

AMY O'DOHERTY

The Seattle Times
www.seattletimes.com
WEDNESDAY, SEPTEMBER 11, 2002

In remembrance
of September 11, 2001, a moment of silence.

The news of today
can be found starting on Page A3

TERROR

Trade Cent
destroyed
hijacked jet

Pentagon also hi

'Horrendous
number' dead

crashes
tsburgh

nediate claim
responsibility

Bush: We will
nt down' attackers

White House
evacuated, U.S.
airports shut down

Space Needle
state capitol
as

U.S. fede
suspects identi

On the day after, stories of heroics on the ground,

Bush vows to
venge deaths

Saw the horror! A 3

Suspect:
ma bin Laden A 5

Intelligence,
predict A 5, 6

Economic
predict

il hijacke

All of us have scrolled through endless text to check the box saying, "I have read and accept the terms and conditions." What fascinating possibilities did we miss in our impatient scroll? What is waiting to be explored and exploited, sources of existential emptiness?

Nothing here, folks; keep moving on. I have seen the future and drawn a blank.

THE
POST
OFFICE
RECEIPT
COMPETITION

Competition encourages creativity, but how much and what kind of competition is appropriate? Too little competition may make us complacent; too much may undermine our self-confidence and inadvertently expose inequality in students' backgrounds and experiences. Where's the sweet spot? You may have guessed it: I won't be answering your question directly, but we will explore the topic! Like many exercises, what purports to be its primary purpose turns out to be a sideshow. But don't take my word for it; read on.

Here's the gist: It's a competition. Go to a convenient post office at a conducive time, spend no more than $5, and keep the receipt. The winner is the participant who procures the longest receipt.

Participants' immediate reaction to the assignment was horror. What will the clerk think? What will those in line behind me think? How awkward. How horribly embarrassing. What should I do? Do I HAVE to do it? These sentiments were followed by the "There must be something wrong with the assignment" phase. But, no, the project's logic is impeccable, even if it appears to contradict the fundamental premise of capitalist transactions: Rather than measuring success by the quantity or quality of products, it is measured by the length of the receipt. What would Adam Smith think?

Like most of life's texts, the assignment possesses an unwritten subtext that's more important: It's not about the money; it's about the quality of the social interaction. The exercise is a social problem, not a mathematical one. So conditioned are educated participants to conforming and behaving that no one asks

the obvious question: "Why?" Perhaps they are too startled, bemused, confused, or intimidated to question the assignment beyond asking, "You want us to do WHAT?" But "WHY do you want us to do this?" remains unasked. As with so much of human life, STEM proficiency won't help. It is the "why?" not the "what?" that counts. The exercise expands our explorations to include creative social interactions. It requires participants to engage with a post office clerk, asking that person to help with a peculiar, but not illegal, request to generate a long receipt. The only problem is that the exercise neglects to make this goal explicit. Participants are led astray, in the hope that the assignment isn't about what it appears to be.

Social interactions are an extremely important manifestation of creativity. Whether it be persuading an army to cross the Alps on elephants or the Delaware in small boats, the act of persuading

Project 3: The Internationally Famous and Not to Be Stamped Out

POST OFFICE RECEIPT COMPETITION

It is better to receipt than to receive.

Proceed, at a time when the stars are conducively aligned to favor your venture, to a post office of your choice. Buy goods or services not to exceed five dollars.

Remember, while you do so: This IS a competition—I must win!

Mot du jour: Win some not winsome or wince on.

The competition winner is the individual who receives the longest receipt.

Note: Receipts must be intact and undoctored—that is, they may not be cut and pasted, twisted and attached Möbius strip–like, or otherwise bent, folded, mutilated, or spindled to make them longer. You are what you receipt.

The competition's governing authority (Tammy, Iain, and any other guests we chose to assign, nominate, depute, authorize, appoint, invest, depose, signify, etc.) reserves the right to award prizes commensurate with receipt lengths as it sees fit. Entrants must be present to win. One prize per contestant. Offer void in states where prohibited. Children, other family members, or friends of governing authority personnel are ineligible to participate.

others to do something that may not seem to be in their self-interest is intensely creative. Effective leadership is creative. It's one of the most highly valued human attributes, so why does most of education ignore the topic almost entirely?

Exercise products are standard government-issued receipts containing standard government text, with the benefit that, in this case, it is unnecessary to read the fine print. To avoid incurring the wrath of the U.S. Postal service, I have only done this project twice. On the first occasion, participants evaded the issue by cutting receipts into long strips or taping ends together to form infinitely long Möbius strips. The later iteration of the instructions closed these loopholes: Receipts, like airplane lavatory smoke detectors, cannot be tampered with. Here's what happened.

One participant persuaded a helpful clerk to ring up five hundred one-cent stamps individually, generating a 4.5-meter-long receipt, a formidable accomplishment but not, unfortunately, the longest receipt. Several participants tried to purchase a roll of receipt paper and were told they were not for sale. Three enterprising participants persuaded clerks to ring up a small transaction and then remove the machine's roll and give it to them—with receipts attached. They returned with fifteen-plus-meter receipts. The suspense as these receipts were unrolled, back and forth across the table, to be measured was palpable, a fitting competition climax. But the longest receipt does not necessarily come to the canniest, for "time and chance happeneth to them all." The receipt's length was dependent on chance, a risky partner.

Nevertheless, successful participants employed persuasive social skills that Willy Lomans the world over would die for. This is social creativity in action! The reflections are so revealing that they are worth quoting at length.

Few participants considered why they were asked to obtain long receipts. Thus they failed to discern the competition's purpose hidden in full view beneath their noses. Had participants been trained to accept every education assignment unquestioningly like Tennyson's Light Brigade, "Theirs not to make reply, Theirs not to reason why, Theirs but to do and die"?

MARY H: *I was very nervous for my receipt assignment. I had a general plan going into the post office but wasn't sure if the employee would go along with it...There was a definite possibility that [they might] look at me with an expression of Really? You want me to do what...I put a smile on my face and tried to be very genial. I explained what my assignment was, and I was wondering if he would be able to give me a really long receipt. I asked if they had any receipt roles I could buy, and he said [no]. I asked if there was any other way to make a long receipt. He thought for a little bit and then said that if there was a used receipt roll, he could probably give that to me. I then asked if there was any way to get my purchase on the receipt. He graciously tried to problem-solve with me, and put the item under "miscellaneous." After printing up the first receipt, it [the machine] automatically cut off the receipt. He thought for a little bit again, and then said he could pop the machine open before it cut the receipt. He did this successfully, and I paid him two dollars. He watched curiously as I cheerfully stuck the roll into my backpack. It was very clear to me that it took the ingenuity and creativeness of this employee for me to get the result I wanted.*

ELLA T: *Thursday I went on my lovely post office trip. I was lucky my second time there and found no line. Two cashiers, one [who] looked all business and the other that looked hopefully more accommodating, and. lucky me, he was. I still can't believe he rang up all five hundred stamps. Hopefully, I can get that receipt back to get his clerk number and write him a delightful thank-you note.*

ANDY A: *To be truly honest, I had not even thought of asking the post office workers to assist me in this project. Perhaps I am not a manipulative person? That, of course, is a lie. I, Andy A, consider myself to be a competent manipulator.*

I suppose the real problem lies with my hesitation at times to ask for help. This is not because I am a supremely confident being, but, rather, that I am, in most senses of the word, shy with people I interact with once in my life.

All these factors led to my (only) idea of trying to manipulate the automated post machine. This glaringly failed and earned me (and I quote) "the underachiever of the year award."

AVEN S: *Job well done…I had no idea what we were meant to learn from the exercise (and am glad that I didn't; if I had, it would have changed things)…I remember thinking at one point that I had figured out how to beat the system! Get a bunch of people together and combine everyone's purchases—I figured that you were trying to teach us something about competitive mind-sets and cooperation, but then I read the sheet, saw that it explicitly said that it was an individual thing, and then gave up trying to read into it.*

…The social turn of this learning experience was good. I guess I'm just learning more and more that engaging with people can be incredibly creative.

Learning to obey orders, focus on the task, and ignore extraneous factors may be unhelpful for developing creative attitudes of mind. Thus participants missed the main point: the nagging uncomfortableness of making a ridiculous request and the embarrassment of holding up the line in a busy post office. Creative insights occur when students realize that "the question I'm asking is not the question I'm asking."

Although all participants reacted in the natural human way, none realized that the project's essence lay in resolving human feelings of awkwardness and inconvenience. Had this been made explicit, it would have impaired the exercise's effectiveness. Concealing real questions beneath plausible but trivial requirements is a common technique in psychological tests and daily life. The question, reframed, asks how to make friends and influence postal workers.

Success in social relations is essential to success in life; surprisingly, the topic is rarely overtly addressed. More surprising is that most participants didn't realize that this was the competition's purpose until it was revealed. Questioning the premise of what we do, think, or know is an essential creative attitude of mind. We must learn to ask "Why?" in every context. Without curiosity and inquisitiveness, creativity shrivels. Beguiling smiles and sweet dispositions help, but they must be underlain by determination—a willingness, when necessary, to be thought not merely as strange but ridiculous. To succeed, one has to be "out there" AND be able to draw others along with you. The Alps or the Delaware River, anyone?

Although all participants reacted in the natural human way, none realized that the project's essence lay in resolving human feelings of awkwardness and inconvenience.

Expansions and Additions

Creativity in human communications and social interactions is perhaps the most useful but least considered locus of creativity. Social expressions of creativity deserve exploration—not just in exercises; they need entire programs. There's so much to think about and try, and the topic's potential for dynamic explorations is unsurpassed. What could be more useful than creative diplomacy and persuasion? In what ways are creative attitudes of mind "social"?

Most exercises possess a social dimension, but the topic is central in this one and the debate exercise. Social creativity is about much more than learning to work in teams or cooperate in the workplace. Social creativity can resolve the warring duality of cooperation and competition and instill cooperative completion and competitive cooperation. Can we develop fluid minds that can switch between competition and cooperation in response to changing circumstances?

The post office exercise only scratches the tip of the iceberg of possibilities. Who would think of entraining the U.S. Postal Service to put its stamp on a creativity exercise? In what other social contexts could we explore creative interactions? An accurate but unhelpful answer might be "the rest of your life," for we can, and should, practice this form of creativity all the time. Where two or three are gathered together, there are opportunities for creative social interaction in the midst of them.

SAM C: *The receipt assignment was the assignment I enjoyed the most this week. I knew going into it that it couldn't be as straightforward as trying to buy as many inexpensive items as I could, and when I got to the counter, I told the woman there about my assignment. Luckily, she had already had several people from our class come by and was more than willing to lengthen my receipt. I didn't really understand the point of the assignment until class, but the ways in which people manipulate each other both directly and indirectly is something that I've thought about a lot during college...I feel like it's a skill that many people don't take full advantage of, and something that is not taught in many majors (business and psychology seem like some of the few majors that discuss it explicitly). Although people do pick it up innately, it would be something useful to teach classes about so that it can be honed.*

Consider social contexts that are ordinary, low-key, and familiar—situations that possess well-understood behavioral expectations for interactions. How might these be manipulated with a simple twist to render them suitable as exercises? Two kinds of interaction come to mind, commercial interactions and interactions with bureaucracies. Social exercises require skin in the game. They cannot be conducted from behind technological shields. One-on-one, face-to-face interactions are essential, NEVER online social simulacra.

This exercise may seem crazy at first blush, but it's absolutely not; the PO competition exercise is far too timid. The time is late; the need for social creativity has never been greater. We must head further out on our exploratory limb, taking heart from Thoreau's ringing assertion: "The greater part of what my neighbors call good I believe in my soul to be bad, and if I repent of anything, it is very likely to be my good behavior. What demon possessed me that I behaved so well?"

What demon possesses us that we behave so conventionally, so conciliatorily, so cringingly obsequiously in the face of what needs to be done? How can we creatively seize the levers and mold society's institutions to make them do the right thing?

ELLIE H: *I think it's interesting that the point was about social interaction, because I kind of caught on to that while I was waiting in line and thinking about which clerk I hoped to get and how I was going to present my request… Having been on the other side of a cash register changes your view of a situation like that, and I think that's the reason I instinctively thought of my interaction with the clerk as two-sided, when maybe others immediately didn't. I think it's easy to forget that customer service people are actually people and treat them as a machine that takes your order and your money, and experiencing that helps you realize to treat people better…At the post office I tried all of that and I think it worked, because my clerk was laughing, and without even asking, she implemented her own idea on my receipt…My receipt paled in comparison to a lot of the others, but I think I definitely got the point.*

I was very surprised by the original intent of the assignment. I think many of us assumed that the assignment was really about the "creative" way of getting a long receipt. And yeah, sure, that was an aspect of the assignment, but obviously not the main intention. You guys are quite sneaky! This assignment in particular made me wonder how you think up and decide upon these assignments. In a competitive setting requiring creativity, my mind immediately thinks. Is there a specific creative solution or loophole that the instructors are intending, or want us to discover…We've been taught at a young age that there is an "expected" creative solution or a "correct" creative solution. And outside of fairy tales, this is hardly the case.

FREYA Z: *As I approached the counter, I smiled awkwardly and said, "U…um, I kind of have a weird question to ask you…." And his immediate response was a big smile and "You don't want a long receipt, do you?" That alleviated my anxiety. I told him that I wanted to purchase the entire roll, [but] he couldn't sell it to me. Luckily, he was nice enough to give me a leftover roll sitting on the desk over.*

CREATIVITY
IS NOT A FIELD
IT'S
THE ATMOSPHERE

VIRTUAL
REALITY
IS SECOND HAND
EXPERIENCE

WHICH?

Supplies, Supplies!
The Material World

I can love a stone, Govinda, and a tree or a piece of bark. These are things and one can love things. But one cannot love words. Therefore teachings are of no use to me; they have no hardness, no softness, no colors, no corners, no smell, no taste— they have nothing but words. Perhaps that is what prevents you from finding peace, perhaps there are too many words, for even salvation and virtue.

—HERMAN HESSE, *SIDDHARTHA*

Creativity is a mindset, but it's not confined exclusively to our heads. As a fundamental basis, stimulate creativity through contact with reality. In other words, in all its wonderful manifestations, the world can lend creativity a helping hand and provide it with timely hints and potent nudges. Our embodied minds think materially; our senses engage in fruitful collaborations with our minds. The deeper and more varied our encounters with the world, the more physical, perceptual, and metaphorical triggers they provide. Some exercises are field trips into the material world. Still, most exercises bring the mountain to Mahomet in the form of collections of materials, the most important characteristic of which is that they are real. Exercises complement rather than replace traditional education's focus on linguistic and numeric abstractions and contemporary education's electronic semblances of reality. They do so by putting us in touch with material reality— physical, tangible contact with real materials and objects. Creative explorations don't subscribe to the view that thinking is an exclusively cerebral activity that can dispense with sensory input. Rather than distancing our heads from material distractions, these exercises suggest that creative inspiration may come naturally from observing and interacting with the real world's substance, forms, and processes. Materiality adds spice and potency to creativity explorations; it lures, catches, holds, and rewards attention.

john **gary** sings

your ALL-TIME
FAVORITE

ALL THE THINGS YO
FASCINATION
AS TIME GOES BY
SMOKE GETS IN YO
STAR DUST
TONIGHT
AUTUMN LEAVES
NIGHT AND DAY
DEEP PURPLE
I LEFT MY HEART IN SAN FR
SOME ENCHANTED EVENING
YOU'LL NEVER WALK ALON

ADMIT

SONY

FM · AM

WALKMAN

FM STEREO/AM
RECEIVER SRF-19W

ON OFF

SOCCER

Radio

Seattle 88
American Society of
Landscape Architects

1099
HOURS F

Education that ignores the material world ignores fertile sources of creative inspiration. The world is ever ready to give our heads a helping hand if we get real.

Look at the diverse collections of natural and human-made materials used in exercises. They are all real—secure lifelines between bodily senses and active minds. Creativity exercises use materials to incite curiosity and to invite manipulation, interaction, and exploration leading to discovery—ignition for cognition. Materials range from common to strange and exotic and from cheap to valuable. The material world's richness is replicated by enhancing experiences and providing materials in small or vast quantities. In addition to sight, materials reward the senses of touch, smell, and possibly taste and awaken all senses. Some materials possess associations and meanings that powerfully connect sensory experiences and mental responses. I be, therefore I think.

Materials should be easy and safe to manipulate. Unpleasant, dangerous, or fragile materials are inappropriate, though messiness may be an asset in some exercises. They should include various natural materials and man-made objects, as they invite a wider range of mental interpretations. Imagine that you are replicating Aladdin's cave's material abundance and the mental stimulation of Renaissance cabinets of curiosities.

Present materials artfully, as participants' responses may be enhanced by packaging and storage containers' characteristics. Seeing afresh aids in thinking afresh, so present materials to ignite sensory curiosity and evoke mental wonder.

The Language of Materiality

Although a metaphor, the language of materiality is real. We may understand our shared experiences of the material world as a language that we "speak," a common ground for understanding. This language is more than just materiality; it includes the languages of form and process. These nonverbal languages are our planetary inheritance, our shared mother tongues. Through our physical being, they connect us to our creative potential. The material world is a potent catalyst for creativity.

Collect materials that range from abstruse, opaque, and puzzling human-made objects to natural objects that are so familiar that we long ago stopped noticing them. Senseless cognition is thoughtless, including trivial inorganic materials, such as stones, soil, and silt. Intriguing organic objects, such as seashells, cones, leaves of varied sizes, shapes, material composition, colors, textures, and smells are recommended to enhance creativity.

Materials may be prosaic, but what we ask participants to DO with them is not. Use the potential of materials creatively: rocks for rock journeys; pennies for abundance; everything for sorting; a ragbag of stuff for connections; and nothing for emptiness. Our bodies help us make sense when our neurons are tied in knots. When regarded attentively and thoughtfully, the material world is never dully prosaic and devoid of inspiration; use its potential. There's more at our fingertips than keyboards. To finger the point: Think tangibly.

The Language of Form

We live in a world of form, a point so blindingly obvious that one feels foolish mentioning/in-forming it. Like words, forms have meanings, so the "language of form" metaphor is not much of a stretch. What should collections of material forms look and feel like? Many collections, such as those of seashells, are already collections of forms produced by intrinsic living, growing processes. Becoming conscious of how pervasive the language of form is to our perceptions and thought processes can enhance creative thought and creative attitudes of mind.

Form takes many forms. Some forms delight us; others repel in their insistence, demanding our immediate and undivided attention. Others are insignificant and fail to attract notice. Forms can be simple and immediately comprehensible, others complex, requiring close attention to unravel their meanings. Forms can be comfortable, reassuringly familiar, and award the senses, while others are unusual, aggravating, and challenging. Living or not, forms may tell stories volubly or require interpretation. Some convey intention and purpose; others, "[y]ou blocks, you stones, you worse than senseless things," are inert. Forms may be fluid or rigid, ancient and formed over vast expanses of

time, or formed in the moment. The world of forms—which is nothing less than the world itself—is infinitely varied, exciting, and meaningful. The forms in which our physical, material world is expressed speak eloquently of material qualities and biophysical processes. Understanding grows as we learn to read the interactions of material attributes and formative processes in the resulting forms.

We frequently respond to the formal world informally—we ignore it. Yet, the language of form is a potent tool for creative comprehension. It is another language in which to think. Pay attention and use it! Unsurprisingly, exercises that increase our awareness of the language of form may take many forms. My bias is an inordinate fondness for the silhouette of glass bottles, but regardless of the materials we use, keep in touch and get in shape.

HINT
ER
ALUDE

VIRTUAL
REALITY
IS A
SILLY CON VALET

EDUCATION
AND ITS
DISCONTENTERS

LET ME REPEAT
IT ONCE MORE =
I DON'T WANT
TO DO THE SAME
THING
AGAIN AND AGAIN

SP9.

BURTON
UNPHY
FREEMAN
ZZARD
HUGH
NEVIUS
FREED
NORMAND
OESCHLE
RITTER

WI 96
BRADY
ONA GREENBERG
HORNBEIN
LINN
MANDEL
TER MARTINEZ
DY SPUSBURY
ND ST JOHN)
SULLIVAN
WAHYUDHARMA
GE KAUFFMAN

MISSIONS 96

CULTIVATING
EMPATHY

I must catch the evening post with this letter. There are a hundred things I must attend to before I start the bore of packing. As for you, wise one, I have a feeling that you too perhaps have stepped across the threshold into the kingdom of your imagination, to take possession of it once and for all. Write and tell me— or save it for some small café under a chestnut-tree, in smoky autumn weather, by the Seine.

I wait, quite serene and happy, a real human being, an artist at last. Clea.

—LAWRENCE DURRELL, *CLEA*

This exercise couldn't be more straightforward: participants are given letters--hand-written in English--and asked to write replies. The only difficulty is that the letters are old; they were mailed in the 1850s and 60s, with a penny stamp bearing Queen Victoria's profile, to a firm of solicitors, in Edinburgh, Scotland. The exercise consists of replying to one of the letters. Better late than never, but better never late.

How might this activity promote creativity? To correspond with someone from a distant country across a span of 160 years stretches the imagination. Corespondents have to develop understandings of each other's culture, place, and time. To compose a reasonable letter, one has to understand its recipient. Such understandings and communications promote empathy. The exercise predicts that empathetic attitudes of mind foster open-mindedness—a prerequisite for a creative attitude of mind. This request, which borders on the ridiculous, may have intrinsic value that fosters the mind's creative attitudes.

There's something powerful about activities that stop us in our tracks, arrest our usual headlong mental rush, and make us pay closer attention. This exercise demands concentrated engagement. Dashing off a mindless tweet won't cut it.

Participants must first interpret the flourishes of Victorian copperplate cursive handwriting. Then they must puzzle through the arcane language of Writers to the Signet and catch the drift of an extended conversation from the evidence of a single letter. To understand the letter sufficiently to form a reply, participants must also understand its context—the culture and social order of their time. Finally, participants must assume a persona appropriate to composing a reply. To do all of this successfully, they must practice skills that are increasingly important in our globally interconnected world: They must understand and empathize with other cultures. Does one empathize fit all? No.

After recovering from their surprise, participants invariably ask two questions: "Are the letters real?" and "Are you really asking us to do this?" Does it matter whether or not the letters are real? Emphatically yes! As twenty-first-century citizens, we spend more and more time embroiled in virtual environments and, as a result, our world and lives appear more and more veneerlike and less solid substances—when knocked, we ring hollow. Creativity exercise materials must be real, with real letters that exude the authority of authenticity. Copies don't cut it. Holding an actual letter in our hands connects us with its writer. Putting ourselves in others' shoes, seeing through others' eyes, and understanding others' feelings expand empathizing skills that foster creativity. But the letters interject stumbling blocks to comprehension: obscure script, obscure language, and obscure times. They are physically unfamiliar. Paper and ink exude whiffs of other times and technologies; unfolding them catches fingers off guard. We slow down and begin to imagine. Replying to Victorian letters requires a temporary cranial transplant, stepping outside our heads and into the heads, shoes, places, and times of others.

That the letters are real is scarcely credible, and even with typed imitations of their cursive script, they are challenging to comprehend. Difficulties highlight that all communication occurs within contexts, webs of assumptions, and associations shared by writers/speakers and readers/listeners. Shared ground rules for communication include understanding the society, the times, and, in this case, the letters' legal context. The letters come to students from an alien culture and a nearly incomprehensible time. Students began to dig into the lives and thoughts of the writers, trying to enter, however imperfectly, into their world. Were they wealthy? Where were they situated in the social hierarchy of their times? The more questions they asked, the more apparent the gulf between the world of twenty-first-century students and that of nineteenth-century Scottish lawyers became.

It was not just a question of bridging temporal distances; there was a yawning sociocultural and temporal gulf to span. "But what," they asked, "if those to whom we write find fault with our English?" The relief was palpable when students were reminded that their correspondents died over a century ago. As part of their search for a common ground, student responses describe current communication modes such as email, texts, tweets, and phone calls. Ironically, these would be even more incomprehensible to the original writers than the letters were to the respondents.

Not surprisingly, the students' cultural background came into play, and you may notice some of this influence in the students' reflections.

Here are some of our foreign correspondents' letters.

After quickly dispensing with the issues in her letter, Raven R gets down to business, trying to bring the "ancestors" up to speed with twenty-first-century developments. Her points provide insight into what's on the minds of those of her generation.

Dear Ancestors,

Sorry we've been too late to reply. It was an accident that I fell to 1991 and landed in China. And now it's 2012, and you know what, no one cares about the property, the inventory, and the stamp thing. So let's all just forget about it. Well?

To tell you the truth, we can hardly understand your former letters. Number 34? Mr. Miller? No one remembers all that! Do you know computer? Mobile phone? Steven Jobs? Chairman Mao? Do you know that Hong Kong belongs to China again? Do you know all Chinese people have to study English and how hard it is to buy an apartment in China? Do you know we don't always write letters anymore? We use emails, Facebook, QQ, and we send messages and make phone calls.

But at least you know the handwriting is horrible poor here.

Sorry, no offense, we just want to bring you some news.

Writing a paper letter is really exciting, but you may also like to try sending a email…. Hope you get a chance somewhere and enjoy your time!

Sincerely,

Raven

P.S.: If you have interest, my email address is…

HUST
Wuhan,
China

Dear Sir,

Are you still alone now? It's the twenty-first century now!!! Things are changing! Your empire has set; the prospects have gone. I am sorry to tell you it. I think it makes you, a English gentleman, sad.

I am a Chinese from China, a county you are not strange, I think. You took a lot of gold, silk, antiques from my land and you burned our palaces. Were you once a soldier? What do you think about your warlike country?

My email address is... Looking forward to hearing from you. Best wishes!

Tang Z.

1037 Louyu Road
Wuhan, Hubei Province,
China, 30th November 2012

Dear sirs,

I was really excited to see your letter after more than one hundred years, and sorry to reply a little late.

I am a Chinese girl and study in Huazhong Science and Technology University. Not seem to have any relations with you, right? However, now the letter is in my hand.

In China, we call this Yuanfen, means "fate." Many stories in the history were in silence, but Yuanfen asked me to reply to your letter.

I don't quite understand the legal part in your letter but still want to invite you to come to China that we can talk about our stories together.

Best wishes,
Suen S.

Huazhong University
of Science & Technology

Dear Sir,

I am very glad to know that Mr. Fraser has allowed your opinion with the lawyer's help. And, it's my pleasure, if you have some troubles again, you can ask for help from me, and I'm happy to help you.

After 156 years, your letter can be received by some students in Wuhan, China, which is absolutely unbelievable. And I'm one of them. Last paragraph is the lawyer's words that I think he wanted to say.

Now we are having creative class. Through the class I am communicating with you; that's interesting. It's the first time I had the feeling of being [a] friend with [a] person from another world, an absolutely different world. That's wonderful.

May you [be] happy and our friendship last forever.

Yours most truly,
HX

Murray & Beth WS
Edinburgh, Scotland
(Bergen office, Norway!)

Dear HX,

Thank you for your letter, I am pleased that the troubles you experienced have been solved and that you were able to offer your assistance with any future problems or correspondence.

It is amazing to know that the letter ended up in China 156 years later, and you might be interested to know that it is currently being answered by an Australian in Norway! The world is much smaller and it is much easier to communicate now that we don't have to rely on the railways!

It has been a pleasure doing business with you.

Best wishes,

J

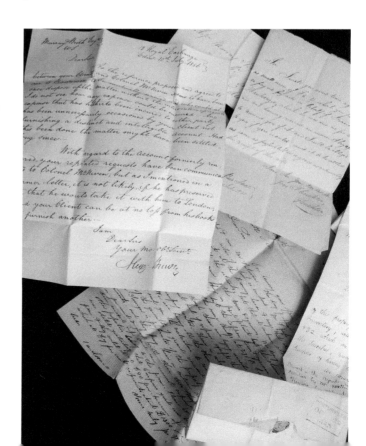

Expansions and Additions

This quirky exercise takes the advice of William Shenstone, a eighteenth-century English landscape gardener, who advised that the driveways to country houses' front doors should "draw nigh obliquely." Sometimes creativity exercises benefit from drawing nigh their goals obliquely. Letter writing is incidental to the exercise's goal of overcoming the impediments imposed by communicating across generations and cultures and developing understanding and empathy for our correspondents.

A leitmotif of creativity exercises is that these activities are fun, but their purposes are serious. The literal, rational mind, perpetually in a hurry to catch up with its tail, assumes that frontal assaults are always the most direct route to goals. Creative minds, by contrast, draw nigh obliquely. Following tangents or digressions may allow them to reach prescribed goals AND unanticipated goals more surely. Oblique routes discourage flying on automatic pilot. Empathy may seem far removed from creativity, but it is a foundation for creative attitudes of mind like knowing oneself.

The need to understand the customs of other cultures and societies and empathize with their social norms grows as global citizens jostle and rub shoulders together. Broader and more expansive attitudes of mind open doors to creative thought and action. What other ways might we explore cultural empathy and understanding? What techniques might we use that would catch the attention and imagination of participants? The Internet is pregnant with infinite positive opportunities. What do you think? Tweet or text when you arrive.

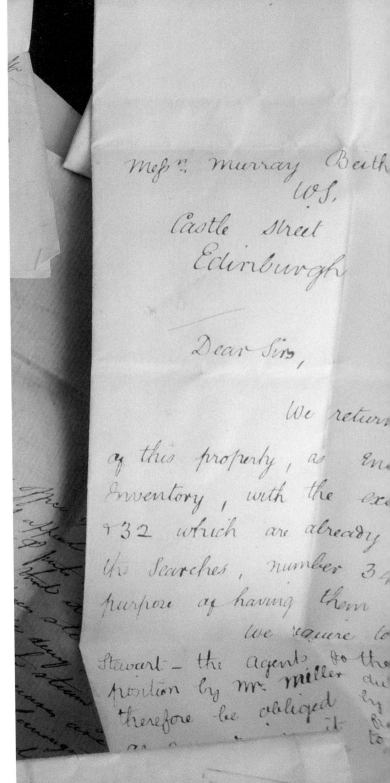

a
**FIELD
TRIP
into
NATURE**

It is not easy to live in that continuous awareness of things which alone is true living. Even those who make a parade of their conviction that sunset, rain, and the growth of a seed are daily miracles are not usually so much impressed by them as they urge others to be. The faculty of wonder tires easily and a miracle which happens every day is a miracle no longer, no matter how many times one tells oneself that it ought to be... Really to see something once or twice a week is almost inevitably to have to try—though, alas, not necessarily with success—to make oneself a poet.

For our natural insensibility, there is no permanent cure. One may seek new sights and new wonders, but that aid to awareness, like other stimulants, must be used with caution. If the familiar has a way of becoming invisible, the novel has a way of seeming unreal—more like a dream or a picture than an actuality.

—JOSEPH WOOD KRUTCH, *THE DESERT YEAR*

Let me repeat a preface I've used many times; this exercise barely scratches the surface of its topic because it is particularly pertinent for the subject of this field trip—explorations of the natural world's potential for cultivating creative attitudes of mind. Nature influences our creative spirit and is boundless and bountiful. As with other field trips, natural settings alter our frame of mind by extracting us from daily routines; second, natural places reward observation and delight our senses. Field trips, like all education, guarantee nothing but provide rewarding opportunities for attentive minds. Experiences knock, and participants must answer. Here are our marching orders.

Our participants lead frantic lives, juggling competing obligations and absorbing more and more information in less and less

time. Stress is ever present. But what shall it profit a man if he understands the whole world but loses the ability to feel and discriminate? This field trip carves out a peaceful moment in the participants' busy lives, a moment to catch their breath, look around, and remember why they are doing what they are doing. It illustrates ways we can open our minds to fresh experiences and how natural places can provide inspiration. Its method is simple—take participants to a garden and turn them loose to explore, experience, and enjoy. Required products are minimal because intangible "products" are what matter: peace of mind, refreshment, and quiet reflection. Encouraging participants to be idle—even indolent—for a moment IS the point. The point for instructors is to have faith that experiencing nature will work its magic. The exercise description repeats the mistake of asking participants to create tangible products. Fortunately, participants made light of this and focused on the experience.

Field trips physically extricate participants from their daily routines and, we trust, jog them out of accompanying mental ruts. New sights, sounds, and experiences will, we trust, stimulate fresh perceptions, thoughts, and attitudes of mind. The more unusual the destination, and the more it contrasts with daily surroundings, the more deeply the experiences will impress us. In addition to being mentally inspiring, natural settings may also be physically restorative. Going to places that participants have never visited will be even more potent. The Kruckeberg Botanic Garden fitted our needs to perfection and met Thoreau's exhortation to slow down and lose ourselves in nature to experience its positive influences:

...and not till we are completely lost, or turned round—for a man needs only to be turned round once with his eyes shut in this world to be lost—do we appreciate the vastness and strangeness of nature. Every man has to learn the points of compass again as often as he awakes, whether from sleep or any abstraction.

—HENRY DAVID THOREAU, *WALDEN*

Field Trip 3: Travel Anew

I have travelled a good deal in Concord.

Today we shall go to somewhere that will be new for every one of you, the Kruckeberg Botanic Garden, located in Shoreline.

In contrast to our earlier travels (stressed by time constraints and inclement weather), we shall today emphasize slowness of movement and quiet, acute observation. We shall (for if only a moment) cease our daily rushing
to and fro,
        back and forth,
               around and about,
here and there,

                 hither   and   yon,
            and

s l o w d o w n

to look closely at these unusual surroundings, a lifetime's collection of plants, many of which are rare or unusual. NOTICE! We shall wander—alone or in groups of two or three—feasting on the freedom of living slowly, something we may not permit ourselves to do often enough.

Why are we weigh'd upon with heaviness,
And utterly consumed with sharp distress,
While all things else have rest from weariness?
All things have rest: why should we toil alone,
We only toil, who are the first of things,
And make perpetual moan,
Still from one sorrow to another thrown:
Nor ever fold our wings,

And cease from wanderings,
Nor steep our brows in slumber's holy balm;
Nor harken what the inner spirit sings,
"There is no joy but calm!"
Why should we only toil, the roof and crown of things?
We shall, of course, not wander aimlessly, bleating
plaintively as lost sheep, but purposefully
getting our bearings
recalibrating
reorienting
grounding
centering
refreshing
AND, we shall create
a dynamite diagram,
a delectable depiction,
a delightful deposition,
a daring dispensation,
a dependable denotation,
and/or
a detoureous delineation,
delectably describing our journeys.
No hurry, no worry, no way, no judgment of your product.
Then we shall return to the vans, travel I-5, and resume our daily lives.

O, rest ye, brother mariners, we will not wander more.

—HENRY DAVID THOREAU, *WALDEN*

Not till we are lost, in other words not till we have lost the world, do we begin to find ourselves, and realize where we are and the infinite extent of our relation... It is a surprising and memorable, as well as valuable experience, to be lost in the woods any time...

—HENRY DAVID THOREAU, *WALDEN*

Taking our chance with a Seattle winter day, we strolled this small, quiet botanical garden. Fortune favored us; the day was brisk but sunny, and the garden regaled us bountifully with fresh, engaging, and fascinating experiences. Singly and in small groups, we opened ourselves to nature, brushing away the cobwebs of routines and allowing openings for inspiration. Botanical gardens are not required destinations; any natural setting that takes us out of ourselves and puts us in touch with nature will suffice. How did the experience affect participants?

Expansions and Additions

Contemporary travel is so easy—slickly effortless—that the experience tends to become facile and disconnected from place. We must learn to slow down. Technology is so insidious that we forget to turn it off. Paradoxically, technological boons make it increasingly difficult to be where we are. But, slowly and inexorably, close attention to nature may suck us in and engage our minds.

Field trips aim to step out of routines, slow the driving pace, turn off the insistent conscious mind, be receptive to external influences, and wander with an open mind, allowing receptiveness to creative influences in a myriad of ways. The literature is littered with examples of creative inspiration striking when we step out of routines. Such moments may be momentous. Others may jog the mind unexpectedly, and, like supersaturated solutions, ideas may crystalize instantaneously. Deliberately jogging the mind is not easy, but field trips may provide effective breaks in routines, and conducive contexts may trigger creative thought. Our field trips illustrate different kinds of destinations—social gathering places, natural settings, cultural venues—and other mods of travel—foot, public bus, and magical mystery tours. Their components may be mixed in many ways and for different lengths of time.

Can we invent a one-minute vacation as a counterpart to the elevator speech? Field trip possibilities, particularly those in natural settings, are enormous, and their horizons are endless. Throughout human history, nature has been a source of ideas, inspiration, and comfort—as well as stress and terror. For those with receptive minds, might the weeds in a sidewalk crack provide a one-minute field trip into nature? Perhaps poking one's head into a lush hedge will do.

Field trips allow us to surface and remember not just what we are doing but why we are doing it. In what other ways might we encourage breaks in routines that synthesize rather than negate their purposes? How can we generate breaks that provide the necessary space to distract the conscious mind from being in charge and allow the unconscious to complete the picture?

The kinds of breaks we create should respond to specific contexts and the content and intensities of routines. Deeply established behavior and thought patterns may be the most difficult to disrupt, but the disruption may provide correspondingly large rewards.

Nature is a bottomless wellspring for developing creative attitudes of mind; nature is the whole world. It begins beyond our classrooms, offices, and home doorsteps and extends beyond horizons into unimagined lands. Ways to successfully explore these lands are infinitely varied—the wide road beckons. We are wayfarers all.

A final compelling reason for seeking creative inspiration in nature is that it highlights our time's defining crisis, climate change. This is THE challenge we must creatively address locally and globally, individually and collectively. Failing to do so, nothing else will matter.

DREW M: *Continuing our grand tradition of field trips designed to force us to examine how we think of place and especially the classroom, the trip to the botanical garden just didn't quite make as much sense to me as some of the others have… it just didn't connect quite as strongly in my mind to the (apparent) bigger ideas of the course as some of the others have.*

It was certainly a change of pace, and from the assignment write-up, I'm tempted to believe that such was the idea, but I feel like that was something that could be done anywhere (a classroom certainly included). Yes, it's an easier thing to do in a separate place, but not nearly as difficult to do in a classroom setting as dissolving formality (à la going to a coffee shop instead of a classroom) or as reliant on the actual journey (à la taking a bus trip).

ELLIE H: *While we were at the botanical garden … at first all I really thought was. Oh, this is pretty, but after walking around for a while I was stunned by how detailed all of these natural things are. Even the smallest leaf or piece of bark is unbelievably complex, and I walk by dozens of trees and things every day without a second glance. Despite the cold fingers, I really enjoyed the field trip.*

WILMA L: *I thought our field trip was really fun but too short. I would love to be able to take twice as much time, or a full day even, to go somewhere and meditate, connect, think, create. Even if that's not possible through this class, that field trip inspired me to go do that on my own once it warms up a bit. I had never been to that botanical garden and I thought it was a very interesting place. Going back to the notion of time briefly, I thought I didn't really get to "slow down" like we were supposed to because I was so focused on finding something to draw and drawing it AND trying to relax, all in half an hour. Obviously, I would've had more time to slow down if we'd HAD more time, but that's always the problem, isn't it?*

FREYA Z: *My first impression of the botanical garden was that I was overwhelmingly underwhelmed. I felt like I had seen everything before, and that everything looked the same. It was very dark and "Northwesty." … But after staring at enough trees and getting over the fact that my fingers were about to freeze off, I starting noticing little details and quirks about each plant—those were the ones I decided to draw…*

But in the end of the day, through familiarity I found uniqueness, though in small ways… So creativity must, then, be a by-product of experience. It's not a tangible thing or something that can be directly taught. Can you teach experience? Not really. I've always imagined that that's what this class was about. Sure, this class isn't designed with any one goal in mind, but what I've gotten … from it was developing creativity through experience— experience from field trips, experience from activities and exercises, experience from discussion.

MATT P: *The botanical gardens were interesting, but I don't think I enjoyed them as much as I could have because I was so cold. I was thinking about this over the weekend and I got to thinking about comfort versus creativity. I decided that a lack of comfort really cuts down on how creative you can be. That isn't to say that if you aren't comfortable you can't be creative.*

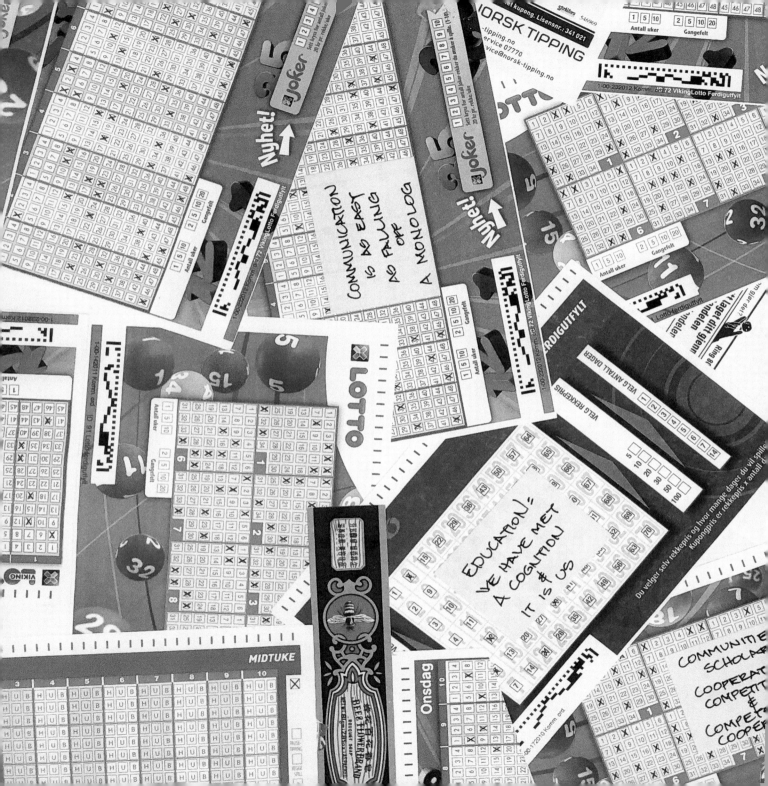

Reflection is Learning

Reflection brings thought full circle, back to ourselves: I am my education. Nowhere is the practice of reflection more pertinent than in creative explorations. We uncover our creative potential not only that we "might have life" but that we "might have it more abundantly." Reflection is fulfilling, a completion without being an ending. If you haven't reflected on it, you haven't made it your own. If you haven't made it your own, you haven't learned it. If you haven't learned it, you can't use it. If you can't use it, you really don't know it. Education without reflection is useless. How can we encourage participants to reflect?

Reflection may occur during and after exercises. Participants discuss their work as it progresses, perhaps comparing it to what others are doing, but, paradoxically, the real work begins after the assignment is finished, when they reflect. How can the reflection process be documented? It's easy for people to persuade themselves that they can complete the reflection cycle in their minds without generating an external record: "Of course I know what I learned and will remember what it means to me." This is usually a self-delusion. To complete the exercises, instructors require reflections in writing, drawings, or models. Most frequently, participants use words—a written reflection at the end of an exercise or in an email later. Reflections done by participants in supportive learning communities may start as a

trickle but can become torrents as they discover the value of recording just how they felt about the work and what those experiences mean to them.

The idea of reflection as the culmination of work is novel for some participants. Instructors start slowly, building familiarity, increasing confidence, and providing reassurances that confidentiality will be respected. The results are all across the map; some reflections are deep, others superficial; some result from internal compulsions; others are pro forma responses to an imposed requirement. Our goal is to instill the practice of reflecting, not dictate precisely how it should be done or what reflections should contain. One size does not fit all, nor does one structure, so there is no correct or required format. The best reflection makes sense to the individual writing it. Reflection time may be built into exercises or done after they are over. The former ensures that they are, in fact, done; the latter encourages more thoughtful responses. Because they bring closure to where participants are now, reflections point to where they might go. Trust participants to do them.

Reflections follow exercises in the cycle described as "Act first, think later" or "Try, then reflect." Reflections on what students did in earlier exercises may influence how they act and reflect on later ones in a never-ending cycle, an iterative process.

A participant in a UW course evaluation put it this way: "I've learned to act first, think later, then reflect … speaking of which, those reflections definitely were the meat on the bones of the exercises." Nevertheless, it's not easy to convince all participants of the value of reflecting on what they've done. This is particularly evident in a participant who has become facile at gaming the educational system and is in a great hurry to complete his or her education and move on. The idea of taking the time—precious time—to s l o w down and reflect may seem like time wasted to those used to measuring success by production, production, and production. Learning that slowing down to reflect may speed us on our way, AND send us in appropriate directions, doesn't always come easily. You own your education, but you're not entirely on your own.

Having dispensed these indispensable and self-evident, in-the-rearview-mirror truths from on high, it remains to be emphasized that reflection is every bit as essential for instructors as it is for participants. Educator Robert John Meehan says, "Be a reflective teacher. Honestly look at what you do from time to time. Evaluate the purpose of your role as a teacher." But enough, let's compare two participants' first- and last-week reflections from a ten-week creativity class. Although each describes individually

distinct experiences, both express observations and conclusions that are common to many reflections: These are honest rather than fabrications, and they describe how each respondent feels and thinks, not what he or she thinks the instructor would like to hear. We start at the end of the first week of class.

The process of reflection provides time to connect the experiences of the moment with our larger life experiences. It allows us to make current lessons, and, by extension, all education, our own. Onerous becomes own R us. Our goal has not been to study creativity, nor to understand creativity, but to BE creative—from which understanding blossoms.

Let me reiterate; reflections are crucial to understanding lessons. Think about it. Reflecting on what we have done, thought, and discussed helps us assimilate, integrate, and synthesize understanding. Synthesis is a foundational characteristic of creative thought. Pasteur's lucid observation that "fortune favors the prepared mind" suggests that reflection is part of our preparation. Reflection results when all the pieces of the puzzle fall into place, revealing an integrated whole that is complete and comprehensive. Asking participants to deliberately and consciously reflect on exercise activities—and record their reflections—is an essential part of the curriculum.

To repeat, reflection is not only essential for participants but also for instructors. It is a medicine that cures a multitude of ills. Performing reflections may be an unusual idea for some participants, but sharing their reflections with instructors may be even more alien and worrisome. Providing honest reflections is risky business. Revealing their thoughts through reflections may make participants feel vulnerable and exposed. As even inquisitors know, honest reflections cannot be extracted by force; participants must feel comfortable providing them. An essential base for honest reflections is trust between participants and instructors. Comfort with providing reflections varies from culture to culture. In some cultures, communicating with instructors in this way may be familiar; in others, it is an extremely challenging idea. In the latter context, it's essential to introduce the idea of reflections gently. To avoid being prescriptive, guidance about how to do reflections is best given verbally rather than in writing. Having said that, let me contradict myself. The advice and comments that follow are written notes provided to a University of Bergen class—vice concealed in the form of good advice.

BEN C (early reflection): In terms of my response to this class so far, I think I should admit that my first reaction has been one of bewilderment. So far, it definitely does not fit any of the norms that I've come to expect from a five-credit University of Washington class. What's expected of us, how to prepare ourselves for the quarter, what books to buy— in short, all the things I try to note on the first day of class—were conspicuously absent. It leaves me feeling a bit lost and, as mentioned before, bewildered. But underlying this bewilderment is, I think, a deeper emotion. I'm afraid that this won't be a class that I can succeed at.

I don't understand how I am supposed to meet the expectations of the class (from what I understand the expectations to be). I believe that I'm not naturally a very creative person. As a child, I never liked arts and crafts, and my mother used to tease me that I was less flexible than a ruler. Drawing in the lines was never a challenge for me. And now I've picked economics as a major, a series of classes focused on learning laws, graphs, and rules. I'd like to bring out my creative side, but I can't help but wonder how much of a creative side there really is to bring out… .

Anyway, my fear is exaggerated. I will be doing my best to open up my creative side throughout the quarter, and I am actually excited to try. But it's not going to come easily to me. So I guess what I'm really hoping for is patience and a hand in guiding me through this process. We'll see how it goes.

BEN C (final reflection): Since we didn't get to submit reflections last week, you can imagine that I've just had to keep my musings all bottled up. Anyway, one of my classmates… made a comment about there being so many different ways that we've played with creativity and that it has made her question her sense of being a creative person, as she has faltered in some of the less traditional creative pursuits. I came from perhaps the opposite perspective—not initially identifying as creative in the traditional painting, poetry-writing, zen-rock-garden-raking way, but being pleased to recognize some creative spirit in myself.

Now, certainly a major theme of the class has been the idea that creativity can be expressed in a diversity of ways. This fact should not be underestimated, and I think it's truly core to the "point" of this class. Not everyone will take pleasure in any individual activity, whether it be constructing a city from boxes or a paradise from earthy materials. Or a trip to a museum, or a magazine diagram, or a life chart, or an article on travel as escape. You have to assume that each of these activities will only connect with a portion of the class. But, as disappointing as that might sound, this is the best you can hope for. Because it's not possible, in a literal sense, to teach creativity. You just have to hope to spark it. And I think each of us has felt that spark/flicker/glimmer of creativity in some of the activities put before us.

What's hard, then, is not to limit yourself to the acts that spark your creativity. To recognize that there are different types of creativity and to see which are natural for you. Writing is one for me, and I've felt comfortable being creative in that realm. Similarly, there are other types of creativity that I'm comfortable with: playing pranks on my roommates, working in martial arts, flirting, discussing movies, joking in class, et cetera. And it's good for me to know that these are ways for me to flex my creative spirit. But, perhaps more important, is to recognize the types of creativity that don't come naturally to yourself. To push that envelope a little bit. That's part of the reason that I think the "paradise" exercise resonated so well with me. I don't know how to sculpt or how to [do] landscape design. But I'd played with dirt before and I could put feathers on top of rocks and I could let go of that part of myself that critiques my "artsy" side. I didn't have to be good at drawing; I could just push around the various pieces of nature until they felt right. It was a good balance for me, finding a type of creativity that I don't normally exercise but also something

that wasn't so far beyond my comfort zone as to hamper me. It was the ignition of that spark.

I hesitate to say with any certainty that this was the point of the class. But I will say that I think much of the class has been focused around exposing us all to various things that might spark us. The difficulty for each of us, then, has been when an activity was too comfortable for us (leading us to boredom) or when it was too far out of [our] comfort zone (leading us to doubt our creativity). The class has showed us what types of creativity are natural for us. In my mind, just showing us the current limits of our creativity, so that we may know those limits and then push against them, that is success.

PENNY S *(early reflection): The first week of Cultivating Creativity, we were introduced to the course and began some of our in-class exercises. At first, nobody knew what the course would consist of, only that we would be using our imaginations through creative projects. I wanted to take this class because it seemed so different from many of the classes I have taken at UW…*

I liked that this class seemed not to fill us with any information, which we would use to analyze and express our thoughts. Instead, we will be expressing our creative sides while given very few directions. I think that these kinds of activities are very interesting, because everyone can head in so many different directions given just a few simple directions.…

Many times when writing a paper, solving a problem, or doing a biology test, although you do not know what the final product will be, exactly, you have a general idea of your strategy to complete a project, and also how to use the tools you've acquired to go about the assignment. In comparison, in an assignment in the creativity class, you are literally going through ideas, picking out a good first step, then continuing to go through more ideas in your head and pick out attractive ones. Creativity is building gradually, with surprises of what you can think of. This is so different from going into an assignment with a plan. It's almost as if half the work and ingenuity is already gone in this usual way of learning. Although I do see the novelty in our projects so far, I don't yet see the applicability of these assignments to what we can do in life outside the classroom. I hope that, as the quarter progresses, the learning that we shall acquire will become clearer to me, and I will understand how this type of thinking will serve as a tool in my future profession.

Penny S *(final reflection): This week we were able to work creatively as a team to make some very interesting final products. I thought both the magnificent cities and the art painting struck me the most by what intricate and visually pleasing products we were to make with such little time. If someone had just seen our final "magnificent city," they might guess that the city was very carefully planned from the beginning, since the city contained most of what a real city would contain, and every object on the table was used as if it had an obvious function. Instead, we started building in small groups, working together among two to five people, and then, once we had already made a part of the city, started cooperating with the entire group. I truly think that if we were [had been] presented with this task early on in the class, or if you took a random group of fifteen students across campus, or even if you took a group of fifteen students who knew each other well, they would not have been able to create something so large and beautiful so quickly and well. I remember talking in class about how it's necessary to build intuition and reflexes about creative acts, and then apply these skills to our studies, and then, of course, our careers. I think this week made me realize that there's one more level in this hierarchy. First is being creative alone, then being creative as a group, and then taking this creativity to apply in life.. Although of course it varies from career to career, I think most things people end up doing just as much or more group creativity as single creativity. And if the creativity doesn't come from a group together, individuals surely are always having to be creative based on what another person does. For example, a doctor diagnosing a patient, a lawyer putting together a case based on the defendant's personality and strengths, a teacher applying her lesson plans to the students' needs, and pretty much all human service jobs.*

I thought it was interesting how we approached the second project of the week, the painting, with the same reflexive strategy as the magnificent city. First we worked in smaller groups, then coming together to put our final product together in the end. The more I think about it, I think this pattern is exactly what results in big ideas in the real world. If everyone is so worried about what the other thinks, and that his work will fit together in some bigger whole, nothing would ever get done and arguments would surely abound. However, if everyone starts to do his own project with the group in mind, he can be creative but still have the capacity, humility, and even enthusiasm to see his own accomplishment as part of a bigger group masterpiece. And really, this is how the world would really run most efficiently and happily as well.

During the magical mystery detour, I think I took a larger appreciation for art in that one room than I have in any other huge museum I have been to, including the Met in NYC. This initially struck me as strange, but the more I thought about it, I realized that when you're overwhelmed by so many pieces of art all together, it's harder to appreciate and understand each one individually. However, if you spend a long amount of time with a limited number of paintings, you can really start to see the detail and meaning in each one. I realized that I never really looked at art more than once until I was at the Frye, where I circulated through the room around three times. My mind seemed to filter through a lot of paintings the first time, focusing on those that grabbed my eye with color or shape. The next time I went around the room, I walked much slower and looked a long time at paintings that might not stand out so much but were really beautiful in their subtleties and emotions conveyed. The third time I walked around, I even started noticing connections! One painting looked a lot like my mother, another had figures in the background I never noticed, and [with] others I started thinking about what the painter must have been thinking about during the process of painting and how he could capture a moment so well, like ocean waves rolling. I really loved looking at others' creative art in the Frye, especially since so many of the paintings seemed so different yet were all from the same time period and a lot were from the same region. I would surely want to go back again soon.

What to Put in Reflections

The reason I don't tell you what to write about is that I don't know what's on your mind. If I prescribed things to write about, then you, as highly conditioned and trained students, would answer only those questions (and provide footnotes and references). But the only reference I want you to check is yourself.

Providing reflections is an open-ended invitation, you can't do it "right" or "wrong" except if you just catalog what we did.

CONFUSED

Confused? Too much ambiguity? Welcome to reality, to the world. Most students experience these responses at least at the start of these classes. If we are truly exploring new terrain, we don't have a detailed map and itinerary. Sometimes we don't know where we are or where we are going.

The only way to get anywhere, to discover, is to try things out and see what happens.

DO THE RIGHT THING

The worst thing you can do in reflections (well, perhaps not THE worst thing, but still pretty bad) is to try to provide me with what you think I want you to do, or do the "right" thing. You cannot fail if you try, because you won't be graded on whether you do the "right" thing, just on making an effort and trying. But avoid telling me what you think I'm thinking or what you think I want you to tell me about what you are thinking.

PLAGIARISM—SHARE IDEAS AND BUILD ON OTHERS' IDEAS

We are trying to become a community of learners—which means a group of people who work together and learn with and from one another. So, by all means, beg, borrow, and steal ideas from one another. It's only plagiarism if you don't acknowledge doing so. The only obligation: If you take an idea or approach from someone else, do it better. That's how we build a robust, growing, integrated culture.

HAVE FUN, PLAY

Is it too silly to say "I hope you enjoy yourselves in this class?"

"But isn't education," you may reply, "serious business, and if you are enjoying yourself, you must be doing something wrong or at least something suspicious?"

"NO!"

I hope at the end of this class you will say, "That was fun; that was interesting. I'll have to think about that some more."

NERVOUS

Nervous? I know the feeling! We are all nervous for good reason: The unknown is full of potential pitfalls. Fall—no, jump—into those pits! Some pits will have sharp, pointed stakes in them. You succeed if you make miss stakes. Make mistakes! Learn from them! Share them with others! Sometimes I will play games with you and try to make you more nervous. Sometimes I will think that my job is to confuse you, other times to reassure you. Why? We shall see. Sink or swim? Think or squirm?

TALK, COMMENT, SUGGEST

Enjoy the creations and efforts of others—TALK IN CLASS—remember, we are a community of learners—and then reflect on these conversations in your reflections.

ONLY YOU CAN SURPRISE YOURSELF

Only you can prevent forest fires. Only you can surprise yourself. So surprise yourself in ways that only you can.

LEARNING OBJECTIVES

Our goal is for you to discover and learn what you want to discover by taking this class. Each of you will take something different from the class, just as you bring different things to it. There is no one "standard" learning objective or body of information/knowledge everyone has to learn. As far as "knowledge transfer" goes, this class is guaranteed content-free.

THEORETICAL FRAMEWORK

You actually do have a theoretical framework for what you do. It's called your values, your experiences, your life. I hope you will become more conscious of these as we progress. The ancient Greek goal "know thyself" is an essential part of being creative.

FULLY PARTICIPATE

Participate as though your life depended on it, which it won't, but your sanity and education might. Participate as a community of learners and reflect on this.

BE PRESENT!

I don't know about plan A, but I do know about plan BE.

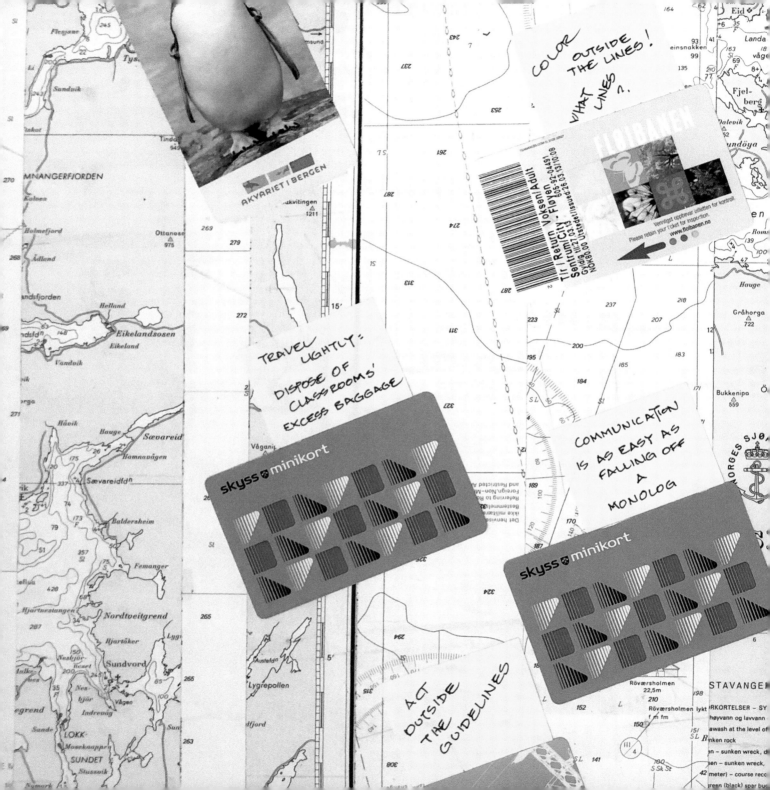

CITY BUILDING and the LANGUAGE of CULTURE

Our culture infuses our bodies and minds; we are the products of our culture. Having creative attitudes of mind allows us both to embody our culture and to step outside it and see its influences objectively. To completely divorce ourselves from our culture is impossible. We can no more evade its influence on us than a fish can escape the influence of water. It is important to become aware of our culture and its influences on our thought patterns.

One way to build cultural understandings is to put language aside and speak the language of culture wordlessly. This exercise invites participants to construct a city out of cultural remnants—shards, masterpieces, and effluvia. Building a city with objects gives physical materials, rather than words, a central place in thinking. Arranging physical objects is a form of thinking.

Instructions for this sort of exercise may be long-winded or brief but must avoid suggesting that there are right or wrong ways to manipulate objects. The exercise couldn't be more straightforward: Build a city with the objects provided. Every city will combine the builders' culture and the culture that produced the objects. It's the matter that matters. The cities will speak the language of culture. Given boxes of strange and unrelated objects, participants have no trouble building a city. The question "What do you mean, build a city?" never arises.

The exercise is reminiscent of childhood play with building blocks, a time when imaginations were less burdened with knowledge and encumbered with the gravitas of experience. Participants jump in with alacrity, exploring the objects' potentials and building with a swashbuckling freedom that would delight Robert Moses. Though frequently maligned, contemporary Western culture permits—nay, encourages, and rewards!—those who take freedoms with it, impose their will on it, or devise fresh insights through it. We live in an open society. The essence of creative cultures is that they permit citizens to take

hold of them and manipulate them—whether by shaking them soundly or caressing them warmly. The invitation to build a city is irresistible. Open cultures accept and reward creative thought and action.

Despite my reference to children's blocks, objects for building a city mustn't resemble conventional building blocks. Collections should consist of random objects devoid of relatable characteristics, so that they can't be assembled in predictable ways: walls, towers, buildings. Create an invitation to inventiveness by providing materials not traditionally used to build things. Creative cities are more, not less, imaginative because of their diverse and peculiar components. Provide objects that possess no discernible script but are intrinsically interesting, but avoid ones that might suggest themes or approaches. Each item should speak, or cry out, its unique story in a cacophony of voices. Some may hint or provoke in the merest whisper: "Perhaps you might want to …". Others may be insistently assertive: 'ME! ME! ME!" All objects MUST be real.

A city grows from a community of learners' shared imagination. Products are invariably marvelous, magical, and metaphorical. No matter how frequently the exercise is repeated with the same materials, no two cities will ever be alike. Originality is inevitable. There will be none of Italo Calvino's invisible city of Trude: "If on arriving at Trude I had not read the city's name written in big letters, I would have thought I was landing at the same airport from which I had taken off."

Creating a city is invariably accompanied by embellishing stories. Yes, we do need verbal language to reinforce the language of culture. As the participants' city grows, stories pour forth, and we marvel, yet again, at each participant's imagination and inventiveness. Why should we be surprised by humanity's infinite imaginativeness? When the city has been completed, encourage

participants to climb on tables for a "planner's view" and crouch beneath them for the "plumber's view." Ask participants to recount stories about the cities in which they have lived. If the participants were asked to write the history of the city they have built, it would generate tomes of dazzling variety without a doubt. What did city-building participants say in their reflections?

Cities provide a physical substrate on which the imagination can take root and grow. While much of our education trains us to be practical, and one of our most important tasks is to rebalance—not totally suppress—this tendency, we must relearn how to be less constrained and become more open to experimenting.

VICTOR J: *There were white plastic bottle caps, shiny sheets of plastic, a metal tin can, rusted paper scrapers, and various other utensils.... Tom P and I took these rejected items and started outlining the infrastructure of an industrial district. As we piled on more and more items, our industrial sector of the city started transforming into a striking and necessary addition, a slum. Even though the scrapers were unappealing, our use of the materials caught on, as Adia N asked for some plastic bottle caps to pollute her picturesque river. When I think of a city, roads, skyscrapers, hospitals, people, and cars are the first things that come to mind. However, [we] accidentally put together a slum. Upon reflecting, we initially just wanted to use all of the materials and did not realize that our creation actually gelled well with the overall diversity of the city. There were areas that were bright, colorful, and charming... [that] contrasted with others, such as our polluted industrial district.*

But that's not enough; we must learn when to let our imaginations loose and when to rein them in. Exercises like this help students distinguish the difference between rediscovering a childlike mind-set and actually being childish. Robust learning communities grow, fun is had by all, and creativity thrives. To construct our city cooperatively, we get by with a little help from our friends. With only cursory prompts, participants jump into this activity willingly and naturally. Yet, from a logical perspective, "building a city" is at odds with the crazy objects provided. The exercise requires a metaphorical response; bricks, mortar, concrete, and asphalt need not apply. Insightful participants may blurt out, "But all we are doing is playing!" Yes, indeed, the emperor's nakedness is instantaneously revealed and subterfuge exposed! Our purpose is play! Humans—and our very humanity—evolved through play. For Homo ludens, all the world's a play.

Creativity exercises are an antidote to tests; they encourage play, which promotes the kinds of activities we attribute to creative minds: making connections, manufacturing meaning, cooperating, building, inventing, and thinking for ourselves. We play with passion and do so naturally. Then, further invigorated, we play all over again. Play comes so easily to us that it doesn't seem like work at all. It's child's play. That we must resort to duplicitous means to encourage participants to relearn to play is a cultural tragedy.

Insightful participants may blurt out, "But all we are doing is playing!" Yes, indeed, the emperor's nakedness is instantaneously revealed and subterfuge exposed! Our purpose is play!

Expansions and Additions

There's no getting away from it; you're your culture. We make our culture, and it makes us. How might the kinds of play that this exercise invites make our culture more creative? Might we do so through creative constructions that express and transform our cultural understanding of cities? How can we encourage inventing purposes and making meaning in disciplined yet playful ways? Our cities, magnificent though they are in our minds, are nevertheless ephemeral—alive while being built, grand when surveyed on completion, but, unlike venerable Troy or the Eternal City, fleeting. Soon materials will be boxed up and stowed. What endures are the liberating thought processes that made an adventure out of creating and dismantling our cities; even as it constrains us, our culture sustains us, and we sustain it even as we transform it.

How might we rebuild this city-building exercise? It's important to keep exercise explorations abstract rather than allowing them to become skill-developing or knowledge-building exercises. Their purpose is not to advance professional or disciplinary understanding or expertise, per se, but to free our minds to think more fluidly. This exercise is not concerned with building "better" cites, desirable though that goal might be.

SAVANNA G: *Our creation of the city was very telling about the things we have discovered thus far as a class and how far we have come in the way we think about creativity. Everyone dived right into the random assortment of materials and instantly began coming up with ideas for what could be what in our city. It was cool how quickly the creativity came to people. It took no time to jump from stamps to roads and handkerchiefs to circus tents. We were able to trust ourselves and each other in a way that allowed for a very free-flowing project. This allowance for letting creativity in and not doubting it is definitely something we have learned throughout the quarter. It would not have felt so natural two months ago.*

I think the fact that our city didn't exactly turn out as a practical living environment showed even more that we weren't letting too much logic inhibit our thoughts.... Instead of worrying about logistics and details, we went with the flow and allowed that current to take us wherever it wanted. This ability to let go and be free is an amazing opportunity that is hard to come by, especially in the classroom setting. Although there are times this type of freedom is appropriate and times when it isn't, the ability to differentiate between these times and allow for the craziest of thoughts and ideas to become real is an extremely important skill. If the rest of the world is anything like me, then we all too often shut down ideas and thoughts just because we don't think they are right. If everyone were to give those thoughts time to develop and become something real, great things could come from them ... or perhaps just an extremely poorly planned city... you never know!

SAM K: *I think I finally got used to this class because I'm pretty sure I didn't even roll my eyes when given the city-building exercise. [It] may have had the most meaningful message yet: the importance of playing and of getting into a "childish" mind-set. It's a great way to remove mental clutter, both temporarily (see problem better) and long-term (overall mental health).*

DREW M: *Imaginative play is something we were all experts at during our childhoods, but [this] is an ability (although "ability" isn't quite the right term—perhaps "willingness" would be a better description) that the vast majority of us (myself most certainly included) either lose or suppress to a very substantial degree over the course of our schooling and growing up. There are certainly times where it can be useful (and probably even essential in some fields) to let a little bit of that willingness to play through, but certainly not at the level that we would have as children.*

As has been the case again and again, [the exercises are] not about learning how to be creative or even discovering one's creativity—it becomes a case of merely uncovering and unsuppressing that which is intrinsic to our existence as humans.

Like all exercises, the goal is to open minds to more ways to see the world. It encourages us to see metaphorically rather than literally. Surprisingly different outcomes are generated by asking participants to build metaphorical cities rather than literal ones. While all cities made from a medley of odds and ends are necessary, metaphorical ones, making the word explicit rather than implicit, induce very different approaches. Metaphors open the floodgates of fluid thinking.

How else might we modify the exercise to foster self-examination of cultures and develop empathy for one another? Indeed, different materials evoke different responses, but that is a difference without a distinction. Might we suggest that cities should be magical or imaginary—or, like Calvino's, invisible? But even that is a minor adjustment. Might we combine the exercise with a field trip and ask participants to reimagine the city in which they live as symbolic rather than real? Might this be interesting and induce fluid attitudes of mind? Can we make journeys down familiar streets in ways that allow us to see them in a fresh light? In what other ways may we step through the looking glass and see ourselves afresh?

HONEST
BOTTLES

This exercise asks participants to perform a seemingly innocent task: to line up a collection of bottles "in order of descending truthfulness,"—that is, from most to least "honest." Like many exercises, this one exudes a whiff of absurdity that dislocates rational thought processes and leaves the mind scrambling for other ways to address the question: How DO, how CAN we relate inanimate bottles to the human value of truth? The exercise resembles dilemmas we commonly encounter in daily life; it requires participants to replace logical, rational, analytic thought processes with more fluid metaphorical thinking.

Like oil and water, bottles and truthfulness don't mix. Instructions cannot be followed literally. Participants must enlist poetry, not prose. They will discover that they are surprisingly agile at ascribing meanings and values to objects; indeed, people do it all the time. Participants switch from literal to metaphorical thinking to interpret the instructions. What can, and do, we do with this remarkable ability to attach meaning? How may we develop it and use it to cultivate creative attitudes of mind? Good questions! But first, an honest appraisal of the bottles.

Candidate bottles should be different enough to allow clear distinctions among them and sufficiently numerous to enable a variety of comparative classifications; from twelve to fifteen bottles should suffice. Glass is superior to plastic, as we associate plastic bottles with trash, which may bias thinking. Bottle forms should invite varied aesthetic responses and functional associations. Consider elegant, narrow-stemmed white wine bottles; round, quarterback-shouldered red wine bottles; sophisticated, square olive oil bottles; squat, practical beer bottles; and uniquely shaped soft drink bottles that brand our minds with product associations. Add plastic bottles to some iterations of the exercise to see what happens, but avoid bottles with labels, as texts provide pretexts for the rational mind to inveigle its way into controlling thought patterns. If participants are properly primed, discussions will range across aesthetic, ethical, and associational issues. They may repeat, in microcosm—and sanitized of attendant lugubrious baggage—

TALLY A: *[The] bottle exercise was amazing! I was fascinated by the spontaneous division of the class... I think it's a rare privilege that everyone in our class got to experience, with such immediacy, two fundamentally different ways of organizing information.*

For the assignment, we were asked to come to a consensus on an ambiguous, subjective value judgment. One group did this by creating a system of more or less objective criteria (physical characteristics of the bottles), while the other group "mind-merged" and used totally subjective reasoning ("trusting" the bottles). Then there was everyone on the periphery, who, I'm guessing, didn't fully agree with either group's methods. It would be interesting to hear what all of these people thought of the exercise...

One thing I do know for sure: People process the world differently, and this is okay as long as we can talk about it and accept the puzzlement. Otherwise, we end up with an "us versus them" mentality.

historical, ethical debates and contemporary culture wars. The exercise incites discussion and leaves us contemplating the role of ethics in our lives and culture.

Products are transient, a row of bottles arranged by one group, rearranged by another, and perhaps modified once more by renegade participants who disagree with the majority. Like "wicked problems," the exercise has "no stopping rule," and participants' "correct" arrangement may be debated for days. As with so-called wicked problems, "there is always more than one possible explanation, with explanations depending on the Weltanschauung of the designer." To this, we must add the unstated corollary that each of us believes "My explanation is, of course, the right one." Because products are ephemeral, we focus on participants' reflections from two American renditions, one that resulted in a heated argument and the other in a more measured, but no less passionate, discussion.

But first, in this exercise of shifting terrain, we foreground a little more background. Even agile participants typically respond with deer-in-the-headlights bewilderment: "What is this all about?" Honesty and bottles? The rug of logic has been yanked from under participants' feet. They must step tentatively onto the ambiguous and contested ground to discuss values and truthfulness.

Physical involvement encourages mental participation, so start by placing the bottles in the center of a large table in order to require participants to stand and stretch or climb onto the table to reach them. Clambering participants lay claim to bottles and inspect them with interest. Discussions ensue.

What IS an honest bottle? How SHOULD we define truth in terms of bottles? Does honesty have to do with shape—which may be beautiful or ugly, depending on prevailing Platonic images of bottleness? Is truth beauty? Are forms that facilitate accurate judgment of their contents more truthful than those that prevaricate? Does truth derive from glass color and transparency—revealing or concealing the contents? Or does it have to do with bottle-manufacturing processes and the purity of glass? Does functional efficiency measure truth in bottling? Is the meaning of the vessel in its emptiness, as the Tao Te Ching suggests, or in its image, as corporate branders might suggest? The exercise loosely connects, or associates, ethical considerations with creative attitudes of mind. Throughout, the bottles remain silent witnesses.

Truth, even in bottles, remains elusive, so the product is a continually adjusted line of bottles. Slowly, attention shifts from the bottles themselves to the meat of the exercise, lively debates about truth, values, beliefs, and meanings. These emanate from the core of our beings and incite deeply held opinions. Some assert their opinions more forceful than others, but everyone possesses a point of view. If all goes well, discussions become passionate. Discussions of "correct" arrangements range from sedately reasonable to stormy.

What did the participants in two different classes make of it? The length and assertiveness of the students' reflections speak volumes about unbottled passions. One group engaged in a knock-down, drag-out argument between two teams; another engaged in a more measured, but no less deeply felt, debate to ascribe values to bottles. Let's begin with reflections from the fire-and-brimstone group.

Most reflections addressed the human dynamics of interactions, the slippery nature of values, and their place in education. Because of the intensity of the debate, reflections from the first group tended to focus on interactions. Tally A discussed how they derived values. Since they were first lined up, the bottles were merely a pretext; this is appropriate. The absurdity of the request did nothing to dampen enthusiasm.

ELLIE H: *I thought the bottle ordering was really interesting. I might have been responsible for the splitting of the two groups, because everyone was already just yelling at each other and being unable to agree, so I suggested we order the bottles twice. I thought it was interesting that it escalated into such a divisive and heated conversation. We all made it so that there were two specific ways of thinking and each [group] thought the other was wrong, which I think really contradicts what we do in class. Maybe if the group hadn't split up, we would have been forced to talk about and compromise on ways of thinking and one way could have come up with one bottle order that everyone was happy with.*

TALYA S: *I found this week's bottle activity to be the one with the most impact on me, and it particularly stands out due to the controversy which it caused….*

Like most activities done in this class, there was obviously no correct answer to the question posed, yet many found it worth it to argue the matter. This led me back to last week's discussion pertaining to unanswerable questions, in which some thought that unanswerable questions were important in life and others thought that they were not worth answering or even addressing. In spite of this, many who thought that unanswerable questions were pointless still felt the need to argue their case.

BRENDA S: *What the heck happened in class? Who were those people who became so argumentative about an exercise in the "truthfulness" of bottles? Seriously, some people came alive… in a way I'd never seen them alive before in class. I loved it!*

[W]hat were we really arguing about? From an outsider's perspective, it sounded like we were having a ridiculous argument about the placement of random bottles on a table. What I think people thought that they were arguing about was how to determine whether something is "truthful" or "trustworthy."… But I think what was really at the core of the argument was a disagreement over how or whether anyone can ever know anything is true at all.

There were basically two camps: One side believed that, in order to order the bottles, there had to be a standard to measure by—some essentially Platonic ideal of "bottleness."… In the other camp were people who thought that the truthfulness of the bottles had to be based on a gut feeling or intuition.… [T]he first camp was arguing for absolute truth and the second camp was arguing for relative truth as ways of ordering and understanding the world. That is basically what epistemology comes down to, right?…

Okay, so what does all of this have to do with creativity?… My initial thought was that the relativists are more creative because they are not "confined" as much by standards and therefore have the freedom to pursue more "lateral" lines of thought. But I don't think that is entirely true. The truth is that relativists still have standards. The difference is that they think that they have come up with the standard within themselves instead of bowing to a Platonic or religious ideal. In reality, their standards are just as externally motivated and produced as the absolutists', since our intuition is largely influenced by our surroundings—they're just not as well-defined culturally (i.e., they're not written down or institutionalized or organized).…

The key to being creative in the midst of that is to know what the rules are to which you choose to submit yourself, precisely so you can bend them or remake their implications to your heart's content.

SAVANNA G: *The biggest thing for me was the passion that this debate ignited. I felt surprisingly strongly about the arguments that were made. I would never have guessed that something like this assignment would have such a capacity for controversy, but as I have thought about it more, I guess it makes sense. When we are given concrete ideas and topics to argue, people can argue them, but also admit defeat, or at least accept disagreeing slightly easier. When presented with a topic like this, where we are forcing ourselves to create our own thoughts based on something that really doesn't have any preconceived notions attached, we feel more strong and protective about the ideas. What we came up with was completely our own. It would have been different for any number of different groups of people, because there is nothing in society to tell us what is right in defining a bottle's truthfulness. I guess we were so passionate about our differing arguments because they were created from somewhere very original, and true to the way we look at life.*

SAM K: *Please tell me we're never going to examine the truthfulness of bottles again. Now I know why my grandpa said he wouldn't last in this class.… When I said that was the hardest thing I've ever done in a college class, I wasn't joking. Reflectively, I think the experience helped me understand apathy a little better. One problem that always comes up in discussions about education is apathy. When kids are apathetic, no amount of great teaching can help (teachers can help through motivation and such, though). My apathy to our little exercise because it made no sense (in fairness to me, it really didn't) allowed me to think that perhaps kids are apathetic because they don't have the tools to engage in whatever it is they're supposed to be doing. Furthermore, it gave validity to the argument of "What's the use?" To some people, math seems as dumb as the honesty of bottles. I'm probably going to start rambling, so I'll just say that fixing our education system is going to take some creativity on the get-kids-engaged front.*

The heated discussion confronted the slipperiness of values. The less stable the foundation, the more rigid the viewpoint. Education that confines itself to delivering facts ignores messy, indefinable, unquantifiable values, and thus omits considerations that are called "life" in the real world. Some students dug deep to find the heart of the matter, which is what the argument was all about—values. Understanding and responding to human values are essential considerations for promoting creative attitudes of mind.

In the same way that bottles were merely a pretext for discussing values, connections about behavior and personality types were made. The reflections are reminders that curricula should address both unanswerable and answerable questions. Does the integration of ethics classes into STEM and professional curricula achieve this goal?

The second class, although less vitriolic, also generated first-class reflections. Although participants' reactions were less confrontational, their reflections reveal no less profound and heated passions. This exercise reminds us not to pass quick judgment on the success of educational endeavors; one never knows whether the seed took root and how, or when it may flower. Let's start with an earful.

The exercise provided several conclusions that removing frustration from education is undesirable. No friction, no heat! A potent reminder that each participant is an individual who responds in personal ways. Education mills that forget this and pour seed into the hopper, anticipating a uniform flour, go against the grain. Some students felt the instructions were "impossible," and, although the task was "unimportant," noted how passionately we promote our perspectives and are annoyed by others' views! A pertinent question—"How does this hypothetical exercise mimic real-world problem-solving activities?"—concludes by pulling the rug from under the exercise requirements. As with most exercises, interpretations vary with each participant. While this left some nonplussed, others found it effective. Learning that the class is being tied into daily life is confirmation of its value. Although frequently ignored, there's no doubt that one aspect of creative thinking is fostering creativity in social interactions.

The exercise provided several conclusions that removing frustration from education is undesirable. No friction, no heat!

CORRIE M: *The bottle lineup was by far the most illuminating activity of the week. The assignment was frustrating, because it felt like the instructions were asking us to do something impossible. How are you supposed to rate bottles on truthfulness?... It was interesting to see the wide array of viewpoints on something that seems so unimportant. I found myself becoming annoyed when someone categorized a bottle in a way I thought was unfair. After we arranged the bottles by their "bottleness," I got caught up in defending our reasons, even though in retrospect I don't think I would have used that model.*

Even though the activity was frustrating, seeing how people reacted and worked together made it interesting. I wonder if people's reactions in a more hypothetical setting like that actually correlate to how they problem-solve in the real world. It made [me] appreciate the difficulty of making decisions, because it took us a long time to come to a consensus in a very small group. At the same time, you can gain important perspectives and ideas through processes like those, like at the end, when Tom P suggested the idea of putting the bottles in the circle.... The activity also opened up questions about definitions, like what is truth? We referred back to the instructions for guidance, but in the end, why are the instructions the bottom line?

Expansions and Additions

"Value-free'" education, like calorie-free hamburgers, is an insubstantial mirage. Just as it cannot ignore reason, education cannot ignore values. This exercise explores individual and group values. It provides a more concrete foundation for discussing values than do abstract debates. It is a tentative but tangible exploration of how to address this important educational topic. To use our minds creatively, we must become conscious that we see the world through the lenses of meanings and values. Because we do first, then talk, we take a circuitous route to this goal, substituting a tangible activity to discuss abstract ideas. In some respects, the exercise is all metaphor and no substance—empty bottles standing in for values.

We may talk about information and knowledge dispassionately, but values turn up the heat. Values, so used to being left to simmer on education's back burner, may boil over when brought to the front burner. Understanding the values that motivate and guide us is essential for creative explorations. Had we addressed the topic in a conventional debate, the discussion would likely have been well reasoned but lukewarm. What is education's value if we sit through classes with flaccid attention, never getting passionate about topics and how they affect our lives?

If it's fun that you're after, this may be the exercise for you! However, it's also serviceable if your goal is to rattle the foundations of participants' value systems, an essential step in making thinking more fluid and less constrained by self-imposed value judgments. Human values are explored in a myriad of ways through a liberal arts education, where attention is given to cultivating values in addition to learning facts and acquiring skills. The exercise draws attention to how understanding personal and broader social values may enhance creative attitudes of mind. Bottles are used to explore participants' values and beliefs in a neutral way. Because they possess no intrinsic values or meanings, they can be physical metaphors for topics often too highly charged to be discussed dispassionately. We can freely judge and debate the "honesty" of bottles in ways that are difficult or impossible to do with people.

Keeping the variety of bottles relatively simple is a constraint that helps focus discussion on specific bottles' qualities and values. Doing the exercise was probably a red herring to add a crushed plastic bottle, a glass fishing float, and small jars. Keep bottles simple and straightforward; try it with very similar bottles. The exercise opens the door to a topic that needs much more exploration. Bottles allow us to address sensitive issues through analogy. Using physical objects to explore deep-seated and emotionally charged beliefs can defuse explosive topics. What other objects might we use?

JULIANA Y: *To be honest, I felt kind of "out of the loop" during the bottles exercise. It seemed to me like everyone else was approaching it logically, and almost overanalyzing the schematics of organizing the bottles. It actually surprised me that this was the way that everyone approached it—maybe I'm weird, but I arranged them in my mind according to the "personalities" that the bottles embodied. I saw them as policemen; some were portly and stout and had an aura of fatherly "truthfulness," whereas others were tall and lanky and not to be trusted; and yet others were obscured by various shades of color, kind of like a cloud of doubt looming over their "transparency."… I didn't speak up in class when you asked if anyone wanted to arrange them differently, because no one else around me seemed to think of it this way.*

ADIA N: *I thought that the best part of this week was… ranking the bottles according to their "truthfulness." After class, I heard another classmate mentioning that it wasn't worth arguing over, but I completely disagreed. I thought that… we got so invested in an idea presented to us, and were able to form such strong opinions about creativity, and for me, part of the exercise was being able to use creativity to get the others in the class to see our point. We needed to creatively shape our arguments to get the half of the class that was satisfied with the original structure to understand why we thought it could have been improved.*

That also ties in with using creativity in our social interactions.… As the class progresses, I love how the concept of creativity is getting more and more tied in with every aspect of our lives, and we become aware of using creativity in the most ordinary situations. At the beginning of this quarter, I would never have listed "social interactions" as places where I use creativity; I would have gone with the more clichéd: in painting, in sculpting, in studying, et cetera.…

A MAGICAL MYSTERY DETOUR FIELD TRIP:

Frye Art Museum and St. James Cathedral

There are times when pressures build, tensions rise, stresses accumulate, and—just when we need it the most—we convince ourselves that we haven't time for a break. For students, this happens at exam times, precisely when this field trip was scheduled. When time is precious and participants work every minute of the day, when they are mentally and physically exhausted, we provide a break from grueling routines and take a magical mystery detour to an undisclosed destination! Our goal is to not to TALK about the value of breaks, but to LIVE and EXPERIENCE how they may enhance creative attitudes of mind. Amid the assignment's cacophony of literary asides and insinuational clutter are unusually prescriptive but open-ended instructions: Wander the museum, drink it all in, connect, relax, and expand. Themes from earlier exercises are repeated: the effects of place and travel on moods and thought processes; the values of culture and close observation; sensory experience as a source of inspiration; openness to inspiration through empathetic frames of mind. The field trip is a break and a summation.

Contrast is a powerful tool: Step outside, away from one's daily routine, and the world can refresh one's spirits. We took a van ride on a devious route to a secret destination to momentarily disorient thought patterns. Throughout the ride, baffled participants desperately tried to guess our destination … until we arrived … at the door … of the Frye Art Museum, where surprise knocked on the instructor's door. Traffic was light; we arrived before the museum opened. All magical mystery detours, not just those with "tangerine trees and marmalade skies," are pregnant with possibilities. We tumbled out of vans, crossed the street, and entered cavernously vaulted, incense-fragranced, flickering candle–lit, organ-reverberating St. James Cathedral in Seattle, Washington, an experience as refreshing as the museum. "Music that gentlier on the spirit lies, / Than tired eyelids on tired eyes."

Poles apart from classrooms, museum galleries and cathedrals are both cathartic; "I gazed—and gazed—but little thought / What wealth the show to me had brought." Art revives us, and fortune favors us with organ music. For a moment, amid these enchanting scenes, our burdens fall away. Participants wandered and experienced. Then it was over, back in the van. Fast-forward to our routines. "Was it a vision, or a waking dream? / Fled is that music:—Do I wake or sleep?"

Field Trip 4:
Magical Mystery Detour

INSTRUCTIONS FOR VISIT:

He's a real nowhere man
Sitting in his nowhere land
Making all his nowhere plans for nobody

Doesn't have a point of view
Knows not where he's going to
Isn't he a bit like you and me?

—THE BEATLES, "NOWHERE MAN"

*READ & DIGEST (Relax! It's a metaphor, not a meatafor.)

(But remember, metaphors and analogies are direct routes to creative thought patterns!)

Because I know that time is always time
And place is always and only place
And what is actual is actual only for one time
And only for one place
I rejoice that things are as they are and
I renounce the blessèd face
And renounce the voice
Because I cannot hope to turn again
Consequently I rejoice, having to construct something
Upon which to rejoice

—T. S. ELIOT, "ASH WEDNESDAY"

*WANDER THE MUSEUM

(Sometimes alone, at other times in the company of a colleague, always gently and thoughtfully questioning, commenting, sharing impressions...)

Our cheerful faith, that all which we behold
Is full of blessings...

—WILLIAM WORDSWORTH, "LINES COMPOSED A FEW MILES ABOVE TINTERN ABBEY"

*DRINK IT ALL IN

(Another metaphor! Unless, of course, you find yourself in the café.)

*CONNECT, CONNECT, CONNECT

(Connect what you see and experience [experience is more than just seeing—involve other senses, attend to them—give them a scratch!] with the rest of your education and with your life and career aspirations. Make a seamless web, a rich tapestry, an intricately woven fabric, a resilient network of your life and your culture.)

(Speaking of the work, which he received in a letter in 1913 from the Hindu clerk Srinivasa Ramanujan, Godfrey H. Hardy, the English mathematician, said, "The formulae ...are on a different level and obviously both difficult and deep ... I had never seen anything in the least like them before. A single look at them is enough to show that they could only be written down by a mathematician of the highest class. They must be true because, if they were not true, no one would have had the imagination to invent them." Hardy quoted in *Biopilia*, by E. O. Wilson.)

*WE LIVE IN A CULTURAL STREAM

(Another metaphor. Will they end only when they debouch into an ocean of letters or ideas?

Our culture is alive, moving, flowing, and we go with it and direct it as we go.

How does this field trip alert us to our culture and its flow?)

"Beauty is truth, truth beauty,—that is all
Ye know on earth, and all ye need to know."

—JOHN KEATS, "ODE ON A GRECIAN URN"

*RELAX AND EXPAND (metaphor)

(Paradoxically, we may grow expansive by relaxing into experiences rather than forcing them to attend to superficial, consciously perceived needs. Dig deeper—metaphorically!)

Where man has not been
to give
them names

objects
on desert islands
do not
know what they are.
Taking no chances
they stand still
and wait
quietly excited
for hundreds
of
thousands of
years.

—IVOR CUTLER, "WHAT?"

*AND, IN THE END, REPAIR TO THE VAN(GUARD) FOR OUR FORTHWITH RETREAT TO UW.

(Resolutely refreshed for the remaining week of the quarter)

*DON'T BE LATE OR BERATE, BE GREAT!

Student reflections are, as usual, more interesting and revealing than an instructor's explanations. They voice clear—and different—opinions on the value and meaning of the magical mystery detour field trip!

BILLIE L: *It was a magical mystery detour, because I think the detour we took was the most magical part of the day…. We stumbled upon the cathedral. It was so impressive and grand; exploring and trying to learn what each object was used for was a great cultural exploration…. Everyone was inquisitive and wanted to learn as much as we could about the Catholic faith we were looking at. I had no idea that this cathedral existed, and quite honestly, I am still surprised that something so breathtaking is in Seattle and not Paris or London. This field trip allowed us to take what we learned [earlier] … and apply it to wandering a city, where we stumbled upon something that made the field trip even better.*

ELLIE H: *The main thing the art museum made me think about was the multitude of ways creativity can happen…. It also made me think about the museum atmosphere and how it's designed more for observing than for creativity itself— my group talked about how intimidating and sterile a white room with a tall wall of pictures felt and that it was hard to take in anything when it was so overwhelming and we didn't know what to turn our attention to first. Of course museums are designed for creating, but it does provide a good lesson in what a creative space should not be - that is, formal, uncomfortable, intimidating.*

To those in a hurry, the gift of slowness can be unappreciated—until it works its magic. To slow down when pressures are most intense—even if only for a magical mystery moment—is magical. The sharp contrast of a serene lifeboat in the choppy seas of finals week made the experience intensely delightful. In education, as in humor, timing is everything. Can one justify accepting the gift of slowness precisely when work time is most precious? Yes. When we're least willing is when it's most needed. This trip suggests that even brief departures from routines can induce our minds to jump productively from one way of working and thinking to another, and then allow us to compare notes. Where are the magical mystery detours in your world?

Expansions and Additions

This field trip encouraged openness and attentiveness, attitudes of mind characteristic of fluid thinking. How is the process of making connections internally—which fluid thinking does—relate to making connections externally? How do momentary disruptions of thought patterns by directly exploring the world trigger connection making and fluid thinking? How do powerful cultural institutions offer inspiring and potent opportunities for connection making? What is the value of field trips like the magical mystery detour for cultivating fluid and creative attitudes of mind?

On the other hand, as we are increasingly being advised to do by powerful media corporations, why not just stay in the classroom and explore an even wider world through virtual technology? Why not dispense with physical travel? There's no denying the enormous power and growing potency of technology. Clearly, it deserves far more attention as a source of creative inspiration than it has received in these cellulose pages. Technology has innumerable promoters and does not need another advocate, while promoters of direct experience are less vocal.

Nevertheless, reality still outperforms virtual reality; analog still beats digital 1–0; field trips still pack punches. Participants' responses to this trip illustrate the power of direct experience for all senses and the immense opportunities for discovery in the real world. Simulacra will grow ever more compelling, but

CASEY Z: *The entire place [the cathedral] was designed to instill a sense of reverence in people who enter. The room with candles and the statue of Mother Mary was my favorite part. I didn't know such a place like that could exist until I visited it; I felt almost like I was floating in a sea of light. I wonder who was behind the lighting design of the place. Again with the engineering: I don't know if video-game graphics (well, that's programming) are advanced enough to reproduce the lighting of the place.*

ANDY A: *The place affects the person, not vice versa. At the art museum, everyone was talking to each other in groups, sharing questions, comments, and general impressions. We were loud... and happy. The chic modern design of the museum contrasted with the art it showed, and we felt open to the ideas it shared.*

This is in stark contrast to St. James Cathedral. Everyone was quiet, on their own and careful not to tread too loud. It evoked a sense of reflection of yourself merely by demonstrating how insignificant we were in comparison to this monolith of gilt. It was contemplative to look at, and the dim light definitely wasn't exactly joyous.

We learned about environments and their affect on our thinking and synthesis. It is very clear that for a group project that requires lots of fun, interactive, inference creativity, museums like the Frye are perfect environments to gain some inspiration.

If it is a more serious, solo project, I would definitely go to a place like St. James Cathedral.

To be able to have these places in our repertoire means that we have to first experience them. To be perfectly honest, without this class I would never have gone to either of these places. So I am very thankful that I took this class and added these places to my newfound skill of picking environments to help me think.

Nevertheless, reality still outperforms virtual reality; analog still beats digital 1–0; field trips still pack punches. Participants' responses to this trip illustrate the power of direct experience for all senses and the immense opportunities for discovery in the real world.

what they all aspire to become is what reality already is. Frescoes and Formica aspire to be marble. Technology desires to create believable simulations of real experiences, but reality remains the touchstone. What opportunities sit quietly on your threshold, waiting to trip creative attitudes of mind by touching, feeling, smelling, experiencing the real world? Find and use them.

An exercise like this one does more than put us in touch with reality. It encourages us to see how our individual lives fit into our swaddling culture, while also providing insights into other cultures. Do we lack resources to explore our culture if museums, art galleries, and cathedrals are distant from our doorstep? Not at all! Magical mystery detours could visit a local supermarket and transform it by asking participants to experience it as an art gallery. Might we invite participants to buy a product, return to the classroom, display it, and explain it as a work of art? Alternatively, could we ask participants to see the local

supermarket as a theater? It has entrances and exits. How do we enter it? How are the aisles lit? Is each aisle a different act in a play that culminates in the checkout scene? Not exactly Chekhov, but you buy the idea. And, of course, the cast in the play is another source of fascination and opportunity for connection making. All the world's a stage you're going through.

Storehouses of art and culture wait to be realized in unexpected places. Can we make our minds more fluid by seeing streets, stores, and businesses as cultural institutions? Take a further step across the threshold of experience and into culture. Encourage participants to compose their magical mystery detours. Detours de force, go outside and see only light and shadow? Warmth and coolness? Exposure and shelter? Familiar and mysterious? The world is a cave, a cloister, out of which we can step at will into wonder.

MARY H: Friday's field trip was fantastic. I had never been to the Frye, and I will have to go back all the time now. The exhibit evoked many emotions. I thought it was interesting how idealistic most of the paintings were. Many had extremely realistic settings but seemed to me more beautiful than any picture that someone could have taken of the scene. I think I stared at a painting of a girl for fifteen minutes, just looking at how realistic the toes were. Somehow, these paintings of scenes or people seemed much more powerful than a picture, probably because they're so deliberate and purposeful. An artist gets to choose the positions, expressions, and angles.

The St. James Cathedral was surprisingly soothing. I can understand why people feel so safe in churches. At the beginning, the organ music was kind of creepy…. I thought the Phantom of the Opera was going to pop out at any minute. Maybe because most of the music didn't have a satisfying melody (there were a lot of themes in minor keys)… . Once it became quiet, I felt very comfortable. Even though the cathedral was large and the ceilings extremely high, I felt enveloped and warm. I think this may have been because there was beautiful light streaming in from the stained-glass windows but I could not see the world outside.

MAKE a MISTAKE

This exercise asks participants to make a mistake. That's it; just make a mistake. What could be easier? Get on with it. Here are the instructions:

MIS, MIST, MIST ACHES

*Put succinctly, surprise, a fundamental reward of all creative work,
is bestowed by the work on its maker.*

—ELLIOT EISNER, *THE ARTS AND THE CREATION OF MIND*

WE ALL MAKE MISTEAKS, I MEAN MISTAKES, YES? SO, MAKE A MISTAKE.

"You must never feel badly about making mistakes," explained Reason
*quietly, "as long as you take the trouble to learn from them. For you
often learn more by being wrong for the right reasons than you do by
being right for the wrong reasons."*

"But there's so much to learn," he said with a thoughtful frown.

"Yes, that's true," admitted Rhyme; *"but it's not just learning things
that's important. It's learning what to do with what you learn and
learning why you learn things at all that matters."*

—NORTON JUSTIER, *THE PHANTOM TOLLBOOTH*

Of course, I know it's a ridiculous request. We all make mistakes, but we don't—or shouldn't—do so purposely. We can't intentionally make mistakes, or at least not real mistakes. Mistakes are, by definition, unintentional. But how else can we open Pandora's mistake-making box? And how can we relate making mistakes to developing creative attitudes of mind? The two are, most certainly, connected. Life is frequently paradoxical, so the exercise conforms to life's paradoxical nature. It's an experiment in learning to respond intelligently to illogical requests. That, not mistake making per se, is the exercise's real point. It might better be described as a "wicked problem"—that is, a problem without a clear definition and solution, which is precisely the sort of issue we frequently encounter in daily life. The unadorned exercise instructions make things worse. They provide no explanations for what kinds of mistakes to make or how to make "proper" mistakes. What part of make a mistake, it seems not to say, don't you misunderstand?

Much socialization and education consist of learning NOT to make mistakes. When young, we learn that making mistakes is bad, and we try, often desperately, not to make them. Then, when we do, we tend to deny that we have done so! The more cultivated and well socialized we are, the more averse to mistake making we become. Despite Silicon Valley's "Fail fast, fail often" mantra, which is presumed to lead inexorably to success, we still do everything we can to avoid making mistakes. We don't step in puddles. We don't walk under ladders. And we try not to open our mouths before engaging our brains. The point of the exercise is that we should become comfortable learning from our mistakes. The exercise is an invitation to take matters into one's own hands, to MAKE mistakes and see how it feels and what happens when one does so. It invites action, rather than vacuous verbosity, about the value of making mistakes.

The dominant theme of participants' reflections is a feeling of liberation. When permission includes giving one's neighbor a helping hand with his or her mistakes, even more behavioral taboos can be gleefully transgressed. However, responding to the exercise requires judgment.

SAVANNA G: *The "make a mess" exercise... dealt with this idea of freedom, letting go, and just allowing things to happen. In group settings, there is always a power dynamic that works itself out so that some people are in charge and others are following. This is an inevitable part of being human, given our differences in personality, and it isn't a bad thing. The... painting exercise... didn't really allow for position taking. Everyone had free rein over everything and everyone did what they wanted and allowed everyone else to do what they wanted. Given that we [were] just supposed to make a mess, and there was no expectation of quality, we were all willing to let things happen, even if the outcome was often large blobs of ugly-colored paint. It was also cool how excited everyone was by the finished product. The fact that everyone worked together so equally made it feel like a true team effort for everyone. It was really fun to see what we came up with individually and at the same time very much cohesively.*

> *When young, we learn that making mistakes is bad, and we try, often desperately, not to make them. Then, when we do, we tend to deny that we have done so! The more cultivated and well socialized we are, the more averse to mistake making we become.*

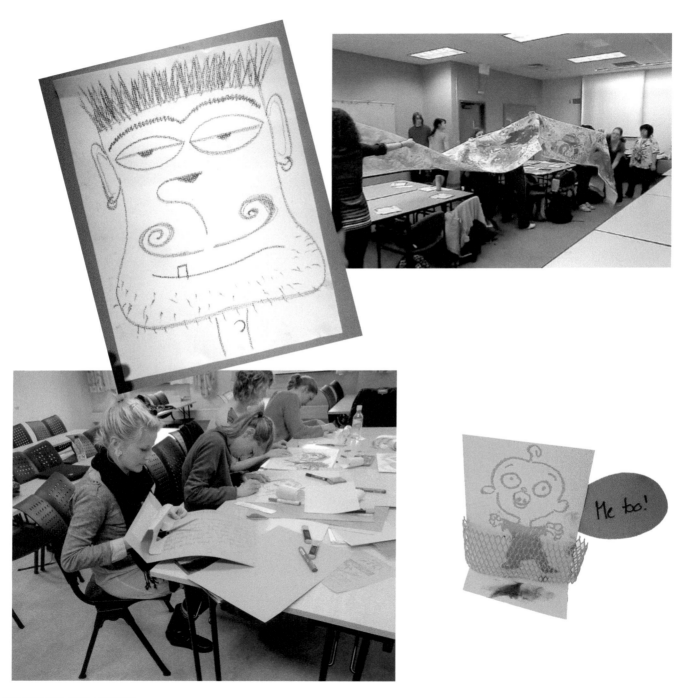

Participants must ask themselves, "What kind of mistake and how big a mistake am I allowed to make?" Responses range from what might be called conventional, and thus acceptable, mistakes to risky mistakes that transgress deeper cultural taboos. Although fun to make, formal mistakes rarely challenge cultural norms deeply—though artists, taking their cue from Picasso, still try to do so.

In an early version of the exercise, called "MESSTAKES," participants were given long sheets of white paper and more specific instructions. They were invited to make creative messes, à la Jackson Pollock. Bottles of colorful paint and brushes reinforced the artistic prompt. Not surprisingly, responses were artistic messes rather than mistakes. Indeed, in a second iteration, participants conspired to make a beautiful and perfect messtake. Perhaps the exercise failed at mistake making, but it did free participants, and they learned that unencumbered experimenting could be liberating and an effective method for exploring ideas. Making messlike mistakes can help us think more fluidly and develop creative attitudes of mind. As with all open-ended invitations, learning varies from individual to individual and often provides lessons that instructors hadn't anticipated. The value of creativity exercises diminishes if we try to have participants all learn the same lesson.

Make a Mistake, Take Two

As I said, the exercise is paradoxical. Making mistakes is both easy and impossible; easy to do by mistake, impossible to do intentionally. The resolution? Cut the Gordian paradox and DO something. Its value lies in giving participants the freedom to explore uncomfortable subjects. Prior education has persuaded them to avoid making mistakes and conceal those that they make. We have a considerable reeducation task ahead of us. Despite all its mistakes, the exercise provides official permission to make mistakes. We learn that mistake making may, of course, be unpleasant and inevitable, but it can be useful. If you can't beat 'em, learn from 'em.

SAM K: *Definitely my favorite exercise yet. Making a mess is a lot easier than a mistake, though, because a mess can look good. We talked about it in class, but really, I still don't think I could intentionally make an actual mistake, and I'm not sure I want to be able to. Two analogies that come to mind: the skateboarders and motocross riders who spend time working on their falling, and basketball players that say they've "never learned to miss."*

Which one is more appropriate for creativity? I like the second one, because I hate messing up, but given the reality of mistakes, maybe the first is better.

TOM P: *The first thing that pops into my mind with this reflection is what we [did] on Wednesday. It blew my mind away that we would explore something as uninhibited as making a mess. Who would have thought that mess making explores creativity? In all honesty, I think Wednesday would be my first time experiencing painting in that manner, even though it felt familiar. What I think I understand from the exercise is that sometimes creativity does not necessary require an intellectual quality all the time to be attainable. Creativity may come from experiences that you gain outside of a classroom environment. Fundamentally, it involves other variables, like emotions such as excitement or intrigue, drawing connections with others, and taking action. None of these elements really requires that you take years and years of classes at college. For one thing, I don't think any of us would have seen just how our paintings would have turned out if we had not actually gotten up and got our hands messy. Imagining just how the paint would glisten against a white backdrop or how each color ... intrudes and joins another person's design wouldn't have sufficed for me. What I know now is that acting on ideas is a must; otherwise, you would just be halfway creative.*

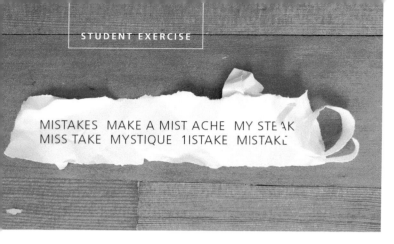

Instructions for later iterations are shorter and sweeter, leaving participants with fewer handles to grasp onto to evade the paradox.

Even when one assumes one is assigning a similar exercise, differences in wording, verbal introduction, and materials can send participants off in different directions. In addition to individual differences and the personalities that groups develop over time, these changes can lead to completely different responses—processes, products, and conclusions. The responses to a later rendition were substantially different and generated more real mistakes, rather than messes. They spanned the spectrum from conventional to outrageous.

In this rendition, participants went to work making mistakes as soon as they received the succinct assignment and materials. There were none of the usual long discussions; participants were in the mood for action. Perhaps, because this was our second-to-last class, they realized it was now or never. Maybe we had finally hit our stride. With exams looming, perhaps they were in the mood to escape. Perhaps I was remiss in not asking why. But the products were revealing.

Politeness requires that we apologize for our mistakes. Participants made mistakes in many ways. Faces with eyes and noses awry might have warmed Picasso's heart, but how mistaken were they? Pictures that were aesthetically less than perfect but, even with smudgy fingerprints, were pretty suggested a brief departure, rather than a fall from grace. A model of a prisoner behind bars and a baby with a full diaper played on the mistakes

of others but called into question the idea of really making a mistake. Too clever? Too elegant? Too contrived? Were these evasions?

Exercise responses indicate how sensitive participants may be to hints, cues, or suggestions. Instructors must take care in how we introduce exercises and respond to work in progress and final products. Mistake making opens a potentially challenging and threatening chapter in participants' education. We must also choose exercise material carefully, as well as any verbal explanations accompanying cryptic written instructions. Explanations may foreclose on deep personal exploration. Enough may be too much. We learn to be creative by getting wet. Swimming is best taught by throwing participants in the deep end. It all deep-ends.

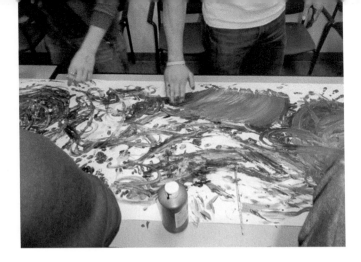

Expansions and Additions

Mistake making is central to creativity, but not in the customarily construed sense, which tends to be superficial. It's the attitude of mind that accommodates mistake making that counts, the degree to which participants are willing to immerse themselves in problems that leave them vulnerable and questioning. Early exercises celebrate the appearance of mistake making but entail little risk. Perhaps that's all we can expect in brief classes in conventional classrooms. Although the freedom of mess making is valuable, as it frees us to explore beyond the trammels of conformity, we should nevertheless try to do more. Perhaps this exercise is too easy and thus flawed and mistaken. How else might we encourage participants to step beyond the confines of cultural mores and break taboos? Can we celebrate progress while acknowledging further boundaries to transgress?

Happily, opportunities to make mistakes abound, and the more we know, the more opportunities present themselves. How can we create environments that encourage healthy attitudes toward learning from our mistakes? Make know mistake, mistakes open not just doors and windows but manholes, too! Learning from small mistakes is the best recipe for avoiding being destroyed by big ones. Silicon Valley's celebrated mantra, "Fail fast, fail often," is "more honored in the breach than in the observance." The gods residing in Silicon Valley are as averse to making and admitting to mistakes as mere mortals with feet in the clay of less celebrated valleys. But we must try.

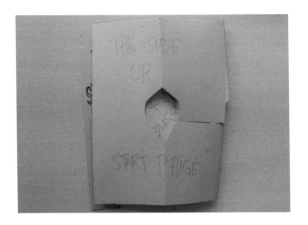

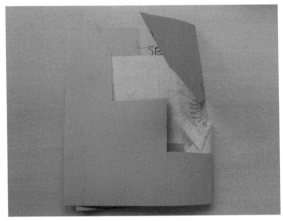

UNWRAPPING
CULTURE

This exercise casts light on a skill commonly associated with creative minds: the ability to think on one's feet—without, we might add, getting them in one's mouth. Seated around a table, participants take turns selecting a festively wrapped object from a pile. They unwrap their objects and describe them from prescribed perspectives, such as those of anthropologists, scientists, and journalists. Each participant is, in turn, put on the spot and must generate a coherent and engaging explanation of, or story about, his or her object. The pile of packages exudes intrigue—what surprises do the packages contain? When opened, the speaker must decide how to portray and present, describe, and explain his or her object while the audience asks, "Is the explanation credible? Does the story draw us in? Am I persuaded?" The limelight requires compelling performances; no pressure, but get it right! T.S. Eliot reminds us, "Anxiety is the handmaiden of creativity." Break a sweat. Where there's a wilt there's away.

Early presenters set the tone for later performances, so getting off to an exciting start with a self-confident individual is crucial. Subtly influence the self-selection of the first participants to get the ball rolling. Unpredictability adds piquancy to the stew, so presenters should be selected randomly instead of in order around the table.

WRAPPED ATTENTION

Today we shall travel further than ever before as we unpack the "otherness" of "untimely" mysteries in the remnants of worldly, or otherworldly, civilizations wrapped before us.

Trapped by the rapt attention of the class, unwrap your package.

Compose and deliver an explanation of its contents

that enraptures us with proFUNdity

and insight

into the alien (or otherwise) civilization that created it.

Transport us to your port of call.

When all objects are unwrapped, construct an exhibit to appropriately display each object.

Discover/create

Explain/innovate

Use/apply

Objects should be interesting, unusual, intriguing, varied, unrelated, unpredictable, and, as always, REAL. There should be enough to ensure that every participant gets a choice. Leaving unopened packages on the table adds to the intrigue. Colorful wrapping may enhance surprise. Theatrical facial expressions, intentional or otherwise, are much appreciated. A bewildered "What the heck is this?" may quickly give place to a knowing smile when a participant conceives an explanation that combines inspiration from the object with her or his life experience. Thinking on one's feet, imagine that!

What makes an outstanding performance? Creative inventiveness and elegant extrapolations from familiar or peculiar objects top the bill. Ordinary, everyday objects prove to be more difficult to work with than unusual ones because one must ignore what one knows about them and invent another reality. But, regardless of whether the object is familiar or unusual, alien or common, the requirement is unchanging: Make it up, make it engaging, and make it convincing.

Locating packages in the middle of a large table requires participants to stand up and stretch to select one—a propitiously active start. Some objects may invite one to play with them, suggesting one kind of explanation; others may exude an aura of seriousness. Inspiration is a gift bestowed on the presenter by the object. As participants become more inventive, presentations grow increasingly strange and fanciful. Explanations may build on earlier ideas but must not copy them; creative responses cannot piggyback unimaginatively on the shoulders of preceding giants. If descriptions begin to fall into familiar patterns, encourage fresh avenues of thought. The unfolding scenarios are not prescribed and cannot be predicted; they depend on each actor's inspiration and performance to make it delightful and endlessly refreshing.

As Willy Loman could have told us, presentations made it clear that how one presents may be more compelling than what one presents. The creative skills honed in this exercise are about quick invention and compelling presentation skills. It is noteworthy that this exercise was performed internationally, and the students' remarks reflected varied cultural perspectives.

TALYA S: *I enjoyed seeing the activity evolve as more people opened their own presents. The discussions changed from literal explanations to slightly more ludicrous ones. The activity also revealed the evolution of our minds and it showed how far we have come as students and as creative beings since week one.*

L. DANYIN: *When people getting together telling stories, there will be a kind of atmosphere in them. I call this "magic of stories." I am a person who is addicted to novels for many years. But until university I finally realized how much I love stories. I read novels day by day in college, even when I paused reading for just a few weeks, I felt very uncomfortable. It feels like something is lost in my life, and maybe that is imagination.*

So I enjoyed this [exercise] very much. I have been looking for a chance for a lot people getting together telling different stories for a long time. All I want to say about this week is OOOOOOOOOOOOH MY GOD.

AMANDA: *This is the most interesting class we've had. I am still in the story about the wizard and the five boys, when . . . Speak out the key words and save them.*

I can see that the class was so different from the start to the end. At the beginning we made [a] story about science to attract other people, but as it didn't work, we tried to make [a] scaring story to shock others and convince them. But nothing can compare with someone who suddenly cried in the class. Nobody doubted it was a real story and deeply believed it. Unfortunately, I'm the one who had to be the "expert" against her—heh. . . .

X. HUIRU: *Long long ago, when I'm a little girl, I had a best boyfriend and his name is Han. We went to school, play, and went home all together. We were just like one person. We were both poor then, and we made money together. I also remembered he said, "I will give you a lot of money when I grow up." We were so happy. However, he fell in a river carelessly on a rainy day, and left me forever. I'm so sad. Till last year, I met a rabbit, it always follow me. We were together no matter where I went to; it felt like that Han was around me. But half one year later, the rabbit died. I cried for two days. I buried it out of my window. The second day I went to see it, there's a box of pounds and a photo of Han and me. Oh, I suddenly realized that the rabbit is Han. He became the rabbit to see me to make me happy. I even can't believe that, it's so magical. But that's the truth. Please believe my story; it's true.*

The lesson is very interesting, to make other people believe me. And I have learned another thing, very important. The very important thing is that we ourselves must believe the story. If you can't believe it, how can you make others to believe it? That's very nice, I think.

Expansions and Additions

Successful performances can foster creative thought and action; these examples merely scratch the icing on the iceberg of possibilities. The exercise is analogous to business workshops where salespeople hone the soft-, or hard-, sell skill of the sale—in this case, during two-minute auditions. Still, our exercise is less single-minded than business presentations and far less pressured than acting or dance auditions. Our goals are to encourage playful and inventive thoughts and actions and to develop the skill of generating ideas quickly—to hit the spot while being on the spot. Creativity may be expressed in the delivery, as well as in the generation of a message. Creative minds are adept at making connections to facilitate such thought patterns. Thinking on one's feet (or, as occasion demands, on one's seat)

is a quintessential attribute of fluid, inventive, creative minds: to make something up as one goes along, to invent a story at a moment's notice using unexpected prompts, to fabricate something from nothing, to weave the emperor's clothing from thin air. What better way to practice these thought patterns than by opening and explaining a surprise package? Lights, camera, action! But don't use this exercise verbatim. Don't adhere to what you hear here; add here.

Who among us has not performed the gymnastic feat of kicking oneself while thinking, Why didn't I say . . . But the moment for the apropos retort passes, and the response always comes to us too late. We associate mental agility with creative thought. Our goal isn't to become quick-witted for its own sake—that's for stand-up comedians. We practice formulating quick responses to increase our mental agility and think more fluidly. Of course, quick responses run the risk of being voiced before thoughts are fully developed and thus being foolish or inappropriate. The element of performance provides enough pressure to increase heart rates but not stifle thinking. Unwrapping packages is playful; it provides time for us to make and recover from mistakes.

How else can we encourage quick and fluid thinking? Having a second participant offer a contrary interpretation of an object can heighten the tension and encourage fluid discussion in the right context. Still, a competitive edge can have negative consequences. Here's a second iteration of the exercise that includes contending participants:

IMAGINE THAT! INTERPRETATIONS

The objects we shall examine today are priceless relics from little-understood civilizations, possibly ancient, possibly from another part of the world, possibly from a distant planet or galaxy. We are immensely fortunate to have been able to borrow them from a museum.

We know very little about these civilizations. Were they advanced, or were they primitive? Opinions vary. The experts disagree. Fortunately, we have two world experts here to explain them to us! They have devoted their lives to studying these cultures intently.

Work in pairs. Unwrap the objects. One expert (selected before opening the package) will interpret, describe, or explain the use/purpose of the object. Then the fun! The other expert will disagree vehemently and offer a contradictory and contrasting description.

As a class, we willl debate which explanation we believe!

Whether successful or not, this iteration illustrates that exercises designed to encourage quick and fluid thinking can themselves be fluid. There is no end to how exercises may be modified and adapted; the context, the kinds of participants, and the specific objectives should suggest appropriate changes. Other than changing the exercise description, what else could be changed? We could vary materials. We could require objects to be interpreted as sacred icons and ask for metaphorical interpretations. Instructors could prescribe a different persona for each participant and alter the presentation requirements as we go along to keep everyone guessing—instantaneous evasion rather than invention, and so on. Not all of these are good ideas in all contexts. For example, the idea of constructing an exhibit of objects after presentations proved to be tedious and detracted from the success of earlier presentations.

Successful presentations are quick-witted, thoughtful, and engaging ones. They interweave cues from objects with the presenters' imaginations. Above all, they are engaging and invigorating. Restricting speaking time and encouraging theatrical performances heighten the tension and suspense and make presentations more exciting. While making adjustments, keep in mind that our goal is to create contexts that foster inventive responses from fluid, creative minds. Quick! All the world's a stage. What's your line?

DEBATE
ABLE

The yeomen, farmers, dairymen, and townsfolk, who came to transact business in these ancient streets, spoke in other ways than by articulation.

Several exercises explore communication as an impetus for developing and expressing creative attitudes of mind, including communication through graphic representation and the language of form. All exercises are punctuated with discussions and reflections. This exercise makes verbal communication, in the form of debates, its primary topic. That communication should be rich in creative potential should not surprise—we are social animals. We talk, talk, and talk in ways that range from formal debates that adhere icily to Roberts Rules of Order to casual chats over steaming cups of tea. This exercise explores a form of verbal communication with deep rhetorical and oratorical roots—debate. Like other topics we have touched on, a debate has a storied history into which one toes trepidatiously. We cannot ignore opportunities inherent in verbal communication as we cultivate creative attitudes of mind.

Not to hear the words of your interlocutor in metropolitan centers is to know nothing of his meaning. Here the face, the arms, the hat, the stick, the body throughout spoke equally with the tongue.

Some of our explorations of varied debate structures are successful, while others are not. Creative explorations require instructors to take risks. It is better to have tried and flailed than to be flailed for never trying. Accordingly, we try different ways to encourage creative discussions among our community of learners and mitigate traditional classrooms' dampening effects. Some participants like the sound of their own voices, while others are scared of what comes out of their mouths. Some participants

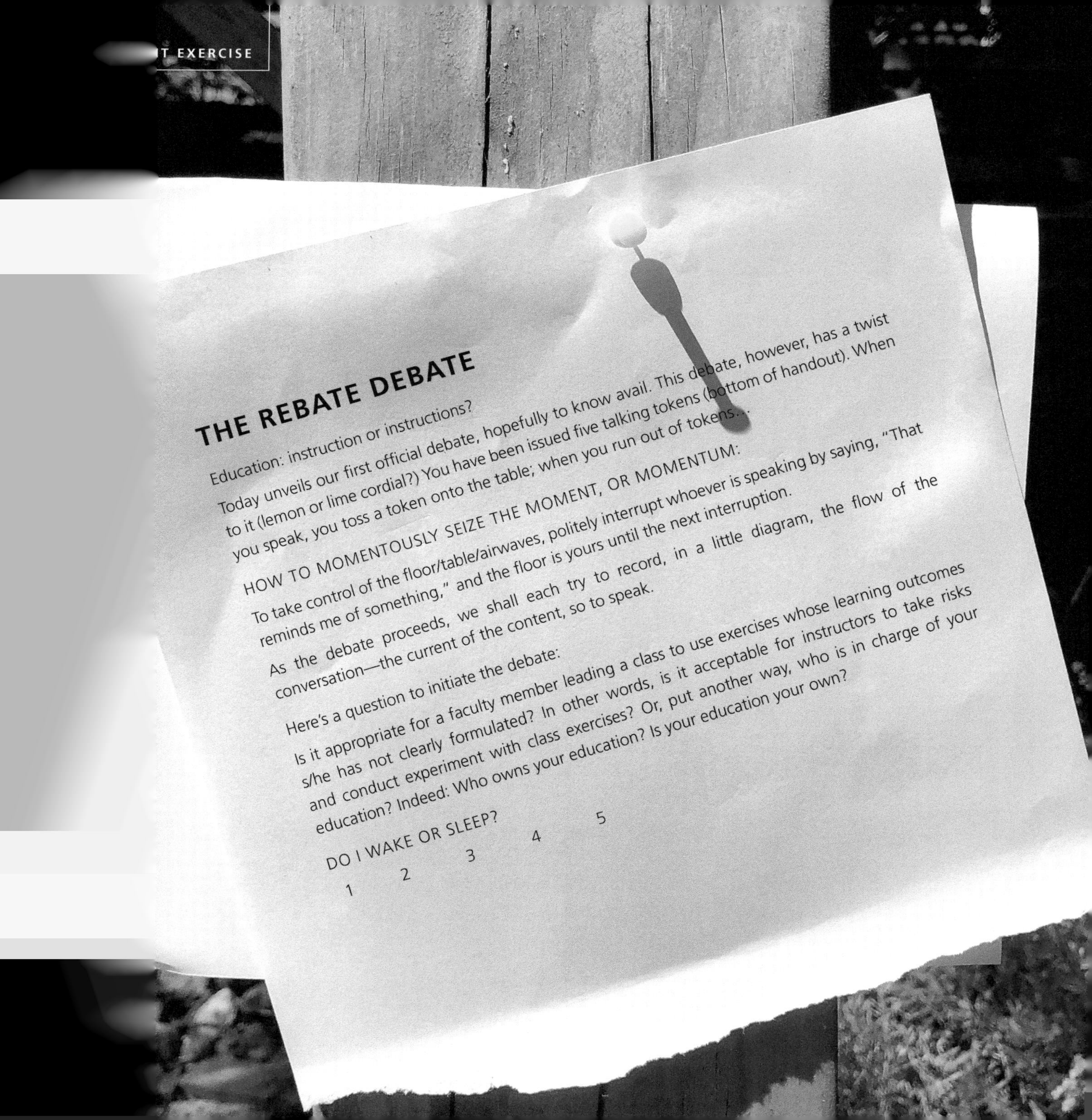

THE REBATE DEBATE

Education: instruction or instructions?

Today unveils our first official debate, hopefully to know avail. This debate, however, has a twist to it (lemon or lime cordial?) You have been issued five talking tokens (bottom of handout). When you speak, you toss a token onto the table; when you run out of tokens...

HOW TO MOMENTOUSLY SEIZE THE MOMENT, OR MOMENTUM:

To take control of the floor/table/airwaves, politely interrupt whoever is speaking by saying, "That reminds me of something," and the floor is yours until the next interruption.

As the debate proceeds, we shall each try to record, in a little diagram, the flow of the conversation—the current of the content, so to speak.

Here's a question to initiate the debate:

Is it appropriate for a faculty member leading a class to use exercises whose learning outcomes s/he has not clearly formulated? In other words, is it acceptable for instructors to take risks and conduct experiment with class exercises? Or, put another way, who is in charge of your education? Indeed: Who owns your education? Is your education your own?

DO I WAKE OR SLEEP?

        5
    4
  3
2
1

talk, talk, and talk; some don't, won't, or can't. How might we attain educational nirvana: open, vigorous, free discussion of ideas in which all participants' voices are heard?

The debate structure described here provides participants with five "talking tokens." Tossing a token onto the table gives one command of the floor until another is thrown down and the baton passes. When one's tokens are gone, it's all over, bar listening. Talking tokens are meant to ensure that voluble talkers are eventually silenced, but they do little to encourage quiet participants—still holding a handful of tokens—to talk. Talking tokens dissolve part of the problem, but lumps remain in this solution. Once ground rules for debate have been set, don't change them. Debates in which I have permitted those who have burned through their tokens to borrow tokens from quieter participants proved disastrous. This method undercut and negated the rules of engagement and is not a creative adaptation. Rules that are fundamental to the activity must not be changed.

This structure produced a lively, although somewhat stilted, discussion. It was considered successful by some but not all participants. As became apparent, classrooms have taught us to act and think in prescribed ways, inducing inhibition in some students and posturing in others. It's difficult to hold free discussions in rooms that carry excess baggage. Although billed as a debate, the exercise aspired to be a free-flowing— an artful—conversation. Conversation is perhaps the most sophisticated and commonly practiced creative art but is widely overlooked as an expression of creativity.

Artful conversations string ideas together. They make persuasive connections and introduce mental leaps that participants can follow, even though generated by individual participants' unique experiences. These "connectivity traits" are expressions of creative attitudes of mind at work and at play. What proves universally ruinous is changing the rules in mid-debate, allowing quiet participants to give tokens to more loquacious ones.

The following reflections illustrate different responses and conclusions. It's not unusual for some participants to respond to an exercise negatively and others to respond positively. If there's a common agreement that something isn't working, changes

BILLIE L: *I appreciated the setup.... . I generally feel that Socratic seminars don't work because the people who usually talk still talk, and those who don't talk still don't. The five papers [tokens] limited how much people contributed (at least at the beginning), which made people say things that were legitimately thoughtful. That is not the same experience as I have had in the past, so I am pleased that it was so successful.*

FREYA Z *(a self-confessed talker): Tearing off pieces of paper in order to talk? Definitely something I'm not used to. But it's probably the best, because I talk WAY too much. What I found interesting was that even with an implemented system with everyone given the same number of "talking tokens," it didn't change the dynamic of the group nor make anyone talk more or less.*

MAN RAY: *The "debate" assignment was frustrating mainly because I didn't care to push the boundaries, but instead played within the rules. This made it incredibly frustrating when people, probably thinking they were infinitely clever, decided to make sixth, seventh, and eighth tokens because they needed to speak. Like many others, this exercise was most interesting when we reflected upon it in class, discussing the different approaches and strategies we took.*

should certainly be made, but various opinions indicate the value of trying varied methods. The "five tokens and you are out" format, intended to encourage participation by everyone, appealed to some but not to others.

Some participants are insatiably voluble; others are perennially quiet. Is it, therefore, reasonable and appropriate to structure a debate to induce equal participation by all? Is it desirable to provide speaking opportunities to those who would prefer to listen? Is it appropriate or fair to try to make everyone participate equally in every activity? Are there cultural conventions as well as personal differences that should be respected?

Another experiment provided participants with "interruption cues" to see if these might encourage more uniform participation. In this format, one could interrupt by saying, "That reminds me of something …" and use this as a connecting thread to carry the conversation forward—or sideways. Results were interesting, but discussions lacked the spontaneity and liveliness of convivial conversation. It was an ordinary conversation on stilts. Experiments that required participants to interrupt with negative phrases such as "I disagree, and here's why" proved ruinous, as

any aspiring improvisational artist could have told us. Keep it positive; provide others with cues to respond to improvisation. Experts use sophisticated methods to stir the communication pot; we would do well to study and emulate their strategies with regard to creativity explorations.

Goaded by the desire to document conversations, I've made more mistakes by asking participants to make notes about how topics connected as the debate progressed. Having participants record the story line while engaging in a debate is ruinous. One cannot serve two rulers, at least not simultaneously. A good discussion requires one's full participation. Either we debate wholeheartedly or we document the discussion carefully; trying to do both is unwise. Because it may be useful to understand how idea threads interweave to form a discussion fabric, we should record this in words and diagrams. Encourage some participants to take the role of participating and others the role of documenting debates. Reversing roles in subsequent debates allows everyone to play both roles. Try debates in which two orators debated while a scribe recorded the ensuing connections, ebbs, and flows—the shuttles that weave the communication fabric. Requiring documentation of conversations produced different responses, some of which reaffirmed that damned requirement was negative.

In another experiment, I asked pairs of participants to respond to each other exclusively in the form of questions. Successful? What do you think? No! This format loosened communication, but it invariably dissolved into laughter. It might be appropriate for suited and tied corporate executive participants in need of loosening up.

Conversation topics will, of course, influence engagement enormously. Topics close to our hearts, or research interests, will engage us in entirely different ways and degrees from those of slight interest. Can we engage in discussing topics about which we're ignorant? Is it reasonable to assume that successful discussions should be measured solely by the passion of participants? In our constructed debates, we didn't adequately consider the choice of topics; we mistakenly thought of topics as vehicles for initiating discussions rather than as fundamental reasons for communication.

WILMA L: *I thought that this debate format was very interesting, though I'm not sure it was effective. I think the people who normally talk more still talked the same amount (because they could tear up more pieces of paper) and the people who normally don't talk a lot still didn't say much (mainly because we weren't REQUIRED to get rid of all our pieces of paper). I thought that it was an interesting format because it seemed more structured than a lot of the discussions we usually have in class and therefore it almost seemed a little stilted because we're so used to just going with the flow and working with very vague constraints. I also thought our discussion itself was very interesting, especially the fact that we kept coming back to the stratification of schools (perhaps particularly because we ARE all high-track, overachieving Honors kids).*

MARY H: *I really liked the communication activity last week. It gave everyone an equal opportunity to speak, and our group didn't feel too bogged down in the rules to be able to follow up on questions and thoughts with each other. The conversation flowed quite nicely. It was good to hear the people speak who don't necessarily get to all the time during class, and I think everyone had (and has) something worthwhile to say. However, I do understand that some people may feel pressured into talking when they really don't feel they have anything to contribute.*

DREW M: *Having us map the conversation was a huge distraction. I found myself far more involved in ensuring that my path was continuous and accurate than participating (or even really listening to) the content of the debate itself. Coincidently, every time I got more into the debate, my map would suffer, as I'd start thinking about what people were arguing instead of who was arguing it.*

CORRIE M: *I did enjoy diagramming the conversation because it's cool to see the connections people's brains make.*

Expansions and Additions

To express satisfaction the Casterbridge market-man added to his utterance a broadening of the cheeks, a crevicing of the eyes, a throwing back of the shoulders, which was intelligible from the other end of the street.

These experiments return us to the questions of what are we trying to accomplish with debates and what this has to do with cultivating creative attitudes of mind. Fundamentally, our goal is to foster open, passionate, engaging, active, unbridled discussion. We hope to encourage debate associated with soapbox orators, coffee klatches, boardroom brawls, used-car dealer's sales pitches, and smoke-filled, beer-slopped barroom politics. Occasionally, such passions light up classrooms, and ideas develop and flourish. These exercises recognize that free-flowing discussions evoke creative thought and responses—the crucible in which many creative ideas are formed.

If he wondered … you knew it from perceiving the inside of his crimson mouth, and a target-like circling of his eyes.

Successful conversations self-generate—the subject is the conversation, so dictating a topic may inhibit free-flowing, animated conversations in which everyone feels comfortable. The context may also thwart an imaginative conversation. Conversations in coffee shop field trips come easily and naturally, while classroom conversations often wither. How might we re-create, in contemporary contexts, a mood akin to the vibrant buzz of seventeenth-century English coffee shops when the New World was opening up in front of the occupants' eyes? How might we foster interactions that will bring contemporary classroom conversations and learning to life? Selecting an appropriate subject to get the ball rolling is crucial. Topics should be universally interesting but should always avoid discussions of creativity directly. The goal is a creative experience, not discussions of what creativity is.

The experiments with formats reveal that somewhere between the precise rules of formal debates, the casualness of coffee shop conversations, and the 140 characters of a tweet lie sweet spots for generating and sharing ideas and making connections. Becoming a community of learners sets the stage on which to explore social interactions that foster individual and group creativity.

I have titled these exercises "debates," but a debate may not be an appropriate model for what we are trying to accomplish. Debate structures, trussed up in Robert's Rules of Order, are disciplined but may be overly formal and inhibiting. Conversations or discussions may be better words for verbal communication that promotes the mind's creative attitudes. Better still might be improvisational theater—improv—a fluid form of communication that actively encourages discussions that feed off one another in positive feedback cycles. Improv seems more attuned to creative attitudes of mind because it involves more cooperation than competition. The purpose of the "Unwrapping Culture" exercise is similar to improvisation, and such conversations thrive in learning communities.

Deliberation caused sundry attacks on the moss of adjoining walls with the end of his stick, a change of his hat from the horizontal to the less so; a sense of tediousness announced itself by the lowering of the person by spreading the knees to a lozenge-shaped aperture and controlling the arms.

—THOMAS HARDY, *THE MAYOR OF CASTERBRIDGE*

The number and forms of ways in which communication may be used to develop and encourage creative attitudes of mind are endless. Consider the opposite end of the spectrum from our verbal explorations. For example, what would happen if we orchestrated a reenactment of John Cage's 4'33" composition—silence? Is it always necessary to get all participants' juices flowing at audible decibel levels? Plays and poetry also offer a plenitude of possibilities. Explore different forms of communication to set minds afire with ideas in different ways. These exercises are exploring a broader question than simply communication: How do social interactions enhance creativity? Communication promotes fluid thinking—creative attitudes of mind may be enhanced by social interactions.

SELF-PORTRAIT WITH CULTURE

"Self-Portrait with Culture" brings us full circle, completing explorations begun in "My Journey to Here." When we completed that exercise, we thought we were "here," but now we have fully arrived. In Eliot's eloquent line, we "know the place," and perhaps ourselves, too, "for the first time." Self-discovery is a lifelong endeavor; there are always more places to look for ourselves. A self-portrait is an excellent place to begin, and end, and begin again. Self-portraits may portray lively young lives full of hope and promise. Look not just at the portraits but at the creators' faces because, unbeknownst to participants, they are the real self-portraits. Here's what the final project asked participants, who have willingly—nay, eagerly—engaged in this educational experiment, to do.

This project asks participants to take one last shot to reveal and express their latent creativity—using a subject about which each is individually expert—themselves. In earlier projects, participants introduced themselves to one other; now they reintroduce themselves to their community of learners. By creating their self-portraits as "exemplars of contemporary civilization," they place themselves within their cultural context.

Participants were given clear-lidded plastic hummus containers to encourage three-dimensional portraits. The artistic qualities of creations were downplayed, while contemplating their lives as products of our shared culture was emphasized. The containers did little to confine explorations that blossomed beyond their confines. Few remained intact. Most became unidentifiable—extended, blown apart, or, like booster rockets, falling away when their inspirational work was done. Participants had learned to think and act outside the container. Self-portraits confirm that, despite jaded elders' head shaking, each new generation is born with the same hopes, aspirations, ideals, and potentials as earlier ones. Creativity is alive and well, living in a youthful cranium near you. The richness and thoughtfulness of self-portraits defy description, but more revealing is the delight on presenters' faces. Without even noticing it, participants again surprised themselves.

YOU WHO? A SELF-PORTRAIT; OR, PORTRAIT OF THE ARTIST AS AN EXEMPLAR OF EARLY-TWENTY-FIRST-CENTURY AMERICA

The point is to enter the dialogue of the times.

—GARY SNYDER, *THE REAL WORK: INTERVIEWS & TALKS, 1964–1979*

If you are born of the artist tribe it is a waste of time to try and function as a priest. You have to be faithful to your angle of vision, and at the same time fully recognise its partiality. There is a kind of perfection to be achieved in matching oneself to one's capacities—at every level. This must, I imagine, do away with striving, and with illusions too.

—LAWRENCE DURRELL, *CLEA*

Piglet was busy digging a small hole in the ground outside his house.
"Hallo, Piglet," said Pooh.
"Hallo, Pooh," said Piglet, giving a jump of surprise. "I knew it was you."
"So did I," said Pooh.
"What are you doing?"

—A. A. MILNE, *THE HOUSE AT POOH CORNER*

We commenced the quarter with a depiction of your journey to here, and with that in mind, we shall conclude our take-home projects with a self-portrait. But not just any self-portrait, for this one you will create a 3-D (yes, 3-D) self-portrait of yourself as an exemplar of contemporary civilization—for, make no mistake, that is what you, I, we collectively and individually ARE—we ARE our civilization as much as the debris and detritus that ends up in museums and collections.

Feel free to modulate, moderate or, if absolutely necessary, immolate (but don't emulate) your container; burst forth.

Usually I carry an idea in my head for years before making up my mind to give it shape on the page, and on many occasions while waiting for this to happen I just let it die… .

Spontaneity also has its moments: sometimes at the beginning—and in that case it does not usually last long—sometimes as a thrust you develop as you go along, sometimes as a final flourish. But is spontaneity something we should value? It certainly is for the writer, since it allows you to write with less effort, without going into crisis every minute; but it is not certain that the work always benefits from it. The important thing is spontaneity as an impression which the work conveys, but that does not mean you can achieve this result by using spontaneity as a means: in many cases it is only patient elaboration that allows you to arrive at the most satisfying and apparently "spontaneous" solution.

—ITALO CALVINO, *HERMIT IN PARIS: AUTOBIOGRAPHICAL WRITINGS*

Expansions and Additions

As usual, the project concealed underlying questions in broad daylight. It invited participants to synthesize a solution—to take that magical step in which disparate thoughts, words, and materials combine into new understandings, new expressions, new products. Synthesis is the flowering of creative thought and work—the leap that transmutes lead into gold. Through synthesis, the old is renewed, the commonplace becomes extraordinary, and—by generating new perspectives—the world is revealed in a new light.

Many of our activities have consisted of reformulating—through synthesis—common, ordinary, unremarkable, everyday stuff, words, or thoughts into new combinations, new relations, new meanings, new understandings. The exercises have explored how to do this not in straightforward, head-on, analytical ways, but tangentially, using synthetic thinking and abductive reasoning. The exercises do an end run around analytical thinking. For our world's "wicked' problems," forthright, head-on approaches to solutions are ineffective; we must employ fluid synthetic and integrative thinking.

As students developed their self-portraits, participants integrated their understanding of themselves with their understanding of their culture personally and thus uniquely. In a very literal sense, throughout the exercises, participants engaged in the process of making and remaking themselves. Nowhere is this more explicit than in this project. We have encouraged our minds to be more fluid and less rigid. We trust that this will develop fresh neural structures and pathways—what Norman Doidge calls "modules" in our "plastic" brains. Of course, all educational and everyday experiences do this, but our creativity exercises focus on encouraging more facile, flexible, and fluid connections across brain structures. Education is the process of making up your mind. The exercises invite participants to make up and then remake their minds to cultivate creative attitudes and fluid minds.

"Self-Portrait with Culture" externalizes participants and their minds, putting them on the chopping block, so to speak. They package and present themselves to one other. "Well, well, well, what a surprise. I'm delighted to meet you!" The best projects are accomplished after participants have come to trust one another—that is, have become a learning community. In Zen and the Art of Motorcycle Maintenance, Robert Pirsig says, "The real cycle you're working on is a cycle called yourself." In this

project, participants give themselves a workout. In what other ways might they get to work on, know, and express themselves?

Conceptualizing and deciding how we wish to present ourselves to others is a form of self-discovery and self-revelation. It's exciting beyond measure to discover that the "ordinary" people around the table, whom we thought we knew, turn out to be extraordinary as they reveal depths and breadths we hadn't imagined. This project is merely an example of exploring the tangle of interactions between knowing ourselves and relating to our culture. In other renditions, the tone was altered and focused by asking participants to create "a shrine to culture." While less individually revealing, those shrines also become personal expositions. A "shrine" is a compelling meme for compressing a culture—lock, stock, and barrel—into a box of comfortable dimensions. Responses are revelatory.

Open-ended and ambiguous questions, such as the ones we ask here, are invitations to the imagination. Their very elusiveness imparts power to explorations. Even as they torque our conventional educational enterprise, they uplift it. It's time to leave the straight and narrow and prepare for the twists and turns of life and its "wicked problems." Creativity exercises are the first steps in preparing for journeys into unknown futures. Thoreau had it right when he said, "I think we may safely trust a good deal more than we do."

AFTERWORD: SILENCE

Over the borders, a sin without pardon,
Breaking the branches and crawling be-
low,

This book celebrates the processes, products, and reflections of students in classes designed to cultivate creativity. Because the exercises were activities conducted both in the classroom and outside it, not structured research experiments (although, of course, creative attitudes of mind accept all life as an experiment), we cannot draw definitive conclusions. A gain, all is not lost. Think of this book not as a how-to manual but as a why-to manual; that the latter goal is more pertinent than the former became evident as each exercise progressed. Participants' responses revealed what I take to be a universal desire: to recover, express, and use our creativity. Ought not this be a central goal of all education? Just asking.

Explorations into cultivating creative attitudes of mind led to a deeper and broader realization: Like all true education, all of our questions were underlain by deeper and wider questions, and those by broader questions still. The more we dug, the deeper the whole we found ourselves in. So many omissions: Creativity itself remains cloaked in ambiguity, undefined. We don't tell you how to do it, nor what we are trying to accomplish. Making matters worse, we repeatedly defy the educational injunction not to cross academic boundaries. The book's enduring legacy may be muddy footprints trespassing fertile but foreign fields in pursuit of a hound, a bay horse, and a turtledove. If these non-experiments have one, the "control group" is the rest of the educational enterprise.

> *Out through the breach in the*
> *wall of the garden,*
> *Down by the banks of the river we go.*

Connections and Synthesis

Our world owes its fragmentation in part to the fragmentation of understanding by our educational systems. These systems seem more interested in gathering and cataloging pieces—analytical thinking—than in preserving wholes—synthetic thinking. Creativity's connection-making encourages the latter by providing the glue to connect the fragments. Synthesis and integration, hallmarks, though not trademarked, of creative attitudes of mind, are connective processes. Creativity may encourage educational styles that in E. M. Forster's penetrating phrase "Only connect!" By connecting or integrating, we may "live in fragments no longer." But to connect, we must break down barrier walls—institutional and individual, external and internal. Creativity sees wholes, where others see holes.

> *Here is the mill with the*
> *humming of thunder,*
> *Here is the weir with the wonder of*
> *foam,*

Curiosity and Observation

It is said that "curiosity killed the cat." Much of education, though perhaps inadvertently, seems to have had a similarly catastrophic effect on curiosity. Curiosity, the wellspring of all searching,

seems stifled by educational systems designed to fill students ever fuller of "stuff," leaving little room for contemplating what to do with it. "Curiouser and curiouser" cried Alice as her height prevented her from entering the Wonderland garden. Girth, resulting from the current emphasis on stuffing us full, may have similarly debilitating effects on curiosity. When curiosity is stifled, the educational enterprise withers. What to do? Curiosity engenders creativity.

Our insistence on honing careful observation is born of the belief that curiosity and observation are yin and yang: Observation encourages curiosity, and curiosity encourages observation. Which comes first is inconsequential. Our methods encourage broad observation and assert that observation is not confined

to one sense, sight, nor one form of intelligence. The exercises encourage observation with hands and hearts as much as with heads. Together, curiosity and observation engender aliveness, awareness, and appreciation of the world, fertile ground for creative thinking. Using the material world in exercises, we return curiosity to planet Earth rather than leave it roaming Mars.

Here is the sluice with race running under—Marvelous places, though handy to home!

Wonder and Surprise

Creativity is the food of life, wonder bred. No wonder, no creativity. Creativity? Wonder full! Do the curious and diverse materials and requirements of our exercises fill us with wonder? We wonder. Mentioning wonder won't work wonders on one's résumé, but its lack on one's CV—and in one's life—may cause creativity to wither lackadaisically. For want of a daisy, wonder was nailed. How do we encourage and incite wonder? A potent method is surprise, a response not easy to orchestrate to order or evoked repeatedly without changing methods. With the goal of encouraging participants to become more nimble on their feet and fluid in their thoughts, our most enduring requirement has been that participants surprise themselves weekly or strongly. Admittedly an ambiguous and perplexing requirement but, surprisingly, one that most, if not all, participants discover, unexpectedly, they have the ability to do to themselves. All too often, we snuff out curiosity and wonder in education and bemoan the darkened minds that result. Surprising ourselves by discovering how surprisingly agile our minds are provides a welcome antidote: delight. The goal of creativity is to live more abundantly. The wonder of it is that we still wonder and, like Ferlinghetti, we find ourselves still "awaiting/perpetually and forever/a renaissance of wonder."

Years may go by, and the wheel in the river Wheel as it wheels for us, children, to-day,

Wisdom and Humility

Finally, wisdom. A shrinelike word toward which we trip-toe trepidatiously. Who but the desperate, the cynical, or the sage dares utter the word—the unacknowledged goal of education and life? Fuels rush in, and climate instability results. We put aside the question of whether our exercises might instill wisdom, along with its sister question of relationships. Out on what limb do creativity and wisdom appear on education's pedagogical tree? We focus instead on one of wisdom's most silent but telling attributes: humility. Humility might seem to be the last thing we need as we strive energetically and passionately to be creative—but lacking its counterbalance, we run the risk of growing arrogant, greedy, and intellectually self-aggrandizing. These lead, willy-nilly, down the slippery slope to self-important and self-satisfied attitudes of mind. But only fools, or the foolhardy, would hang signs on their door saying WISDOM TAUGHT HERE.

In our paradoxical world of ambiguity and confusion verging on chaos, humility seems a likely ticket to success. The more we know, the larger the enveloping ignorance. Our exercises' ambiguity encourages humility. We are also rendered humble by the responses and products of our peers. Invariably, these cause us to exclaim, "How did you do that? I would never have thought of that in a thousand years of nights." Contrary to the clangor of contemporary conventional wisdom, humility may induce creative attitudes of mind and support the childlike freshness of a "beginner's mind."

Wheel and keep roaring and foaming for ever Long after all the boys are away.

—ROBERT LOUIS STEVENSON "KEEPSAKE MILL", *A CHILD'S GARDEN OF VERSES*

Pertinent and Personal

Creativity may be personal, but its results keep "roaring and foaming" long after we are gone. How do we retain the personal in mass educational systems that seem hell-bent on contrary journeys and on growing increasingly impersonal? We stretch the point, but creativity may be the cure for the common curriculum. Thoreau reminds us: "We commonly do not remember that it is, after all, always the first person that is speaking." Pertinently, it is also "the first person'" thinking, learning, and creating.

The products and reflections that enrich and illustrate this book are the work of exceptional "first persons," as all ordinary individuals become when they recover a creative attitude of mind. To these students, from the University of Washington's Honors Program, Huazhong University of Science and Technology's College of Design, and the University of Bergen, I owe an enormous debt of gratitude for their personal commitment and faith, initially in me and latterly in themselves, for this work. Thank you, thank you, thank you. We explored together, taking delight as much in our journeys as in our discoveries. Thanks to all of you, whether you read this or not. Without you, I would have been a noisy gong or clanging cymbal. You rendered the journey musical.

In respect of the personal, a confession: I began, and now end, with two poems from Robert Louis Stevenson's *A Child's Garden of Verses* and photographs of the Water of Leith, which inspired the poems. Rivers are fluid and regenerative; they suggest journeys; they are bringers of floods and fertility, worthy bookends for creative explorations. The Water of Leith flows from the Pentland Hills, winds sinuously through Edinburgh, and debouches into the Firth of Forth. Stevenson's grandfather was a minister in Colinton Parish Church, around which the river makes a great bend and along whose banks the poet played in his youth. I, too, grew up near this river and have family roots entwined with the church. One must make personal connections. As you read this, may the Water of Leith's fluidity impart to you also an effusion of creativity, a fluidity of mind. Say. Know. More.

IAIN M. ROBERTSON (1948–2021), an internationally admired landscape architect and educator, was Associate Professor Emeritus and former chair of the University of Washington's Landscape Architecture Department, as well as adjunct faculty in the UW School of Environmental and Forest Sciences. A native of Edinburgh, Scotland, Iain earned a Bachelor of Architecture from the University of Edinburgh and a Master of Landscape Architecture from the University of Pennsylvania. Iain's design methods and teaching approach emphasized the spatial, functional, aesthetic, and ecological uses of plants within the framework of creativity. He was active in the design community, frequently presenting on topics such as design studio pedagogy at the Council of Educators in Landscape Architecture's annual conferences and authoring articles for *Landscape Journal*. Iain was well known for his ability to foster the self-discovery of one's creative capabilities and to inspire students, colleagues, and professionals to push beyond their preconceived boundaries to imagine the unimaginable.